WOLF BENEATH THE FLEECE . . .

We were to raid in seas a world away from home. We were to sail against England by way of Greenland and the Cape of Good Hope. The *Atlantis*—Ship Sixteen, as she was known to Berlin, or Ship C, as she was classified by British Intelligence—was one of nine disguised merchant raiders operating in two waves.

We called her the *Atlantis* because it was a name that would distinguish her from an oceanic Pandora's box of concealed torpedoes, guns, and mines. It symbolized something of the mystery and the strangeness of life upon the waters. Thinking it over, Captain Rogge felt vaguely pleased.

They'd first allotted Captain Rogge his wartime post when Mr. Chamberlain had gone back from Munich promising "peace in our time." At the time, the role had seemed an extremely hypothetical one, for chances of conflict between Germany and Britain had appeared remote.

Well, the worst had happened—to Rogge, war with England was really *the* worst—and it was up to him to do his duty. Not even a hint of the intention to use commerce raiders must leak out. Security was essential. The main weapon must necessarily be that of disguise. The *Atlantis* must pretend to be what she was not. No enemy eye must discern the purpose of Ship Sixteen's furtive transformation into what the Allies were later to call the Nazi Q ship, or less flatteringly, the *Rattlesnake of the Ocean* . . .

SEA RAIDER ATLANTIS

ULRICH MOHR
& A. V. SELLWOOD

PINNACLE BOOKS   LOS ANGELES

SEA RAIDER *ATLANTIS*

A Pinnacle Books edition, published by special
arrangement with New English Library, Ltd.

First printing, February 1974
Second printing, July 1980

ISBN: 0-523-40961-3

Cover illustration by Ed Valigursky

Printed in the United States of America

PINNACLE BOOKS, INC.
2029 Century Park East
Los Angeles, California 90067

SEA RAIDER *ATLANTIS*

NOTE

by Admiral Bernhard Rogge

THIS BOOK, dealing as it does with the story of my old command, the commerce-raider *Atlantis,* has brought back to me the most vivid and poignant memories; both of an incredibly fine comradeship and, far less pleasantly, of the collective tragedy, unsurpassed in all human experience, that brought that comradeship about.

To the men who served their countries at sea, World War Two provided no lull, no breathing space. The British Blockade was continuous. The German commerce attack was also continuous. Like the tide itself the battle for the control of the sea-routes might ebb and flow, but it was always in a state of movement.

Certain former adversaries have been good enough to give me credit because I tried to fight with respect towards them. As one who joined the Imperial Navy at fifteen and was attracted at that impressionable age by the noble conduct of Captain Müller-Emden, and was later by the teachings of Grand Admiral Raeder, I find it a sad reflection on this epoch that such behaviour should be considered as anything unusual.

But War is an exacting task-master, greedily insisting upon the honouring of ever heavier demands. The more successes obtained by the raiders the more did the British Admiralty understandably insist that merchant ships employed on its service should send radio reports of the 'enemy's' presence and position, and the more was this instruction followed the less opportunity had we of implementing our original decision to employ the chivalrous technique of a signal to heave to, followed by a shot across the bows.

As a result life was lost that could in more leisurely

days have been spared, and yet it is hard to see how either protagonist, once having accepted the tenet that it was serving a war effort, could have done other than it did.

It is true to say however that in other respects we of *Atlantis* were more fortunate than the men of the submarines and bomber, in so far as that, by the nature of our warfare, we had many opportunities of saving life when our task was done. And those opportunities—I say this in fairness to my crew—were never neglected, even at considerable risk.

In the story of *Atlantis* you will read of the courage of British merchant sailors who obeyed their Admiralty's instructions regardless of the fact that they knew their action would force us to open fire.

You will read also of my officers and men—several of them later killed on other fronts—who, separated from civilisation and home for nearly two years, stood together in fair weather and foul, so well that not once did I have to cope with a really serious case of indiscipline.

In general, the men who fought the battle on the Ocean—whether German or British, Scandinavian, Dutch or French—were sailors who had little use for fanaticism, and found little attraction in the so-called 'glamour of war'. They were men who quietly did their duty because they felt it was the thing to do; yet, in so doing, they faced not only the chance of destruction by their enemies, but also combated continuously with the monotonous, unrelenting onslaught of the Sea.

It is my hope that this book, by conveying some idea of the unspectacular devotion of those who served the War upon the oceans may raise a thought or two regarding the value of finding a formula to harness such energy and comradeship to the far more worthy cause of Peace.

ROGGE
HAMBURG
January 1955

FOREWORD

by Captain J. Armstrong White

*'And I 'eard a beggar squealing out for
Quarter as 'e ran,
And I thought I knew the voice—and it was mine.'*

IT IS unpleasant to realise one has been caught in a trap, and that the innocent fellow-merchantman is a sea-wolf in disguise. But it is even more unpleasant to feel his fangs strike home, and find oneself at the receiving end of a row of 6-inch guns, all blazing away at practically point blank range.

Yet such was the predicament in which I found myself on a July morning in 1940, with my ship the *City of Bagdad* caught beneath the suddenly unmasked guns of the German raider *Atlantis* and with nothing more effective to answer back with than a single anti-submarine gun. To use a Stanley Hollowayism 'I thought nowt of it at all', and although we did not 'squeal for quarter' as the enemy's shells came over we most certainly squealed for help—and vengeance!

But our effort was in vain, for scarcely had our radio sent out the R sign that meant raider attack and hammered out our position in a desperate attempt to warn others like us to escape, and call in the Royal Navy to the hunt, than down came the fore-topmast about our ears, bringing the aerial with it. Then, with the next salvo, a shell hit the wireless room, wounding the Wireless Operator and wrecking the set. And that was that.

Such then were the unpleasant circumstances in which I, and my officers and men, made the acquaint-

3

ance of the ship that sails again in the pages of this book.

After that fierce overture in the morning we were to watch the *City of Bagdad* slide beneath the water to join other faithful merchantmen upon the ocean bed, and for one hundred and seven days we were to be the prisoners of Rogge, and have as our immediate 'jailer' his A.D.C. Mohr, who now tells the story of *Atlantis* as it seemed through German eyes. Our ship was the third victim of this raider-in-disguise, and there were more to follow, many more alas, and all of them taken by Rogge's technique of surprise, effrontery, and superb seamanship.

On board *Atlantis* we British prisoners endured a by no means pleasant existence, and abroad the 'Hell Ship' *Durmitor*—described by Mohr with commendable frankness—things were very grim indeed.

Whenever *Atlantis* went into action, which was unfortunately all too often, we had naturally to be shut up below, and, equally naturally, became at such times the prey to the most harassing speculation. For one thing we knew that, if there was no return fire, then some of our fellows at the other end were 'getting it', and if there WAS—well, our prison flat happened to be situated right over the magazine.

I do not think that I shall ever quite escape from the memories of those tense occasions—each one of us attempting to busy himself according to his individual temperament, each one of us trying to to outdo the other in the pretence of offhandedness. Those games of chess, where the pawns shook as the guns cracked and rolled; those games of cards where many a partner's ace was trumped as the whine of the ammunition hoists and the echo of the boots of the German sailors overhead prefaced what we knew would be the start of another attack; those books that so often you'd notice the reader was studying upside down . . . such moments are indeed impossible to forget, as are the memories of the wounded and the dead.

But there were other aspects to the picture as well,

aspects that, to many former *Atlantis* prisoners, are equally unforgettable, and to me the *Atlantis* story is unique, not so much for the extent of the 'successes' she obtained—such 'successes', as Rogge would be the first to admit, being but empty things when the final count is taken—but for the fact that, through all the ugliness and filth of war, and despite her employment of all the ruthless efficiency which war requires, a chivalry existed upon that ship; a chivalry between man and man that left respect instead of hatred.

A lot of water has flowed under the bridges since those early days of the conflict, and many of us in Britain who survived their many experiences during it must have sometimes wondered at the strange realignment among the nations; seeing the once powerful European countries who waged it now impoverished and other countries rising to power in their place, to see the world still an armed camp with all spending more than they can afford on armaments, and all racked with hatred and suspicion. Now our one time allies are our 'enemies', and our strangely recent enemies our 'friends'.

Often during my long sojourn on *Atlantis* I used to ponder the strangeness of circumstances where one moment one wreaked destruction and the next risked one's life to drag to safety the survivors of one's 'success'; where one wounded and then spared no effort to repair the damage. I used to ponder too—we had plenty of time for pondering—on the destiny that caught good men up with a Bad Man's Cause. For while the concentration camps were full ashore and innocents perished beneath a vile tyranny, the sailors of *Atlantis,* Mohr prominent among them, risked their necks on more than one occasion to battle through the full force of gale and sea to round up our fellows and bring them in to safety.

When the *City of Bagdad* was attacked Rogge ceased action the moment we had been rendered *hors-de-combat* by the smashing of our only real weapon, our wireless installation. Our wounded were extremely well treated. Such scant fare as there was was shared fairly.

The attitude of her crew was 'correct'. The attitude of her officers was actually courteous. Such facts as these formed a marked contrast to the happenings in other ships, and, however much we hated our captivity, we at least conceded that our discomforts after all were but the result of Rogge crowding his prison holds rather than leave us to the 'freedom' of the Sea.

I little thought, when I prayed so desperately for one of our cruisers to give *Atlantis* a taste of her own medicine, that I would one day be on terms of friendship with my captors. Yet I, and officers from other ships as well, both British and Norwegian, were to acquire such feelings despite our adverse circumstances, and have since met both Rogge and Mohr on the most cordial of terms. And THAT, I would think—a fact, I feel, that makes the *Atlantis* story a very different one from that which would normally obtain.

In the pages which follow you will read how unfortunately, only too slowly, the tables began to turn against the German raider. You will read how the hunter became the hunted. You will, I suspect, reflect at the end of it all how both hunter and hunted are of much the same human material, albeit fashioned by the clash of nations into different guises.

Further, you may reflect that, if we humans do not accept the truism that nothing is gained by war our race is likely to become as extinct as the Dodo, and this applies to whatever people are reckoned as the enemies of the moment, whatever their colour or creed or class.

Otherwise it is going to be a case of:

'Some little talk a while of Me and Thee,
There seemed—and then no more of Me and Thee'

CAPTAIN J. ARMSTRONG WHITE
T.S.M.V. *City of Durban*
(*Maiden Voyage, August 1954*)

PREFACE

MY VICARIOUS association with the adventures of Ship Sixteen began with a mild sense of curiosity; a curiosity stemming in all probability from little more than a journalistic appreciation of the alliterative qualities of her name, and resolving itself only slowly into a determination to find out just what she was, and what she had been up to in the course of her long adventure.

On more than one occasion Mohr has commented that to him one of the most remarkable things about *Atlantis* the Ship was that she should ever have succeeded in reaching the sea. 'The frustrations were so numerous. There were times when we despaired of even starting'.

The same holds true of *Atlantis* the Book. When I first made Ship Sixteen's acquaintance (through the safe media of captured enemy documents) it was 1947. When I began to ponder on the possibilities of writing something about her it was 1949. When fresh evidence of her activities came to hand it was 1953. And, after various false starts, it was not until Christmas of that year that I received the impetus to go 'Full Ahead' and obtain this eye-witness account of her activities from one of 'the other side'; one deep in the confidence of her Commander, and responsible for several of the ruses and subterfuges that enabled the 'phantom raider' to carry out the longest sea-cruise in naval history.

My interest in the *Atlantis* arose when I was studying the 'Führer Conferences on Naval Affairs'—minutes of meetings between Hitler and his naval chiefs that, cap-

7

tured towards the end of the war, have since been admirably collated and edited by the Admiralty.

Somehow or other a phrase in a report by Raeder seemed to stick in my mind. I do not know why, for it was possessed of the brevity expected of a C. in C. with weightier matters on his mind; a C. in C. moreover who was later, according to the minutes, 'to discuss with the Führer, in private, details concerning the Invasion of England'.

'Ship 16 is to lay mines off Cape Agulhas and to carry out warfare against merchant shipping in the Indian Ocean . . .'

Ship Sixteen? I had not heard of her. *Bismark* and *Tirpitz, Scharnhorst* and *Gneisenau, Hipper* and *Eugen*—when recalling the surface aspect of the War at Sea the mind automatically wandered to these, the Big Names, that, even in retrospect, seemed so eloquently to symbolise the grey might against which the Royal Navy had for so long been pitted, and had eventually so decisively overcome. *Graf Spee,* and her smoking ruin outside the Plate . . . *Scheer,* and the heroism of the immortal *Jervis Bay* . . . *Deutschland,* and the changing of her name to *Lützow* because the Führer could not accept the risk to morale of a 'Deutschland' sinking—of the pocket-battleships we had heard sufficient. But of Ship Sixteen?

In the 'Conferences' I discovered repeated references to ships that, at first labelled as enigmatically as Sixteen herself, were later to bear such names as *Komet* and *Thor, Orion* and *Widder, Pinguin* and *Komoran.* Like the *Atlantis* these vessels also were Armed Merchant Raiders, the converted cargo ships that we, so preoccupied by the vast and pitiless onslaught of the U-boats in the Atlantic, or the occasional spectacular sorties of the 'battlewagons', knew so very little about; the Ghost Fleet that, in 'emulating the cunning of the Serpent', was to provide the successors to those well-known marauders of World War One, *Seeadler, Moewe,* and *Wolf.*

A subject for further research, I thought, to trace the

8

activities of the raiders and their equally evasive merchant sisters, the blockade runners; how they operated; their disguise; their luck . . . good or bad. Here indeed was rich material for a book.

But what had happened to Ship Sixteen? Somehow or other the name tantalisingly persisted. I started to check up. One thing was speedily evident. There was no mystery about the nature of her End. Her bones lay beneath the waters of the South Atlantic, shattered by the guns of H.M.S. *Devonshire*. But the date of her sinking was *22nd November* 1941, and *Atlantis*, according to the 'Conferences', had left Germany in *early* 1940. What had gone on in the near-two-years between? I tried to find a reference to a return to Germany, followed by a second mission. I could not find it. *Atlantis*, it appeared, had been roaming the oceans for 622 days, and her Ship's Company had kept together for 655.

The temptation to Do Something about her was strong, but Doing Something was a different matter. To find out what had happened during those 655 days would entail considerable research. There was other work to do. I just could not afford the time. So, no sooner was the idea formulated than it was shelved, and might have remained so, were it not for the result of a very peculiar coincidence: a coincidence that occurred nearly five years later.

This new phase in the *Atlantis* Story began when I received for review a book devoted to the wartime experiences and ordeals of various merchant navy men, among them Captain A. Hill, who had commanded the freighter *Mandasor*. Epitomising as it did the plucky, almost cocky, attitude of those who travelled beneath the Red Duster on the lonely sea roads of the East, I found the story of *Mandasor* particularly interesting. She had withstood repeated attacks from the seaplane of a German raider and then, having seen the Arado 'off the premises' in such a condition that she sank on landing, led the raider herself a pretty dance; capitulating only when her radio had been destroyed and every member of her gun crew had been killed or wounded.

9

Captain Hill gave the name of the raider as *Temesis*—which was a new one to me. But the name of *Temesis'* Commander bore the name of Rogge!

Rogge! This most certainly rang a bell. I blew the dust off the notes I had made in 1947-48 . . . Ship 21 (von Rucktesehell) . . . Ship 36 (Weyher) . . . Ship 16 (ROGGE)! So *Temesis* was a *nom de guerre*, and the story that had so intrigued me related to the ship that had originally aroused my curiosity regarding the A.M.C.s. One seemed fated somehow to be denied excuses for idleness in this affair, and with a half-grumbling enthusiasm I resumed my search for clues.

The quest began promisingly enough. The 'unknown' *Atlantis*, I learned from the Admiralty, had been credited with the highest 'score' of all the German raiders, and had destroyed or captured over twice as much tonnage as the notorious *Graf Spee*. But details of her wanderings were hard to get. Her War Diary was still inaccessible to the outsider, for it was the object of study by naval officers engaged with more serious affairs than the writing of books. Nor did the newspaper libraries, normally so rewarding, prove of much assistance. Most of them had very wisely undergone a thorough purge since 1945, discarding in the process thousands of cuttings relating to the so-called 'minor' episodes of the war. Furthermore, the search was considerably complicated by the fact that *Atlantis* changed her name so often that very few of her victims—at least those interviewed by the press during the War—had known her real identity, and as a result one had to pick one's way through accounts of actions against 'A Merchant Raider', and even then find oneself confounded by a false scent that led, say, to *Pinguin* or *Komet*.

Not that the search was entirely fruitless. 'Life' had covered the *Zamzam* episode most comprehensively. An Australian newspaper had run a long story by a seaman taken on *Commissaire Ramel*. From the Admiralty I had learned that *Kemmendine* was another *Atlantis* victim, and, as her survivors had been sent to East Africa and later released by our armies, I was able to trace an

10

interview with them, published by the *London Times* in June 1941. This latter was a most valuable discovery, in so far as that the survivors' names and addresses had also been published, but still the objective remained elusive.

None of the prisoners had been with the raider for more than a comparatively short period of her career, and no one was in a position to record the 'inner story' of her exploits. Doubtless one could, if one had the time, piece together a fairly comprehensive chronological account by tracing and interviewing the survivors of successive actions, but an attempt or two in this direction convinced me reluctantly that this was a process so laborious as to be impossible to reconcile with that of efficiently performing one's regular job, and thus, in late November 1953, I decided once and for all, I thought, to abandon the project. It was a decision made with great reluctance and after much heart searching, for meanwhile it had become increasingly obvious that the *Atlantis* story was better, far better, than I had ever imagined . . .

Her successes seemed to have left so little bitterness among her victims. THAT surely was surprising—indeed almost unique. Rogge was ruthless enough in action— 'after all,' said one seaman: 'You can't expect a bloody war to be conducted like a bloody tea-party—but, for all that he was a gentleman, and appreciated as such. Instead of bitter complaints I was surprised to hear ungrudging tribute. He was just, humane, and endowed with a genuine consideration for the feelings of his "guests". He behaved like a decent seaman'.

This evidence of respect opened a new line of approach towards the story. Maybe one should attempt to get her story 'from the other side' . . . ? The idea, at first rejected out of hand, grew upon me as I learned more of the calibre of the former 'enemy'. Just how did our men seem through German eyes? Just how did the crew of *Atlantis* view the avenging *Devonshire* and *Dorsetshire* from the receiving end of the British fire? And the strains and stresses and manoeuvres of the crew . . . Who better to relate them than the men who experienced them?

But there were snags, first and foremost among them the difficulty of finding the teller of the tale. Fourteen years had passed since the cruise of the *Atlantis*. Where in a Germany that had endured defeat did one start to look?

The answer came three weeks later when I had occasion to call on the *City of Paris*, whose Captain—Captain J. Armstrong White—was shortly to take command of the crack new Ellerman liner, *City of Durban*. This meeting was (to me) momentous for not only had the Captain been a prisoner of *Atlantis*, but he had also, through chance, re-established contact with his former captors, and was, in fact, now a close friend of both Rogge and Mohr. *Atlantis*, it seemed, was destined to be written after all.

Owing to the passage of time since the actual event, the fallibility of human memory and the War Diary not being available for reference, both Mohr and myself felt it necessary to double check, where possible, to ensure accuracy. And in this connection I, being responsible for the English end, am grateful for the frank and willing manner in which several British officers did their best to help.

I am particularly grateful to Captain A. W. S. Agar, V.C., D.S.O., R.N, Retd. This distinguished officer, who presided in H.M.S. *Dorsetshire* over the 'second shipwreck' of the *Atlantis* crew, possessed the most decided convictions regarding raider warfare, and yet was kindhearted enough to read the manuscript and correct the more obvious of the landlubber gaffs that had slipped into it as a result of my interpretation of Mohr's adventures.

I was interested to observe, during my research, how differently an event can appear when viewed through the eyes of two equally honest men, each on different sides, each telling the truth as he sees it, and not always realising the full circumstances.

12

For example, the liner *Kemmendine*. As soon as I had heard Mohr's account, I got in touch with Captain M. M. Ramsay, formerly an officer on *Kemmendine* and now with a command of his own. In reply he wrote, 'You mention that Rogge or Mohr said we opened fire after throwing in the sponge. This in effect was quite true, but the circumstances were peculiar'.

And he explained. 'In the first salvo a shell splinter burst a deck steam pipe close to the bridge, and the terrific roar from this made it impossible to even hear yourself talking. It was during this time when the telephonic communication from our gun to the Bridge was dislocated, that the Second Gunner, without orders, fired. We did not hear the gun going off, and so WE wondered why the raider had opened up on us for the second time!'

Just what did Ramsay feel about *Atlantis*?

'I must say that one and all were treated with due deference,' he states. 'During the four months we were on the raider, Commander Rogge treated us very justly and as far as P.O.W.s were concerned kept strictly to International Law. Food was good and plentiful, and the living quarters clean, and as comfortable as the circumstances would allow. The only shortage was water and that was very strictly rationed, but this rationing also applied to the German crew. The vessel carried a very clever surgeon, and on one occasion he went as far as making an artificial limb for an officer who had lost his leg'.

When I asked Captain Hill, of *Mandasor*, for his impressions of the raider he had so stubbornly resisted, he said, 'She gave us a pasting, but given only half the chance we would gladly have pasted her. That's war for you. But as prisoners we had no complaints at all. Rogge and Mohr were decent people, likeable people even. They did their best for us, and the doctors looked after out wounded as if they were their own. We had no kick about our treatment on *Atlantis* or on the blockade runner, *Tannenfels*, to which we were later transferred. It was only in the prison camp that our real troubles

13

began. Only then did we encounter the Hate Brigade'.

I think that any reader of this book will soon realise that neither Mohr nor Rogge was ever a member of this most international of organisations. Nor had they any connection with the Nazi Party or the two hundred associations affiliated with it. Since the end of the war five out of *Atlantis*'s fifteen British captain-prisoners have gone to the considerable trouble of locating their former enemies, both of whom, significantly, were left at liberty when hostilities ceased.

Rogge, one of the few senior officers not interned, was appointed to an official post by Allied Military Government, and Mohr, after helping to arrange the surrender of Kiel, acted in a liaison capacity between the Royal Navy and the German Navy during the process of disarmament.

The agreement that made the book possible was made in Rogge's house overlooking the Elbe. It was an appropriate setting. In the hall was a large scale model of the raider that had for so long pursued her weary and destructive course across the seas of war, but down the river that lapped the lawn a sturdy British freighter made her way to the North Sea, and we, all of us, drank to

PEACE

A. V. SELLWOOD
St Anthony's Cottage
Shirley, Surrey
Christmas 1954

CHAPTER ONE

AT BREMEN

THE BREMEN docker mopped his sweat, then washed down the dust in his mouth with a tin mug of ersatz coffee. He felt he'd earned his break. After an October day spent in unloading the neutral Swedes and Norwegians who, sneaking south along Denmark's coastline, had managed to dodge the grip of the British blockade, a man began to tire, especially when he was over the fifty mark, for the youngsters had gone to the Front to a war that was six weeks old. And all because of the English! The docker spat.

Out on the Polish plains the heel-clicking emissaries of the Wehrmacht were offering the fruits of victory to The Presence. In Cologne the guardians of the people were sweeping up the pamphlets dropped by the Chamberlain Air Force. And in London, so the docker had read, the population had been seized with utter panic, fleeing the cities against the wrath to come. This last snippet of news had puzzled him a bit—he had experience of the English in World War I. But the truth, namely, that they were preoccupied with pasting bits of brown paper over cracks and crevices in windows and doors, or buying by the yard lengths of black cloth for black-out purposes, would have struck him immediately as a Goebbels lie. For the docker, who had stopped one at the Somme in the first lot, could better understand people getting out of the way of something so frighteningly formidable as the Reichsmarschall's air armadas than he could imagine them wasting their time in devising such childish precautions. Machines. Those were the things that won wars today. And a poor devil of a mere man never stood a chance.

Impressed by the thought, the docker took another swallow. Nigger's Sweat they called the stuff in the Navy, but his mates gave it another more picturesque title.

Funny sort of war, this war at sea. The dockyard scene around him would probably look normal enough to a visitor who didn't know the circumstances— winches clattered, cranes swung outward, cargoes hovered over open holds, and every berth was full. The visitor, of course, wouldn't wonder why all this activity was only around the Scandinavians, or query why so many other ships were idle and empty. The docks of Bremen were nearly full—but for the simple reason that most of their occupants were German, unable to resume their trade upon the oceans, silent and helpless, and hopeless as well.

And all because of the English with their solemn talk about the Freedom of the Seas, and their grey stronghold on all that passed thereon from the Channel to the Bergen Straits. THEY were the people who barred Germany's front door. THEY were the people who were keeping stomachs empty.

Although he'd often said that not all of them were bastards, the docker, applying himself again to his Nigger's Sweat, hoped they'd come unstuck this time. Wait and see. The Führer would teach them a lesson yet. . . .

It wasn't often that the foreman found himself in the neighbourhood of the cargo liner *Goldenfels*. Her berth was a bit out of the way and his duty seldom brought him in her direction. Yet it was to the ship, 'stranded' like so many others since 3rd September, that he now turned his eyes, and to the man who strode towards her gangplank.

He had noticed the chap once or twice before. You couldn't help noticing him. Not that there was anything exceptional about his dress—a white silk scarf, a suit obviously well pressed and a heavy overcoat was the

16

accepted 'off-duty' uniform of merchant skippers, although the bowler really was a little old-fashioned. Nor could it have been merely the man's gigantic stature. After all, the foreman topped the stranger's six foot three and had shoulders equally ox-like. Maybe, he thought, it was the voice. He had heard, once, its Prussian harshness relieved by softer cadences, low and slow and full of confidence, the voice of one of the quality.

The foreman sneered. Of course we were all herren now. Everyone was giving themselves airs these days, even the dockers.

He watched the chap approach another of the skeleton crew that had stayed aboard the Fels ship since her furtive arrival. Airs and graces! To the foreman's stupefaction the other fellow slammed his heels down and, as the stranger neared him, whipped his right hand to the peak of his cloth cap, in a meticulous, dazzling naval salute. . . .

Fancy that crazy P.O. being such a damned fool as to salute. What the hell was the good of regular sailors dressing up in civvies, if they couldn't disguise their parade ground manners.

After giving the offender a piece of his mind, Kapitan zur See Bernhard Rogge, doyen of German Naval Yachting circles, late Captain and Commander of the élite German Officers' Sail Training Ship, removed the bowler with relief and placed it on the planks that lay jumbled across what would one day be the mount of the stern 5.9 inch gun. His fingers, capable, square tipped, and immaculately manicured, loosened the irritating silk scarf, and he prepared once more to get to work on his new command.

In the archives of the Berlin Admiralty, archives marked 'Top Secret', the innocent merchantman, *Goldenfels*, had become Ship Sixteen. Rogge smiled a little. Necessary for security reasons, of course, but he intended to re-christen her as soon as possible. A number might be all right for a U-boat, but it was pretty soulless for a ship.

Atlantis . . . that's what he'd call her . . . a name that would distinguish her from an oceanic Pandora's box of concealed torpedoes, guns, and mines, and symbolise something of the mystery and the strangeness of life upon the waters. Thinking it over Rogge felt vaguely pleased.

They'd first allotted him his wartime post when Mr. chamberlain had gone back from Munich promising Peace in Our Time. Then the role had seemed an extremely hypothetical one for chances of conflict between Germany and Britain had appeared remote.

Well, the worst had happened—and to Rogge war with England really was THE worst—and it would be up to him to do his duty. He was at least glad that his job was such that he wouldn't have to keep turning round every five minutes to ask permission to do it. Not that the going was easy. Rogge brooded for a moment. So much to do, so little time to do it. He wondered how Cecil Rhodes would have fared had *he* been placed in command of the first commerce raider to leave the Reich. How would he have dealt with the snags that seemed to surround the project everywhere? His, Rogge's, the dramatic task of attacking British trade in the manner made famous in the first show by the disguised surface raiders, *Wolf, Moewe,* and *Seedler,* yet the opening atmosphere of the drama was almost comic opera.

Not a hint of our intention to use commerce raiders must leak out, they'd said at Seekriegsleitung. So perhaps that was why Bremen Barracks carried a huge hoarding on which, for all to read, was the inscription 'Headquarters for Armed Merchant Cruiser'.

Extraordinary, he reflected, how red tape tied itself into knots. When he'd applied to the Officer's Personnel Branch they said, "What! You want nineteen officers for drowning?"

To get even a bubble sextant he'd been obliged to apply direct to OKM, and modern fire control equipment was refused because, they said comfortingly, there was too strong a possibility that it might be sunk before

18

he had an opportunity of using it! And as for everyday security! Well, Rogge's sense of humour had reasserted itself as he thought of the panic at the dockside when the packing case had split open to reveal a store of tropical helmets.

Still, no doubt about it, security was essential. His main weapon must necessarily be that of disguise. To get out, to break through the screen that the British had placed around the gateways to the outer seas, *Atlantis* must pretend to be what she was not, and once through must be ready to alter her disguise convincingly, and at frequent intervals. Hence the stage props and the 'make-up'! No enemy eye must discern the purpose of Ship Sixteen's furtive transformation into what the Allies were later to call the Nazi Q ship, or, less flatteringly, the Rattlesnake of the Ocean. Hence, also, his annoyance about the salute from the overzealous Petty Officer. Such mistakes must not occur again. Rogge called for his A.D.C. . . .

And that's where I came into it.

No one could call Ship Sixteen a thing of beauty. I realised that from the moment we met. Quite young as they went but a bit too stout for grace, and at the dockside, without her make-up, an untidy sort of slut for a man to trust his life to. As I viewed the chaos of her decks not an anticipatory flicker of the love I was later to feel for her stirred within me and for a moment I wondered why on earth I hadn't stuck to mine-sweeping instead of wangling, via my Regular Navy father's friendship with Rogge, this berth on a high seas raider.

Not that influence alone had got me the job. Rogge was not that type of Captain. It was just that he had seen some future in my reasonable command of languages, and my background of travel in the States, Japan and China. Even the fact that I was an erstwhile Doctor of Philosophy did not necessarily disqualify me from office, as his then A.D.C.—who wasn't keen on the post—was far more academically brilliant, a Professor of Historic Art!

So there we were—the professor recommended by Rogge as a man who could surely be more usefully employed ashore—being posted by a deaf officialdom to a minesweeper, while I, fresh from such hardships, took over a luxurious cabin complete with chintz curtains, soft carpets and radio, plus, had I but known it, the unsought distinction of taking part in what was to be the longest sea voyage in the history of the world.

CHAPTER TWO

WOLF BENEATH THE FLEECE

WE WERE to raid in seas a world away from home. We were to sail against England by way of Greenland and Good Hope. Ship Sixteen, as she was known to Berlin . . . Ship C, as she was classified by British Intelligence . . . or *Atlantis,* as it were, of nine disguised commerce raiders, operating in two Waves.

Rogge sat at his desk, thoughtfully staring at the globe in front of him, his left hand absently cupping his square clean-shaven jaw, his right hand, equally absently, toying with a fountain pen.

The tranquility normally associated with a warship captain's stateroom was not very evident today, and the hammer of pneumatic drills, the clang of hammers, and the infernal shouting and cussing of the dockyard mateys—chosen to help in *Atlantis's* initial conversion without knowing what the devil it was in aid of—were not the best aids for concentration. Yet to Rogge, as he pondered on the future of his command, they formed as much a part of the symphony of the ship as would the crash of the waves against her hull; and were as vocal of her mission as the wild cry of the seagull, the rhythm of the diesels. Rogge longed for the open sea again, but was not so blindly impatient that he could not appreciate the efforts of the shore in assisting him to get there. Although, God knew, nearly 400,000 man-hours, and so far 80 days of labour, should have been sufficient, he wryly reflected, to have equipped a battleship!

Great are the folk of the land
But greater still are the folk of the sea. . . .

For a moment Rogge pondered on the words of the old Hanseatic poem. Through the half-open scuttle he could hear the fussy puffing of a steam train, the jerky clang of the wheels of the goods trucks along the railway lines, and only faintly, melancholy and redolent of his true love, came the wailing of a ship's siren, outward bound. And yet, he thought, we here in Bremen all belong to the sea, are governed by its unseen pull as ships awaiting its tides. On the work they put in on *Atlantis* depended the hour at which the dockers got home to their wives or mistresses; the extent of the pay packets they'd take with them, the food they'd eat and the booze they'd drink; all these, the normal domestic needs, would be met by their labours on the ship. But later? The ship, unseen by them and probably forgotten, would exert an even greater influence, for the bombs that would one day menace them—Rogge had few illusions regarding Goering's promises—would rely on sea transport to provide their component parts, and the engines of the enemy aircraft must draw their life blood from the tankers just as the pilots relied on the freighters for their bread. All that Britain could use to hurt Germany had first to travel by the ocean highways, and it was his, Rogge's task, to do his best to lay obstacles in the way. To *Atlantis* the destruction of enemy shipping was only a subsidiary. Her main purpose was to launch sporadic and widely separated attacks, designed to cause diversions and delays, and force the hard-pressed British fleet to spread itself further afield in hunt and escort work.

A man in overalls peered around the door, mumbled an apologetic 'Sorry, sir', and disappeared again. Rogge sighed. A carpenter no doubt. People were always getting themselves compromisingly lost aboard this ship of a thousand secrets and he couldn't help thinking that, despite all the security precautions, some of them must by now have made a pretty shrewd guess regarding the purpose of the ex-*Goldenfels* metamorphosis.

Kapitan zur See Bernhard Rogge switched from a disturbing mental survey of the decks outside—that conglomeration of confusion of fittings and cargo, of greasy swabs and red lead, of paint pots and stage props—and concentrated again on the task of compiling his diary. He grinned as he remembered young Mohr's remarks about his ship's appearance. What had he called her? A bit of a slut? Carefully, neatly and purposefully, the hand with the officer's signet ring upon it completed the day's entry with the words, 'We will be proud of our ship by the time she has put her make-up on. But like so many ladies she takes an interminable time preparing'.

Peace has been described as one and indivisible. A similar definition can be applied to the seas at war. An action fought in the Indian Ocean may affect events in the North Sea or the Arctic. An attacker at large off East Africa can effect the diversion of important forces from the Western Approaches. For every ship sunk by a single raider in the course of hours, scores of others may be re-routed or harbour bound for weeks, and the decisions of armies battling from Libya to the Volga can be governed by the fortunes of humble merchantmen to whose existence they have hardly given a thought.

Although most naval planners in the thirties believed the AMC* had had its day, Rogge backed the contrary minority, arguing that the increased threat from the air would be countered by the skilful employment of disguise; and that the advantages bestowed upon the raider by the diesel engine more than compensated for the enemy's increased facilities for detection. He used to point out to us that while in World War One the *Kaiser Wilhelm der Grosse* had an endurance of less than three weeks, *Atlantis,* on diesels, would be able to cover 60,-

* Armed Merchant Cruiser.

23

000 miles without refuelling. Therefore, he said, not only was the modern raider far less fettered in her movement by considerations of where and how she could be supplied, but she would no longer have to call on tankers or colliers to risk destruction or capture in ministering to her needs.

Although quite obviously all his professional inclinations were opposed to the mincing machine type of battle that was later to be waged between the U-boats and the convoys in the North Atlantic, Rogge's belief in raider action was based on far stranger grounds than conservative prejudice. The U-boats of 1939 might strike at the well-guarded heart of the enemy, but we alone could reach far enough to attack the less protected arteries.

In this kind of diversionary activity the attacker holds most of the trumps. His choice, the hunter's choice, of place and time. His also the advantage of knowing that almost every ship he meets will be an enemy, while the forces that would track him down must search for one ship among many, treat everyone as suspect.

Finally, in case you should still wonder, as to why we, at the commencement of this total war, should have felt so confident about the future of a 17-knot merchant ship equipped with 40-year-old guns, let me quote our Commander himself . . . Said Rogge, concluding a wardroom discussion about the sort of modern techniques we might expect our enemies to use: 'At the risk of being trite, gentlemen, I would emphasize that the ocean is vast, and that for several hours out of twenty-four the ocean is dark!"

'And that, sir,' I said, as I wearily laid down the telephone, and flung my pencil on the desk, 'constitutes the fourteenth call to our warlords, and the third day of an all-out effort to coax a mere four flare pistols out of them! And all, mark you, because they don't see why we need them. They're extra to their worships' fitting-out list, and that, as far as the desk boys are concerned, is that!'

Rogge smiled. 'Let's see,' he mused. 'I suppose you really have gone through all the appropriate motions?'

'Sir,' I said hotly. 'I've telephoned Berlin. I've applied direct to the Admiralty. I've been through to Coastal Command, Baltic, and even the Admiral commanding Naval Dockyards. Wherever I go they refer me to somebody else. Doesn't anyone appreciate we might need the flare pistols for our prizes!"

'Prizes? Maybe they think we're being over optimistic,' said Rogge drily.

Well, we got our pistols—eventually—all four of them! But, before officialdom could finally be persuaded to entrust us with such supremely valuable material, a report on the situation was actually sent to the C.-in-C., Grand Admiral Raeder himself.

As the days passed our patience began to wear thin at the queer goings on of the shore, and we began to realise that however conspicuously the much vaunted Nazi efficiency might have shown itself elsewhere, it was by no means evident in OUR sphere—the preparation for the merchant cruiser aspect of the war at sea. Despite the admirable theory of our Operational Planning Division, the divergence of opinion between those who really believed the AMC had a future and those who did not was reflected in the half measures with which the Raider project was surrounded, and contrary alike to Allied belief and our own anticipations the Raider Fleet in September 1939 existed only ON PAPER. The strategical theory had been approved, and the men had been earmarked to carry it out. But that was all. Our crews had been forced to spend weeks of idleness before the ships were even brought to the dockside, and although, pre-war, a secret Government subsidy had been paid to the Fels line it had covered only very minor items such as the strengthening of the deck for gun mounts. We were impatient at the fact that it took ninety days for *Atlantis* to be fitted out. Yet this—thanks to Rogge's establishing good relationships with the yard engineers over many a sly glass—was a record! One raider was actually 18 months preparing . . .

Five hundred books for the ship's library. That was all I wanted. Five hundred miserable books.

The 'Silver Ringer' was genuinely puzzled. 'Books? For a ship's library? But surely your crew won't have time for READING? . . .'

Iron Crosses—these at least were in plentiful supply. Categorically Rogge turned down the suggestion that he should take aboard a stock of them for 'distribution' when the occasion arose.

Coldly he retorted, 'Let us get out to sea first, and wait for the occasion to arise.'

Men who would be good comrades, and fit to bear the stresses and strains of a long and hazardous voyage; these were what we needed. So the ships' captains and Admiralty clerks alike conspired to send us the most disreputable and most easily expendable of human material.

'Bad characters . . . reprieved criminals . . . inefficient. I won't have them!' And Rogge didn't.

But it took a violent demonstration on his part before eventually we got our team together.

On the lighter side I soon discovered that fitting out a man-of-war for what we still had the temerity to pretend might yet prove a somewhat protracted cruise, had aesthetic aspects that the books of reference had ignored, aspects such as the most suitable type of picture to adorn a wardroom wall, a matter upon which there was wide divergence of opinion. Irritatedly we formed a committee to decide.

Said one officer firmly, 'No pictures of home. No trees. No meadows. No mountains. It's bound to make us homesick.'

'Right,' I said. 'Then what about some pin-ups?'

'No girls, for Christ's sake,' protested the Admin. Officer. 'You know what that's going to cause. No. Definitely no girls!'

'Very well,' I said at length, after we'd compromised on a fine sea piece portraying a full rig sailing ship, 'We'll see if the Commander approves this.' And feeling rather proud of our choice I showed it to Rogge.

The crowning blow!

'Good God,' he exploded. 'I can't have THAT aboard my ship. The topgallant stay sails are braced the wrong way!'

This rejection of one idea which had been unanimously approved depressed the committee sufficiently for them to pass the job of selection on to me. So I brought a piece from Marc—'The Red Horses'. As regards the ship, my choice was a happy one, subsequently evoking plenty of intelligent interest (and comment!) from both visitors and captives, but in Germany itself the picture was classified as 'degraded art' and finally banned.

The pictorial decoration of the seaman's quarters created infinitely less controversy.

'Flowers!' decided Rogge firmly. 'Flowers are definitely the best thing for the seamen. Flowers, after all, are so decidedly neutral!'

So flowers it had to be.

Meanwhile we continued with our dock-side charade.

'No uniforms will be worn,' Rogge had warned us at the start. 'Officers and men alike will dress in civilians. Nor will saluting be permitted, for although the dockers must realise something of what we're up to it is important that they should know nothing at least of the identity of the Commander, or of the officers, or the number of personnel we are expected to carry.'

I don't suppose we fooled everybody—you can't get away with it all the time—but in the main the precautions were wise and served their purpose. Some of the crew, entering into the game with enthusiasm, selected the most extravagant of styles and I, for my part, was only too pleased to feel again the unaccustomed freedom of my favourite suit. But Rogge's bowler amused us all until, when taxed about it, he retorted: 'Observe the average captain of a sailing ship. You will notice he invariably wears a bowler . . .'

'But this is no sailing ship?'

'No,' agreed our captain, 'but the theory is the same—the theory of the hat, I mean. The bowler's brim

27

creates little resistance to the wind. It is streamlined.
AND YOU NEVER KNOW WHEN YOU MAY BE ONLY TOO
GRATEFUL TO RUN!'

We were to sail against England, and most of us felt
we'd been at anchor too long . . . but not until 28th
December did we leave Bremen, when we received orders to proceed on the first lap of our journey, a short
run to Kiel, for final adjustments to our ship's make-up,
and the reception of naval stores and ammunition for
the battles ahead.

A dark night, a sudden jolt, a gentle stagger, and then
the engine's silence, followed in seconds by the maledic-
tions of nineteen humiliated officers. The blasted ship
had run aground!

Atlantis, the raider in a hurry, the cruiser that could
scarcely wait to get out to the big, big sea, was ignomi-
niously stuck in the mud of the Weser, with her discomfiture the subject of comment, usually rude, from every
quarter. It had not been Rogge's fault; the ship had
been under the control of a pilot at the time; a pilot who
did not know the new lights. But, regardless of where
the responsibility lay, the fact remained that this was
scarcely the sort of start we had envisaged, and naturally we were extremely depressed.

Fehler, our lean, impulsive demolition expert, had, of
course, to chip in with a word of cheer.

'What are you all worrying about? It's a good omen.
Don't you remember that *Wolf* went aground at the
start of her career, and look what a wonderful career
she had.'

It wasn't a happy analogy. The bald head of Kamenz,
our veteran Navigation Officer, reddened with anger.

'Yes, imbecile,' he said, 'and look what happened to
her captain. They FIRED him!'

This sombre reflection put the seal on our unhappiness. The parallel was so horribly close. *Wolf*'s accident, at the mouth of the Elbe, had also not been due to
any error on the part of her commander. Nevertheless

the Admiralty of the day dismissed him with the phrase, 'It is not enough for a raider captain to have skill. He must have luck as well.'

If that sort of thing happened in 1914 then what could we expect in 1939, we pondered, from a Führer who believed in the stars!

The thought of losing our Captain gave us no pleasure. Like many other big men Rogge was big in character, and had little use for the hysteria of the Nazis ashore. He was a man possessed of all the old Prussian virtues, and perhaps on account of his religious upbringing, few of the new Prussian vices. A rigid disciplinarian, he never bullied. By birth and breeding highly conscious of his position, he accepted with his rank the responsibilities of command. Already we had seen for ourselves that he was both just and efficient, and that he, in return for our loyalty, gave us all of his generously, unquestioningly. We were HIS men, and we spent six miserable hours considering the undesirability of contemplating possible successors, before the rising tide carried *Atlantis* free.

But nearly a week passed by before it became obvious to us that somehow the accident had been excused.

Rogge's star, it seemed, remained in the ascendant!

CHAPTER THREE

'WARE OUR PROPELLERS

It was the month of March . . . March, 1940. It was the third week of the month, and a day of bitter cold. The Kiel Canal was frozen; the shore a ridge of white. It was the last month of a winter that had seemed without ending, the prelude to the War's first spring. The rest of the world had sixteen days left, just sixteen days before the thunder of conflict, breaking the silence of the phony war, presaged the massacres to come.

March 22nd . . . A Naval Depot ship appeared off the Elbe; twin funnelled, a hull of grey, guns fore and aft, ensign at stern.

March 24th . . . A Norwegian freighter lay anchored off Suederpiep; single funnelled, hull of green, superstructure of glittering white, and flying a yellow quarantine flag.

April 9th . . . Through the Bergen-Shetland Neck ploughed the Russian Fleet Auxiliary, *Kim*; hammer and sickle on bridge, red star on Number Two hatch, and over her counter the inscription CTEPETANTECG BHHTCB—Keep Clear of Our Propellers!

We hoped the Royal Navy would take the hint!

For only we, and the men who had sent us, knew that the German, the Norwegian, and the Russian Auxiliary were all one and the same ship—the Raider *Atlantis*; now out to break the grey blockade, and driving to the north on the first lap of her ocean-raiding mission.

It was back in Kiel that we had perfected the details of our masquerade; had heaped the sheep's clothing over the old wolf's back, and hidden her teeth behind a three-ply mask.

Six 5.9 inch guns . . . four torpedo tubes . . . cannons . . . machine guns . . . and scores of mines.

These were the weapons of our raider, the 'ironmongery' that the 8,000 ton freighter would not only have to carry but conceal, and not only conceal but have ready to hand, ready for use in seconds.

But how to get out . . . Rogge had always said that would be the worst problem of our cruise, the major headache. Give him elbow room on the outer seas— 'There's plenty of elbow room, aircraft or no'—and we'd do a good job, whatever its ending. But at the start, the break out, our wits must be at their sharpest, and our disguise impeccable. It was around our own shores that the enemy was strongest, an intelligent enemy at that, wary and wise in the ways of the sea, and with his listening posts in Germany as well as upon the ocean. The start. That was the problem, entailing as it did our passing through waters heavily patrolled both by ships and aircraft, while even in base itself we would be exposed to enemy air reconnaissance. Once caught in the North Sea and there could be but one ending, an abrupt ending to all our hopes and toil, for, whereas the battle wagons had an odds-on chance, we would have no chance at all. Therefore, said Rogge the methodical, our weapon must be disguise. We must 'imitate the cunning of the serpent'—or, at least, the wolf in Red Riding Hood.

The sailor in the dungarees laboriously finished painting a name and address on the large workmanlike crate. Straightening up he glanced for a moment at his handiwork with the satisfaction of a craftsman at a job well done, then pasted a huge label across the box.

I watched him with interest.

'Well, sir,' he said with a grin. 'The label's honest enough anyway!'

Contents of the crate . . .? A heavy machine gun

31

ready to go into action at the moment the wooden sides collapsed.

Inscription on the label . . . ? PERISHABLE!

What an incredible pantomime, I thought. And here am I, a player!

The deck was a dummy, a 'lid' to conceal four 5.9's from the air; the hull, at this point, was an extra, a 'wall' to conceal them from the sea. Not even from the quayside could you detect without effort the joints of the flaps behind which they lurked; yet, operated on the counterweight system, these masks could roar up within two seconds, and the guns themselves could open fire in five.

So much for the forrard battery. Aft a huge packing case labelled 'Industrial Machinery' concealed the fifth of our 'heavies', while the sixth had been transformed into a 'crane'. It is astonishing, truly astonishing, what you can do with a little wire . . . and paint . . . and imagination . . . and attention to detail! That 'crane' really looked a crane. That 'packing case' had the name of the consignee and all the other details usually expected by business etiquette most prominently displayed.

Yes, the fleece of *Atlantis* was really pretty thick—from the range finder disguised as a water tank to the hold where a seaplane hid—and it would have needed a shrewd eye, a vivid imagination and a 'ringside seat' to detect that our masts—so normal and 'Merchant Navy' against the driving sky—served also as foundations for observation posts, for periscopic spires from which our lookouts, hanging precariously on rope cradles, could sight an enemy over 20 miles away.

So did *Atlantis* gain the advantage of seeing without being seen; of stalking her quarry, or dodging her hunters, while keeping herself beneath the horizon's rim.

Fragments from my diary:

January 10th . . . *Goldenfels* died long ago and we are now a very respectable Depot Ship; extremely professional as we lie greyly in the Navy Yard at Kiel. To remove all traces of our mercantile past we have acquired a second funnel, compounded of wood and canvas, and some quite convincing 'guns'. To make up for the 'genuine article,' which we do not show, these home-made timber masterpieces bristle prominently, while to conceal our plan to relapse into a 'civilian' role the 'packing cases' have been themselves disguised. It's hard at times to realise in these transformation scenes just what is reality and what is fiction.

January . . . Admiral Inspector General of Artillery visits us. Much impressed. Says he couldn't distinguish us from the 'real thing'. No, not even at ten yards! Gratified, but wonder if perhaps this praise is not just a *little* exaggerated. Astonishing how heavy Navy searchlights on crossbeams can give a ship an important warlike appearance.

January 31st . . . We are much honoured. The Grand Admiral (Raeder) himself has travelled from Berlin to wish us goodbye. Presents us with de-luxe edition of Operational Orders. All the 'trimmings'. Expensive red leather, deep gold block, and special for us. But note prominent display afforded four words therein. YOU WILL NEVER SURRENDER.

February 28th . . . C.-in-C.'s goodbyes on Jan. 31st rather premature I feel. We're still here. We seem likely to remain so. 'And what did *you* do for the Fatherland?' . . . 'Oh, just froze my feet in Kiel!'

The worst of the winter had fallen hard upon *Atlantis,* mocking the efforts of her crew and the strategy of her captain. Rogge, anxious originally to have been out in November when he could have employed the seasonable darkness of the north to advantage, chafed impatiently at the delays that Nature had added to the backlog of frustrations created by Authority.

The ice clasped the hull of the ship with broken jagged fingers, hung from the rigging and superstructure like a myriad stalactites, lay like a gleaming slide along the quay. Rogge began to hate the sight of the flat, monotonous shore line, the bleak jetty piled with snow, the black and now silent cranes alongside.

Glittering white and blue in the northern sun, the ice burned and seared the hands of the crew as they chipped and scraped the cordage free, sending shivering echoes across the frozen bay. The winds of the east burst upon the ship, winds laden with snow and sleet; buffeting the crew as they trod through the slush of the decks, reaching with frosty fingers to their bones. Nothing seemed to go right, and everything seemed to go wrong. The cold froze the torpedo valves, and the ice, preventing the towing of targets, made gunnery trials impossible. Already, reflected Rogge, there had been leakages in security, and there were times when one's patience reached breaking point when confronted by the pomposities and smug indifferences of certain of the comfortably installed pen-pushing warriors ashore.

It was necessary, said Rogge, that *Atlantis* should have a telephone. I agreed, enthusiastically. The nearest box was far from the ship, and whenever we wanted to make an official telephone call, which was several times a day, the merchant raider's representative (usually me!) had to sprint 200 yards through the snow and humbly join a queue.

But when I called on the Silver Ringer—the glorified civil servant installed in the heated office block on top of the jetty—with a polite request that *Atlantis* be permitted to borrow one of his (20!) telephones, you would have thought the world was coming to an end.

'Impossible. Absolutely impossible,' he said. 'My telephones are needed for Very Important Work.'

'But the one we're suggesting is down in the cellar,' I protested. 'The cellar housing the central heating plant. Surely . . .?'

The Silver Ringer bristled fatly. 'The telephones are under my command,' he said pompously. 'You will have to make your own arrangements, Lieutenant.'

I did! . . . Our complaint, direct to the Admiralty, resulted in my fat acquaintance receiving the shock of his life. Berlin came on the line to him . . . We got our phone!

During six weeks of our stay at Kiel I received 285 top secret documents to study, acknowledge, comment on or reply to. The Paper War was certainly waged with great enthusiasm.

The sequence of disguises to be adopted for our break out had been fixed many weeks in advance. We had 'buried' the *Goldenfels* by now we hoped, but there was always the possibility that enemy agents might make a 'routine' report on the departure of the Depot Ship from Kiel and two and two might be put together. Accordingly we decided to stage a double bluff. *Atlantis* would show herself, as the Depot Ship, off various parts of the coastline, before emerging, north of Cuxhaven, in her Norwegian role. But even while she waited for the final word to go she would be dictating a string of Naval signals to Kiel still using the code signs of the Depot Ship! So by asking tugs to stand by after trials, and by requesting dockyard facilities for repairs, by reporting as due for passage through the Canal at such and such a date, and by conducting, in short, the sort of portentous conversation about nothing that is the characteristic of a vessel engaged on routine operations, we aimed not only at persuading the British that the Depot Ship's return was imminent, but also at guarding against the unlikely, but by no means impossible, risk of a 'leak' arising from our own Naval Authorities. Presupposing the success of such manoeuvres, however, there was still the danger that the weather might force us to spend several days off the coast, in which case the enemy might become sufficiently interested in the 'Norwegian' to watch her re-appearance in the North. What to do? And what should be our final guise on the crucial outward run? Rogge's decision to adopt a Russian rig astounded us all by its audacity.

The Russians, he reasoned, were always the most secretive of people, and so much in the habit of moving their ships unannounced and how they chose that there was always confusion in identifying them. Similarly, he felt, the friction then existing between Great Britain and

35

the Soviet made it unlikely that a British warship would take the responsibility of using really violent measures to stop, on suspicion alone, what purported to be her Russian opposite number. But there were other advantages as well, said Rogge.

'The ports of the Soviet are free of prying eyes, so the British are not likely to be able to pin-point the whereabouts of the "genuine article", and then, of course, there is the language barrier . . .'

Rogge grinned 'I wonder just how many Englishmen have mastered the energy to master THAT!'

Once we had realised its implications, we greeted the scheme with enthusiasm, but Berlin's sanction was given with misgivings, for at that time the Wilhelmstrasse was very anxious to avoid irritating Russian tempers, and when Rogge asked for a Soviet Naval Ensign they agreed only on condition that the transaction was conducted in absolute secrecy. THE FLAG, they planned, would be carefully wrapped in vast quantities of brown paper, secured by masses of string, addressed to the Chief of Staff, High Command, Baltic (an Admiral), and then handed over only to Rogge in person.

This arrangement suited our captain very well, for Rogge—for reasons less political—was equally anxious to avoid publicity. Yet when, very tardily, the ensign finally arrived it came through the normal ship's post, and was discovered to have been opened on the way!

For all their elaborate planning, Naval Intelligence had omitted a vital detail. They had actually forgotten to inform the Chief of Staff.

Said the latter to an enquiring Rogge, 'Oh, that Russian flag? Yes, it came in a parcel addressed to me, so I opened it, of course. But it all seemed so unimportant that I passed it on to the mail office for delivery. Incidentally, just why are you collecting Russian flags . . . ?'

As Rogge returned from the Admiralty he noticed, with inward amusement, how desperately his young officers were trying to suppress their curiosity as to what had transpired. Well, he'd keep the suspense alive for a little longer yet. It was all good training in the gentle art of camouflage.

But the time came when even he found it difficult to keep his tone casual and laconic.

'Well, gentlemen,' he said, 'it is impossible for us to carry out gunnery trials in the frozen Baltic. Instead, we will have to conduct them in the North Sea!'

The NORTH SEA . . . !

There was a pause . . . You could almost hear the tick-tock of their brainboxes. The North Sea? Was this merely to be an exercise? Or were we going on our way? But Rogge said no more.

A few days later . . .

'Sailing on Monday' . . . the buzz went round the ship . . .

'Monday? But that's the thirteenth!'

Rogge grinned. 'Don't worry,' he said. 'I've obtained permission from the Admiralty to weigh anchor at 23.55 on the 12th!'

For us, no Battle Ensign streaming in the breeze; no quayside kisses; no half-said farewells; no smiles, no tears, no cheers, no fuss . . . The *Atlantis* odyssey began with a crawl; just a slow, monotonous crawl; her path preceded by the ancient *Hessen; Hessen,* the pre-dreadnought; *Hessen* of the Kaiser's youth: *Hessen,* now employed to clear a path through the ice . . . and going about her task with the contemptuous dignity of a master forced to serve an upstart slave.

Meanwhile, back in the Navy building at Kiel, my father eyed rather sadly a pile of mail and parcels which lay stacked in the room next to his office.

To conceal the identity and date of departure of our ship we had left a rating behind, with the specific task of going daily to the Fleet Mail Office to collect the post. Then he dumped the lot in that hitherto unused 'back room'.

My father, a parent who DID know what was in the wind, often used to regard this evidence of the love and labour of those who did not, and he told me afterwards that the sight of it had struck him as one of the most pathetic sidelights of the war. For little did the loving ones who wrote and waited in vain for answers know of their wasted effort, or of how far away were the address-ees.

Atlantis entered the North Sea to find that the tugs originally detailed to tow her targets had been diverted on a melancholy and ultimately fruitless attempt to rescue the crew of a U-boat sunk by a British aircraft only a few hours before.

This forbidding welcome was in keeping with the date (the Fatal Thirteenth!) and the superstitious were not unduly surprised when the tug eventually offered us as substitute proved too small to tow the targets at speed against the current of the Jade.

As a result of such difficulties our gunnery exercises proved by no means as successful as we had expected, although on their last night we enjoyed the malevolent satisfaction and exceptional distinction of creating a general coast alarm; our use of tracer—the type that ejects a flare above the target—being so enthusiastic that Berlin was informed, 'Very heavy naval engagement taking place . . . possible the BRITISH FLEET IS ATTACKING IN FORCE!'

But all was well again by the 19th. Until then we had not known whether or not our move was to provide a prelude to the dramatic or merely be climaxed by a re-turn to Kiel but our doubts and fears were quickly scotched. Said Rogge: 'Permission has been granted me to make ready to break out.'

So this was it, the moment we'd been working for through seven weary months, the final prelude to the word to GO. Within the hour, *Atlantis,* her crew's morale again at peak, set course for Suederpiep, to make-up in colours that would be suitable for her Norwegian role and, with only slight additions, the Russian part she would play in the North.

38

Suederpiep would be so quiet at this time of year . . . no visitors . . . plenty of privacy . . . or so we hoped . . .

March 23rd. When night fell and the cold ice-laden wind came whistling over the sea and across the dykes and flats; when the good folk ashore went gratefully to bed and the flickering, distant searchlights wandered palely across the heavy-hanging sky, a certain very ordinary-looking 'Naval Depot Ship' commenced some very extraordinary manoeuvres . . .

'All right, you perishing artists. Look alive there! Slap it on thick, and slap it on fast . . . !'

Out came the paint and the paint brushes. Down the trim sides went the scaffolding and joists. And up from the snug crew quarters came the shivering, complaining working parties, cursing the bite of the weather, and less audibly, the C.P.O.'s who goaded them to their tasks.

'Double up, there!'

'Look alive . . . !'

'You over there . . . who do you think you are? You've no time to be as fancy as Mister Bloody Rembrandt. Slap it on thick, and slap it fast I said!'

So throughout the night, beneath the cautious, shaded, uncanny, low burning lights, the men, hands raw and numb, swung from cradles around the hull, or swarmed up masts and rigging bestowing on the brushes their malicious confidences and the impact of their muffled blasphemies; the general chaos in which they worked belying the very real efficiency that, within hours, would make the 'rush job' a success.

Among these, the suffering, self-pitying 'handmaidens' of the ship, was one called Hell. And, at the moment he felt like the English equivalent of his name. An artist, and possessed of all of an artist's sensitivity—he recoiled from the coarseness of the task as much as he wilted beneath the language of his fellows.

'My God,' he thought. 'So THIS is the glory of war! So THIS is the poetry of battle!' For a second Hell looked back over a vista of shattered, romantic dreams, and then, muffled to the ears, his taskmaster bawled, 'Get off your bloody back . . . Mister . . . Michael . . . Angelo . . . YOU haven't got seven years to admire your ruddy canvas!'

A dutiful titter arose from some of the men around him. Savagely Hell thrust the clumsy vulgar brush into the enormous pot containing the sticky mess these Philistines called paint. His slender fingers ached with cold, and they were blistered before the night was out.

No visitors at Suederpiep . . . except, of course, I reflected, for that infernal British aircraft. But even he had gone on his way without paying us much attention (maybe he had submarines on his mind?) and now we were fortunate again for the fog, swirling up from the still, black waters, hung upon us like a grey-green blanket, shrouding us in a protective gloom that enabled the crew to get busy on lowering the dummy funnel—the final adjustment for our Norwegian rig.

The skipper of the fishing trawler jammed the helm hard over as out of the fog loomed a black and menacing silhouette.

'What the hell's that? And what the hell's she playing at?' he bawled to the mate, then the trawler's bows swung round and the stranger dropped back into the murk like the ghostly Flying Dutchman itself.

But the skipper was not the only man in the fishing fleet to sight the fog-bound ship that had lain so silently in its path, for, five minutes after his blasphemies had died down, the mist suddenly, unexpectedly, lifted revealing *Atlantis* to all—*Atlantis* caught like a player betrayed by the curtain's premature lift!

'Strange. Very strange indeed,' said the fishermen still talking it over when eventually they reached the shore.

'Did you notice the funnel, the ship's second funnel? What the devil was wrong?

'Yes. And did you notice the size of her crew! That smokestack was swarming with 'em . . .'

The fishermen were puzzled. For when they had come along to offer their help a Navy launch had come tearing up in a fine old lather and sent them packing . . . !

Suederpiep was so secluded at this time of the year . . . or so we'd hoped . . .

'A close shave,' said one of the seamen back aboard *Atlantis*. 'Wonder what sort of a story they'll take back with them?'

We soon found out! Our next visitor was the Cuxhaven lifeboat! But by the time she arrived we were Norwegian; very disconsolately Norwegian; and lying 'under arrest' with our quarantine flag limply—but prominently—displayed, and our escort launch simulating the duties of a 'policeman'.

The picture was not an unusual one; not off these coasts in wartime. The Norwegian had obviously been stopped and searched. She had been carrying timber for England—the lifeboatmen agreed on that. But where, just WHERE was the two-funnelled ship in distress of which the fishermen had been talking? Oh well, they shrugged, when they got back to base they'd give a hint or two about the effect of Schnapps and fog on some folk's imagination! So home they went.

The lifeboat crew were at least partly correct in their assessment of one aspect of the situation, for we were certainly carrying timber, though NOT for England.

Ours was the timber of the dummy guns, now dismantled and safely stowed until, in the months to come, they should emerge in diverse guises, shaped and fashioned according to the scene-shifter's whim and the vagaries of his script.

It was the month of April, April 1940. It was the first week of the month, and a night of heavy fog. The waters of the North Sea were troubled, and a bitter wind blew from the land. It was the start of a voyage that was to carry us the equivalent of over four times round the

41

world. It was the start of the most damaging and far-reaching sea raid in human history. For nearly two years we were to know no home but our ship. For nearly two years we were to bear with the caprices of our friend, and enemy, the sea.

Below, the radio switched to a fierce, provocative Marching Song; shouted, staccato, exhilarating, sending a secret shudder down one's spine. But on deck the fog wreathed the masts and superstructure, moist and clinging, and cold, while the silent men moved like ghosts among the shadows.

No harbour lights to blink our ship farewell . . . no distant necklace gleaming from the land . . . the symphonic accompaniment to the start of our adventures was the pulse of our progress through the water, the melancholy, distant braying of the foghorns of other wanderers.

We sailed on 1st April. We sailed on All Fool's Day.

CHAPTER FOUR

RUNNING THE GAUNTLET

INTO THE trough she plunged, straining and shuddering like a dog in a fit. Up on the crest she rose, shaking the waters free like a dog from a swim, and showering the surface with a cascade of glittering, crackling globules of ice and foam.

We were out of the minefield gap; we were driving through the drizzle and the murk; our eyes straining at the skyline for the smudge that could be a foe; our ears deafened by the pounding of the wind, and our hands stiff, unreal. Up on the bridge the odd mug of tea became a thing of unimaginable luxury, setting our flesh a-tingle with its welcome warmth as we bunched together, oddly excited, despite our discomfiture, by the Wagnerian thunder of the seas and the winds, and the violence of the roaring waters strange after so long a sojourn on the land.

There were three main points of danger in our path . . . The Gap—the channel through the gigantic minefield that now reached from the Frisians to the north; the Neck—the narrowest stretch of the sea between Norway and the British Isles; the Denmark Strait—the entrance to the North Atlantic, that mist-shrouded passage between Iceland and the Greenland Ice Pack. We would be Running the Gauntlet, for British submarines had an awkward habit of lurking outside the 'gaps'; British cruisers exerted their main pressure in The Neck; British auxiliary cruisers patrolled the Strait; and British aircraft spread their web out from the Shetlands.

For our first lap—the Gap—we were impressively

accompanied by a torpedo-boat escort to shield us from attackers from the depths, and by fighter patrols to guard us from the menace of the skies. But afterwards? We would be provided with a U-boat for close escort, and a Do.26 seaplane, so they promised, would fly a reconnaissance up the North Sea. It was the best the Admiralty could do and we were honoured by their interest. But in the long run, as Rogge said, 'It all depended on us. And luck, of course—Raider Luck— *Atlantis* Luck.'

'And the last,' he added, 'is bound to be good!'

'Somebody will sleep soundly ashore tonight,' grunted Kamenz sourly as our escort, having completed their 'delivery' turned away, and, with the roaring sea behind them, tore home like a pack of youngsters racing back from school.

'Well. What are you bleating about?' laughed one of us. 'You know you'd never swap.'

And Kamenz, meditating on the first few hours of our mission, and the indescribable sense of relief that had swept over him as *Atlantis* ploughed to the open sea, had to admit quite secretly that he wouldn't.

For this, and this alone—the surface raider business—was what we'd signed for. Owing to security restrictions we had enjoyed all too few of the amenities of the shore to be unduly fond of it, and indeed our major sensation, in these, the first hours of our mission, had been one of relief, an indescribable sense of freedom sweeping over us, and even the regrets for the au revoirs unsaid, the pangs for leave-taking unmade, were temporarily forgotten in the tempo of this, the start of our new life upon the ocean.

Come back though they would . . . haunting . . . exacting . . . as things remembered, but to hurt through the long nights ahead, through our half incredulous dreams, all these, our 'yesterdays' we left behind us on that April Fool's Day, their echoes drowned, yet struggling still for hearing; confused as our own voices in the increasing whipping of the wind and the rhythm of the screws that, churning the water into foam, now drove us willy-nilly to the North. . . .

'There it is . . . ! Red. Forty-five, sir,' said the obliging signalman.

Drifting and spherical, black and menacing, the mine rose high on the wind-swept wavetops; the horns on its surface and the slime and rust around them giving it the appearance of some grotesque creation of the depths.

We were to see several of these unwanted intruders before we finished our drive to the north, but this was our first day out, and the monster, running with foam as it bobbed up and down only forty yards away, was very much a novelty. A group of ratings gathered to have a look, or rather a 'close up'.

'Obviously British,' said one young seaman knowledgeably, his voice shriller and louder than usual either through excitement or the desire to impress.

'Son,' said the older sailor heavily. 'It doesn't matter a damn. If it was born in the Ruhr and flew the Swastika on top it'd kill you just the same . . .'

Came evening and an excitement of a different nature.

'Mastheads in sight!'

Faint in the gathering dusk towards the Norwegian shore we discerned the outline of three small vessels, all sticking very close together.

'Trawlers,' said Rogge. 'But I don't like the look of them. No, not one little bit.'

Gradually they dropped out of sight, but not out of hearing, for Helmle, the wireless operator, reported to us, with evident delight in providing a sensation, 'The trawlers are sending on W/T, sir.'

What were they saying? We never knew. For the message from the peaceful trawlers was going out in BRITISH NAVAL CODE.

My diary for the period refers, I notice, to 'A somewhat uneasy night!'

Astern, the escort U-boat ran awash, her conning tower swaying like a huge cork, the insignia on her sides, when seen, bows on, winking through the spray like a skeleton's eye, and her exhaust pushing upwards clouds of smoke.

Hartmann, this raffish craft's Commander, was feeling pretty sour, and eyed with a certain truculence the lumbering wide girthed mercantile matron it was his duty to chaperone. What an end to a career that had promised so well. What a tedious last mission before moving to the Baltic as Instructor and Flotilla Leader (Training). Hartmann glowered. He had wanted to sink just a few more tons before taking up this non-operational assignment; just a few more miserable tons; just sufficient for him to obtain the Knight's Cross. Until *Atlantis*, that coveted award was almost within his grasp and his record as a ruthless and efficient U-boatman was so well known in submarine circles that he'd felt he was expected to climax his career with spectacular success. Bitterly he regarded the slim pencil of grey awash below the conning tower. Well. He was out of his element, and U-37 was out of hers, each deprived of the liberty of the hunter, driven up from their natural environments of the depths, forced to endure the discomforts of what, he had no doubt, would be a perfectly bloody sea. Not that he would have felt quite so aggrieved had he believed in U-37's ability to be really effective in the event of somebody taking a poke at Ship Sixteen. But he had few illusions. If the weather turned out to be as filthy as he feared, U-37 in a scrap would be about as much use as an outsize whale. It was all too bad.

The storm fell upon *Atlantis* as she was nearing the 'bottleneck' of the Shetlands-Bergen area. Rogge had planned to be out of this unhealthy area by dawn but now saw no hope of maintaining his schedule—not in company with a U-boat labouring against a Force Ten gale.

So he decided to dispense with her protection and sent the disgruntled, faithful U-37 beneath it all, with a brief signal to rendezvous with us later. But when dawn came the murk had flown, and although the seas still climbed we found ourselves beneath a steel cold sky unflected by any cloud . . .

Rogge read the Intelligence Report. Its substance was to the point . . . Three British cruisers operating in the Neck . . . three auxiliary cruisers beating up and down the Denmark Strait . . . enemy aircraft active . . .

'Well. As long as we don't collide!' he said.

The lookout saw them first—two slender needles of black rising out of the sea to the west.

For a moment he hesitated before warning the ship. It's difficult to hold binoculars steady above a pitching sea and the dawn light and the driving wind makes fools of burning eyes. Riding precariously his cradle at the masthead he looked again. No doubt about it.

"Masthead in sight!' His bawl from his icy isolation came through the telephone line that connected with the bridge.

'Action Stations!'

As the buzzer sounded an excitable, volatile man with fiery temper and teeth that bared frequently as he joked or swore, ceased to fulminate against 'the bastards ashore' and jumped to it. You'd have thought, if you didn't know him, that Kasch, our gunnery officer, was Latin-like in his changeability, too sensitive in his reactions to triumph or setback. Now, short, wiry, and dark visaged, he crouched by the range finder above our heads, his apparent effervescence no longer concealing the fanatical efficiency of an artist.

'All guns manned and ready!'

Only a slight quiver at the tip of his long thin nose, and the pitch of his voice, slightly higher than usual, gave a hint of the emotions aroused within Pfeilsticker, as he took up his role of I/C gunnery communications. When the war had called him from the village classroom local parents had been much distressed. The schoolmaster, their schoolmaster as a humble rating! But Pfeilsticker was happy enough, when off-duty bestirring himself to form study groups among the crew— one mustn't let one's mind go to rust he thought—when on duty welcoming the unexpected such as a moment-like this, calling as it did for the clear thinking demanded of a man of learning.

No, thought Rogge, outwardly unmoved. That red light on the foremast of the leading ship was *decidedly not* a navigation light, and both of the strangers were turning quite suddenly in an obviously concerted move in our direction. A black smudge began to form behind the taller needle—the smudge of a funnel. Rogge had little time to lose and knew it.

'Chief Engineer to the bridge,' he'd ordered, and now Kielhorn, having laboriously climbed the companion ladder, stood beside him, panting a little beneath the double handicap of his bulk and the transition from the engine room heat to the outside cold.

'Well, chief? What can you do for us?'

Kielhorn's round and cheery face puckered wisely, then, in his rich Bavarian accent he answered with slow consideration, 'Sixteen, maybe seventeen knots. Doubt we can do more, sir. But the old tub'll give her best.'

Luck . . . Raider's luck . . . the luck of *Atlantis*. For the double ring on the engine room telegraph preceded, to our surprise, the slow, almost painfully slow, disappearance of the strangers' funnels, the gradual sinking of their mainmasts beneath the horizon as *Atlantis,* without pursuit, ploughed on towards the north.

A lucky squeak. But rather an anti-climax, thought Pfeilsticker, pretending to re-read *The Conquest of Gaul,* but for once finding that the written word had lost its magic, his mind reverting to the stimulus he had experienced during the past hour. The unemotional studious Pfeilsticker was beginning to realise that beneath his calm and tranquil disposition lurked the romantic imagination of a poet.

A lucky squeak? Kasch supposed it was—if the Englanders were regular warships. But if A.M.C.'s . . . ? At the thought of engaging his opposite numbers the clever, logistical Kasch gave place to Kasch the fighter.

Well, thought Rogge, sleepless and tired through the rigours of his watching, it had been a close thing and they were well out of it. The job of *Atlantis* was to break out unobserved and not to fight action that, even if victorious, would lead either to speedy retribution or a precipitate departure home.

It was perhaps fortunate for our peace of mind that, although suspecting that the strangers had boded us no good, we had no idea of the extent of the trouble we had avoided.

Several days before the German invasion the British Government had decided to force Norway to accede to their demands—re the ore ships—by sending a powerful Naval force to mine the Leads, the channel lying between the mainland of Norway and the islands off the coast, and used extensively by ships engaged on trade with Germany. It was the fringe of this force that we had sighted, and as it consisted of a battleship and sixteen destroyers the odds might have been a trifle high!

Lonely Jan Mayen Island lay to our starboard before U-37 rejoined us.

The centre of the depression had by now passed over us. There was no wind, and through the short Arctic day the sun set the sea shimmering like a mirror, the vastness of these waters emphasised by their unstirring flatness, their silence and their solitude; a silence unbroken by the cry of any bird, a solitude undisturbed except by us, and the U-boat's turbulent emergence in a welter of noisy, threshing water hurled aside in a wash of cream-white foam.

In my diary at the time I recorded: 'Fresh rolls sent to U-37 and chit-chat interchanged. Hartmann's ambitions *re* sinking of ships, typically submariner. I wonder if the position should be reversed, and *Atlantis* be sunk by some British submarine what exactly the gallant submariners would make of the odd flotsam left behind. Gay summer frocks, the latest creations of the Berlin milliners, and those perambulators!'

What a colossal mess these products of our ingenuity would have made upon the cold sea's surface! And how they would have intrigued the British adversary, as, together with the prams—Rogge tantalised us by refusing to explain the part THEY were to play—they drifted among our other 'effects', White Ensign, Norwegian Cross, Red Star and Rising Sun.

So our voyage proceeded, the days growing shorter and the nights growing longer, and the strangeness of the setting casting its spell upon us all as the Northern Lights set the sky ablaze with their magic, and the ship, and the lives of those inside her became to us the earth, all else seeming as distant as the stars themselves.

Two hazards surmounted, the third lay ahead—we'd passed the Gap and we'd passed the Neck, and now for the Denmark Strait.

To lessen the chances of an awkward meeting, Rogge chose that *Atlantis* took the northernmost route she could, planning to hug the Greenland Ice Pack and, regardless of navigational difficulties, keep as far as he was able from the Icelandic shore. Maximum vigilance was maintained throughout the ship, half of the crew being permanently at Action Stations and few of the officers, least of all Rogge himself, enjoying much sleep or comfort.

Our sense of tension had meanwhile been intensified by news of the outside world . . .

My diary for 8th April records: 'There is an ominous quiet about the Norwegian question. Too quiet. I regard it with suspicion.'

'9th April . . . We have marched in first.'

I heard of the invasion of Norway from the B.B.C.— as Rogge's A.D.C. I was, of course, exempt from the strict rule that listening to enemy broadcasts be punishable by death! The German High Command communiqué followed much later, and was broadcast through the ship's loud hailer system. Our major sensation on hearing this historic pronouncement? I will be candid. It was one of infinite relief at having so narrowly escaped being entangled between the opposing forces, a relief tempered by apprehension of renewed British activity in the North Atlantic, and the realisation that our chances of return, if our break through should fail, seemed, to say the least, remote.

Pigors, the Quartermaster, summed up my thoughts. 'Going to be rough for us, sir, but hell for them.'

I nodded. Bad enough for *Atlantis,* but, as the veteran of the sail ship had said, hell, sheer hell, for the U-boat.

The glass was falling. The seas were rising and ten minutes later we were hit by the full force of a howling Arctic gale, the gale I shall never forget.

One moment tranquility, the next, a screaming anarchy of waters driven by the Furies of the heavens, sending sea mountains sliding towards the ship, hurling men flat upon their faces, battering beneath their terrifying impact a hull that strained in agony. The wilderness cried out around the topsy-turvy ship, shouting at her, bruising her, savagely plucking at masts and rigging, rolling with the noise of thunder across hatch and companionway.

Through the crevices of the gun flaps the seas poured in, the water freezing solidly around the guns, creating a perpetual agony for the men who, sleepless, seasick, exhausted and numb, hacked and burned the ice off breech and sights, only to return to their task again within minutes as the white coat reformed. The thermometers recorded 17 degrees below. Our stomachs strained, our legs lost all strength and feeling, our heads buzzed and the driving spray carried ice that lashed and stung our cheeks, forcing our aching eyelids into slits.

She pitched like a bitch did *Atlantis,* and when she didn't pitch she rolled, with the frozen waters pummelling her, aiming blow after blow at her panting, struggling body, making her shudder, and jump, and wilt. Yet still she carried on, dazed but still fighting; blindly fighting as though, although the sense had died, the will remained, the desire to survive activating her in her crazy course.

Then, when the seas dropped the cold still reigned;

51

our breath steaming against the metal of our binoculars, and every gasp a painful stab as the gale struck home into our lungs. Our fur caps, Russian officers' style, became more than mere disguise; salt-caked, sodden, stinking from the perpetual mists and the spray, they kept our ears from freezing and muffled the stridency of the wind, wailing from the south like a discord of Valkyries.

Bad enough for *Atlantis,* but, for the U-boat, sheer hell. Her turret was covered by tons of ice; yes, literally tons. And she endured such a battering that it was a source of hourly wonder to us that she managed to survive. Yet still she obeyed her orders, her lookouts enduring the foulest of tortures as, more like a roller coaster than a ship, she blundered from one peak to another and another with a sickening smack in the valleys between.

When the storm finally passed our Russian 'props' had been sorely tried, and I found that the Red Star, that the engine room staff had so meticulously manufactured to promote me to a Red Navy rank, had been ripped from my uniform without my even noticing it. Surgeon-Commander Reil, and young Sub-Lieutenant Sprung, were coping with a toll of broken limbs, torn flesh, and frostbite too, yet, in one respect the weather that had hurt us so hard had saved us from wounds more tragic.

The gale had driven back the loose ice which strews the fringes of the Strait, driven it back to the ice belt of Greenland itself; given us the chance of 'sneaking through' by using an area that, known to be normally ice-infested, could be expected to be empty of British searchers. In effect, by blowing the floes against the pack the gale had broadened the channel for our passage, and Rogge made the utmost of his chances, steering *Atlantis* only fifty yards from the treacherous edges of the white and glittering fields that now stretched to starboard.

Once again, this time for good, our submarine parted

company with us. Two words, flicked from her signal lamp . . . 'Good hunting!'

The worst of our journey was at last behind us. I quote my diary: 'One day the ice pack, jagging upwards and as impartially austere as the mountains of the moon, the next, and I see the Gulf Stream. Yes, actually SEE it. For, as the warm waters hit the cold, a steam rises from the ocean giving us for a moment the illusion that the waters are boiling. As the off-duty Watch chatter about this strange phenomenon we realise we are leaving the winds of the north behind and have succeeded in the first and most complicated sequence of our voyage.'

In the next few days we traversed the trade routes of the North Atlantic, seeing many British ships that paid no heed to us. One of them passed us so close that her gun was clearly visible, but our instructions were explicit. We were not to attack anything in these waters unless attacked ourselves.

The borders of our hunting grounds lay thousands of miles to the south, and having run the gauntlet of the North *Atlantis* headed for the sun . . .

CHAPTER FIVE

CORSAIRS AND KIMONOS

I STILL wonder who she was. We identified her at the time as Scandinavian, but as Rogge said later, 'If she'd been British, if she'd been packed with contraband, I still couldn't have sunk her. For what manner of man could sink a sailing ship these days?"

A sailing ship beautiful in the sun's first rays. A thing of infinite grace and delicacy—a three-masted barque, with every curve of her snow white sails swelling before the breeze; as fastidious in her path as a lady in a crinoline stepping through a muddy street.

Down in the wardroom we chivvied our Commander on his attachment to the barque—knowing his love of anything that moved by sail in preference to steam or oil. But perhaps, fortunately, the decision to leave her alone had not in any case been ours to make. Quite apart from the barque's neutrality, *Atlantis* was still in the 'closed' North Atlantic; still with orders not to shoot unless attacked; and still with instructions to avoid any incident that might attract attention to her. So the vision passed us by. Blissfully ignorant of the havoc we might have caused her, with her prow parting the waters like a silver knife and the tracery of her cordage spread like a glittering web, she seemed in all her deceptive fragility a thing of nature and not of man.

By now we were passing through the violet-hued waters of the Sargasso, and no longer was *Atlantis* masquerading in her Russian disguise. Our Soviet Ensign and the Red Star on our hatch had gone for good, and instead we were impersonating a ship of an almost equally unknown and enigmatic nation—sailing beneath the Rising Sun as the motor vessel *Kashii Maru,* of 8,-400 tons, carrying 'passengers' as well as crew—and possessed, of course, of a status most decidedly neutral!

The process by which we had assumed this character was somewhat involved. Back home, to decide which ships *Atlantis* could best impersonate, I had first checked through thousands of names in Lloyd's Register, preparing a list of ships built after 1927, and possessing—this was most important—a cruiser stern. The list was a very long one—I remember shuddering as I looked at it—but after a tedious and lengthy search I found that there were but 26 ships which resembled us, and even these 'candidates' had to be whittled down. We had to exclude all those which would have been known to officers on board the British auxiliary cruisers, and as the latter very often belonged to the P. & O. Line we also had to eliminate all ships serving South African and Belgian ports in Africa. Even then my work was by no means over for there were other considerations—we could not for instance, employ a ship possessing a white water line, for this would be too difficult to keep in paint.

Eventually, therefore, I was left with a very small selection from which to choose, but after due deliberation we adopted the role of the Kokusai vessel, *Kashii Maru*—principally because she was the only Japanese ship that qualified!

Before the battle came days of sheer delight . . . We entered the Trades—above us a majestic procession of white clouds crossing a brilliantly blue sky from which the sun never ceased to shine. Slow and sedately they passed, these cloud argosies, ignoring the minute speck of a ship beneath them, and the shadow so swiftly cast and lost in the shifting landscape of the sea. The waters glittered a cobalt blue, laced by the low and white-flecked wave tops; highlighted by the minute sails of the jelly fish; and broken by the sportive leaps of the dolphin; while, after the rigours of the north, the breeze blew gently, refreshingly, setting our cheeks aglow, making tired muscles live again, and inspiring men to go about their duties more briskly, more cheerfully and self-reliant in this strange unaccustomed beneficence. For, by day, this happy conspiracy of sea and sky and sun gave us all the beauty of the tropics without any of the life-sapping heat and humidity we were later to encounter, and by night the world became cloaked in a different beauty—the interplay of phosphorescent fish upon the moonlit waters, dappling the fringes of our golden wake with myriad colours, ever changing, ever more enchanting. Yes, for the moment ours was a world of beauty without blemish and I am often astonished on looking back to recall this strange tranquility, following as it did so much nervous anticipation, and preceding so much monotony and bloodshed.

Not that we were exactly idle. To adopt our Japanese disguise more was needed than my solemn poring through Lloyd's Register. Our biggest problem concerned the water line. As no self-respecting ship would allow herself to be seen on the ocean wearing a frayed and rusted belt of iron where a neatly defined line and loading marks should be, Kuehn, our second in command, was given the responsibility of producing a water line. This sort of operation, which later became a positive nightmare to him, meant working for days on the side of a ship that was given an artificial list. It entailed one hundred men climbing about on scaffolding and joists, secured to *Atlantis* by manilla ropes, while a selected few were given the unenviable job of trying to paint the overhang of the stern from a dinghy which might be bouncing as much as ten or twelve feet up and down between her strokes. It meant that sentries, armed with rifles, had to be stationed every few yards along the deck, watching the surface for sharks, while an extra sharp look-out was maintained in case of visitors of a human, yet even more formidable nature. As quite often, and always at the last moment, a rising swell would wash off the paint and the whole process would have to be repeated, you can well imagine that this was not the pleasantest of jobs—the men cursing and complaining, the officers bawling, and everybody's tempers

56

getting shorter and shorter. Yet, somehow, our switch to the *Kashii Maru* role was not accompanied with quite the usual annoyances, or rather, I should say the contrast between the weather on this occasion and the icy atmosphere in which we had adopted our Russian rig made annoyances seem infinitely more bearable.

As the nights passed and the Southern Cross rose ever brighter ahead of our racing bows, the battle loomed ever nearer, though no sense of excitement stirred within us; indeed, our objective seemed to have ceased to matter. Today, the fact that the sky and the sea were around us seemed the only real and worthwhile thing, and the shores from which we had sailed appeared infinitely remote, removed far more than 6,-000 miles in space—in fact, divorced from the present by 3,000 years in Time. So, portentously, presumptuously, did the romantic picture himself as one of the original Argonauts; the trappings of our disguise, and the fact that we had (practice) 'action stations' every morning, appearing to him merely as incidental, tiresome formalities; vulgar intrusions of the commonplace and ugly . . . And thus ran on our thoughts, until a sudden, sharp clamour of the klaxons broke in on soliloquy, jerking us back to reality, and bringing us stumbling to the guns.

'Masthead in sight!'

It was the Ellerman liner, *City of Exeter*, steaming up from the south, heading for England and home and carrying many passengers as well as her crew . . . Our first target? We all thought so and as the distance between *Atlantis* and the liner steadily diminished, and the gunnery officer kept ordering distances, and issuing corrections for range and height, a hush of expectation fell among us on the bridge; every eye turning towards the Captain. We waited and watched until Rogge, lowering his binoculars, said crisply, 'There will be no attack.'

No attack? We gazed at each other, then back at Rogge. 'No,' he repeated, 'No attack,' explaining that he had no wish at this early stage to burden his ship with scores of prisoners, maybe hundreds, some of whom might need special care, and a diet very different from the rough fare to which we were now becoming accustomed. And, even apart from the humanity of the situation—he reminded us that there might be casualties among the women and children—a premature alarm would divert us from our established objectives.

'Only one thing for it now,' I thought to myself. 'Let's hope the disguise withstands the British scrutiny—especially that damned title.' Indeed, I'd some very good reasons for having misgivings about the Japanese letters on our hull and stern. I had copied them from a magazine picture, a picture which had portrayed, not a ship, but a sign hanging outside a house in a crowded Japanese street. I had no indication at all as to what the real *Kashii Maru* chose to wear, and when the brush work was completed the wiseacres among us, rightly or wrongly, alleged that I had merely succeeded in rendering in Japanese the certainly intriguing invitation to 'Come here for full enjoyment of the joys of the red light district'.

A few days earlier we had witnessed the solution of a mystery that had considerably puzzled us when we were fitting out in Germany. Rogge had asked for perambulators and despite our amusement an unfortunate headquarters officer had been given the job of providing them. Only in the dress rehearsal of the play we were now so tensely enacting, had we really seen their purpose—as 'stage props' to convince an audience that we had peaceful passengers—and now, as the *City of Exeter* approached, the fruits of the rehearsal became apparent. One of the prams was wheeled solemnly along the deck by a slim, short cook's apprentice dressed in a gay frock with a printed flower design (we had originally suggested a kimono, but this had been ruled out because of the modern Japanese woman's habit of dressing in Western styles). To add verisimilitude to our ruse the pram even contained a 'baby'—an enormous doll—and there was a civilian-suited 'proud father'. What a setting for a comic opera role! Idly, over the stern rails, leaned half a dozen of the shortest members of our crew. Their heads were covered by a German imitation of the 'tenui', a sort of towel and to the ribald and obscene jests of their concealed companions, each had as his main garment a shirt—its tail flapping, Japanese style, in the breeze.

For my own part I stood outside the chart house, grinning ingratiatingly at the advancing *Exeter,* with a straw hat on my head and an oriental gown around my shoulders, while dark glasses completed an effect that was certainly sinister, if, by Japanese standards, just a bit bewildering.

But amusing though it seems to me in retrospect this burlesque was by no means lighthearted—not at the time. Our guns were manned and ready and, if the Englishman had rumbled us, then it would have been too bad for him. We just couldn't afford a raider warning—not at this stage in our journey. From the spick and span *City of Exeter* we caught the glint of binoculars, trained upon us. I wondered curiously as to what they were thinking over there, and reflected on the ordered and comfortable routine that had been interrupted for a few minutes—the passengers aboard the British ship diverted by our arrival, and probably watching with an amused curiosity. What sort of conversation were they having? I could almost guess. 'Just fancy that, my dear! Actually a Japanese ship. And those ghastly little yellow men . . .'

On the immaculate bridge of the Britisher a little group of officers were observing us very closely, but as we passed they split up and went to their normal stations again, evidently quite satisfied. In the end, so obviously was the *City of Exeter* disgusted at the appearance of our unseamanlike looking collection (and well she might be!) that she steamed aloofly on her way without even wishing us the courtesy of a good morning.

We were more than gratified. This indeed was a fitting reward for all our labours, and we were not to know it would be a report from the *City of Exeter* that some weeks later would cause us yet again to go through all the painful process of a new disguise!

There were all sorts of things one had to think about when adopting camouflage. As a Japanese, *Atlantis* wore the Rising Sun, painted in huge squares across her gun flaps. But this additional cover had problems of its own. The flaps had a tendency to rust along their 'secret' joints and draw attention to their shape by thick red streaks—a drawback, that although fortunately not obvious when we met the City liner, was to require plenty of attention later on.

Such problems were to be a source of perpetual worry and chagrin to our Captain. He would consult for hours with Kamenz, our navigation officer, a Merchant Captain himself and a very able man, to think up ways and means of our appearing still more harmless and 'normal'. He would order his launch and ride round *Atlantis* in sudden trips on which I had to accompany him and take pictures that he could study extensively and compare with the details of the 'genuine article'. For Rogge realised that the smallest details were of importance, from the spelling on the dummy box that hid a gun, to the height of our stanchion posts, and insisted on accuracy, sparing neither himself nor others . . .

On several of these trips we watched the effect of our 'trick lighting' . . . a source of gratification to us all because it was so thoroughly effective. The trick lay in the fact that a flick of a switch in the pilot room could 'change' the navigation lights—there being a set of alternative lights at both sides and on the masts. Thus we could show a red light on our starboard, a green on our port, two steamer lights showing aft on our masts and accordingly, while appearing to pursue a certain course be steering in just the opposite direction.

It was on the morning of 3rd May, quite suddenly and cutting across the everyday routine, that the cry came from our lookout of 'Masthead in sight!' And a few minutes later we were steaming towards the British *Scientist*—the first of our twenty-two victims.

CHAPTER SIX

BAPTISM OF BLOOD

KAMENZ screwed up his eyes a little as he looked at the approaching Englander. As an old Merchant Navy man he couldn't quite understand the attitude of the professionals on occasions such as this.

Older than most of the officers, and with a wife ashore, Kamenz regarded the war as a necessary but infernally irritating business, and he for one would be glad when it was over. He bore the English a grudge for starting it, but hate, the sort of hate that really stirred him to fighting madness, he reserved for the Freemasons and landlubbing Germany's favourite radio singer. Whenever anything that troubled him occurred in the world Kamenz would grunt, 'It's those Freemasons again. They're the root cause of it all'. While the sound of Hans Albers's rich vocal invitation to participate in the joys of the life at sea would result in Kamenz stamping out of the wardroom like an angry bull, or rushing to switch off the radio.

He took another squint at *Scientist*. Oh, yes, an Englander in every line. A ship with long cross trees and long funnel, with vintage stern, and sombre superstructure, English in her deliberation, and English, too, in her antiquity. Kamenz felt quite depressed as he watched her for it didn't seem such a long time ago since the coincidence of a German and British ship in port together had meant a mutual spree.

It was with feelings considerably less nostalgic that the admin. officer watched the stranger approaching. A serious minded man, and a Party member, he had been as surprised as anyone when the war had resulted in his transformation into a Commander of the German Navy. He was faithful to the Führer, and eager for service. In his bouts of seasickness, which were plentiful, he retained (if nothing else) at least a warm feeling of dedication to the cause. He could scarcely lower the binoculars from his eyes, such was his excitement in examining every detail of our adversary. But it was the reddish blob on the staff at her stern that stayed focussed the longest in his lenses; this he realised was her certificate of ancestry, the symbol of her service, the Ensign whose presence in the ocean The Leader had vowed to erase.

So this was the start, the sequal to our months of training and preparation, the beginning of the ultimate realities of war.

As the alarm bells brought us to the guns we realised, even the dullest of us that, with the advent of the Britisher, a new sequence was beginning. This, I remember thinking, was to be the dividing line in our lives, the difference between pretence and actuality, the experience that the matador calls the moment of truth.

Even after 15 years I can still remember the acute sense of anti-climax that followed the initial thrill of our encounter with *Scientist*; the tempo of events seeming to slow down, and almost mocking, by the gradualness of their development, the urgency that had so inspired us at the initial sighting.

I looked around me. We had worked out a drill for such an occasion long before our sailing, relying for procedure on precedents outlined in the histories of the raiders of World War One. In certain respects the information they yielded seemed comprehensive enough—first a signal to stop; next, because it was deemed good form, a shot across the bows; and finally, a polite reception of gracious surrender. But we had an uneasy feeling that the historians had not devoted sufficient attention to explaining what went on between the initial sighting and the arrival of one's 'guests' upon one's decks! In total, at least, we were prepared for something more, something different to fill up the interval between preface and epilogue, an interval on which the historians observed a discreet silence.

Well, we would see, I reflected, but so far the mechanics of the game were certainly working to formula.

To the English only two men would be visible on our bridge, the Captain and myself, who, as officer of the Watch, was responsible for transmitting his orders and supervising their execution. Not a glimpse would they catch of Gunnery Officer Kasch and three ratings who lay crouched behind the canvas rail of the range finder. Not a hint would they have that on our innocently under-populated bridge was the Q.M. with his staff, the torpedo officer with his, the navigating officer, and a group of signallers.

So this was it . . . Was all our preparation really necessary? Was this how I had imagined things would be—a summer's day with the sea very calm, and the sun very bright; a rather restful period of the day—post lunch, when ashore in peace time the idle could relax. Ours but the business of waiting for the range to close; to endure two hours, slow in passing, with nothing more momentous to enliven them than the sight of our adversary ever nearing. No great drama here I thought. Just a little steamer approaching you as you approach her, the whole thing developing so steadily that it was almost possible to predict the moment of our warning shot.

On the boat deck below the aircraft personnel masqueraded in skirts, pushing the prams which originally fooled the *City of Exeter,* and while Bulla, our flying officer, who had been chafing at his temporary unemployment, sedately promenaded as a passenger in a grey flannel suit. The stage was set, the ambush prepared.

I listened to the monotonous sing-song of a seaman's voice calling the ranges . . . Eight thousand yards, seven thousand five hundred yards, seven thousand four hundred, seven thousand three hundred . . .

A leading signalman stood by a cluster of bunting, the traditional flag signal of XL (stop or I fire) ready to flutter to our mast head, and another signal, which read, 'Don't use your wireless'. This was a bright afterthought on our part, entailing the use of several flags.

The Englishman came on. We listened to the range calling. We glanced at our watches, I lowered my binoculars and glanced interrogatively at Rogge. He nodded. The moment had come.

'Fallen Tarnung!' (drop camouflage.)

The flaps roared up. The 'crane' became Number Three gun, and the 'hut' on our stern collapsed to reveal the grey menace of yet another 5.9 incher as the flag, the battle flag, shot outwards in the breeze. The whole operation occupied precisely two seconds.

'Just like clockwork,' said someone.

'He'll die of shock,' said another.

But for my part I was gripped by a curious sense of detachment, as if I were watching a film for about the fifth or sixth time.

Up went the signal, bang went the small gun we carried in our bows, and over went the shell ahead of our enemy to emphasise our warning, and all in less time than it takes to tell.

But no reply came back to our signal. This surprised us. At last the unexpected.

Leading Seaman Helmle—to his fellows known as The Frog—was a wireless fanatic in peace time, and *Atlantis* had provided him with a wartime paradise. So far he had found plenty of scope to indulge both his keenness and his capacity for being the life and soul of the party for quite apart from being responsible with his colleagues for the transcription of the eagerly awaited communiqués from home—one of the bright products of our Admiralty's Radio Division—his was the distinction of founding Radio Atlantis. In the course of his activities he had devised not only caustic commentaries and news items regarding the habits and characters of his colleagues, but he had also perfected an ingenious disc jockey system whereby you paid a mark to have your favourite record plugged over the amplifiers, and those who didn't like it paid five marks to have it smashed.

But such organisational masterpieces—'All for the

Red Cross'—were far from Frog's mind now as crouching over the radio he listened intently on the wave length of the Englander. The first intimation of a signal from this silence, and the group on the bridge above must be alerted. Absorbed in his duty he'd scarcely heard the crack of the warning shot, thanks to the close-fitting earphones, so anxiously pressed to his head, and the broad hot hands that covered them.

A sudden hum, and the scream of a morse key. 'Q.Q.Q. . . . Q.Q.Q. . . . Unidentified merchantman has ordered me to stop.'

Helmle's hand clamped down the key in front of him, jamming the Englishman's cry for help, even as his voice snapped up to the bridge, 'Ship sending!'

Funny, he found time to think, how two words from a humble seaman could bring a ship's company into immediate action. Leave it to the Frog—that's what they all said. Always the life and soul of the party.

The enemy hadn't replied to our XL because he'd never even bothered to read it. One moment, except for this noncompliance, everything appeared to be perfectly normal, with still no sign of life aboard her except for the solitary figure on her bridge. The next and her silhouette had begun to change. Before our eyes it grew smaller and smaller, thinner and thinner. She was turning. She had turned . . . and the froth churning ahead of us was the white foam of her stern water. She was making a run for it.

'Frog's' voice roused us from our surprised regard. Rogge turned: *Feuerlaubnis'* (permission to fire). Kasch's white teeth flashed approval from his perch; and so, with surprising suddenness, our war began.

The guns opened up, and a sharp pain pierced my ears as the broadside broke; the soles of our feet jumping beneath the impact of the shock; the acrid reek of the cordite filling our nostrils. Momentarily the target was obliterated, as the gunsmoke poured back upon our bridge. When it cleared I saw four white jets of foam rise, almost slowly, from the sea around the steamer, to stand like columns until they fountained down and Kasch's voice screamed 'Again. Again . . .'

'Still sending sir, Still sending!'

'Again . . . Again . . .'

'Poor bastards,' said someone.

'Poor bastards,' mimicked someone else.

'Silence your men,' said Pigors.

Two brilliant red banners fluttered upwards from the steamer's deck. A great cloud of dust followed; dirty black and grey as from a carpet being beaten. Quite unlike anything we'd seen rise from a practice target it soard into the sky. Our shells had registered.

'Again . . . Again.'

But his time, as the salvo roared across the sea, the voice of our signalman called: 'Sending stopped.'

Following the dust came a cloud of steam, virginal white, pouring from the target's funnel, forming itself into a pattern, fantastically neat, against the blue and tranquil sky.

'Halt batterie, Halt,' Rogge shouted, and a sudden silence fell. We could see that the merchantman now lay stopped. Her decks had suddenly become alive with men rushing to climb into the lifeboats as the steam became tinged with the smoke of her burning. But now our drill resumed its interrupted course. I was to accompany the boarding party, and set foot on 'British soil'.

Fehler climbed into the boat beside me, easing his long legs over the gunwale, then leaning back to drag one of the thirty-pound boxes of dynamite into position beside him, the ginger beard he had cultivated so assiduously to match his flaming, rather untidy hair, jutting with a degree of importance not hitherto noticeable. Our dynamiter had at last come into his own. His was to be the task of placing and firing the explosive charges that would finally sink our enemy, and he had the enthusiasm of a professor about to demonstrate and prove at last a scientific thesis derided by all but him.

Fehler had the adventurous spirit of a buccaneer, and

66

an approach to buccaneering embodying the inquisitive desire for research and experiment of a laboratory professor. A practical joker, who enlivened his leisure hours by such pranks as injecting quinine into other people's toothpaste tubes, he carried a flair for the handling of high explosives and a delight in big bangs to an excess that somehow endowed him with the absent-mindedness as well as the brilliance of the professorial caste.

His conversation as our launch got under way was exclusively confined to the technical. He had decided to place his explosive charges 'according to the book', namely, manhandling them through the ship itself to two strategic points, the bulkhead between the engine room and the forrard hold, and the bulkhead between the engine room and the aft hold.

'But I don't see why we should have to go through this laborious business of carting the charges through every ship's innards' he said, adding speculatively, 'maybe in future I'll try 'em on the outside, and lower them by rope from the deck.'

This, in effect, was the procedure he later adopted, but at the moment we wanted to make quite sure. Oh yes. We were doing it all 'according to the book'. I, for example, possessing the quite unnecessary impedimenta of a large Mauser pistol strapped to my belt, while the rest of the party were bristling with long handled potato masher grenades, side arms and tommy guns. Only much later was I to discard such an imposing armament as completely superfluous, retaining only a canvas bag in which to collect captured logs, papers, and other documents.

As we cast away *Atlantis* made a lee for our boats and those of *Scientist*, and soon I had my first real glimpse of our victims. Candidly, my main impression was one of surprise; surprise at seeing so many dark faces, for I had never encountered Lascars before and somehow I had expected to find an all English crew.

One solitary figure remained on *Scientist*, and as I clambered up the side of the ship he gave me a cold look and a short but correct salute. A certain embarrassment seemed to possess us both. I broke the tension. 'Can I see your papers?' I asked.

I discovered that *Scientist* was a Harrison steamer. She was carrying a cargo of ore, chromium, copper, hides, tanning bark, maize, flour and jute, and was on her way from Durban to Freetown where she was to have joined a convoy for England.

The formalities disposed of, Fehler attended to his charges and I set about the job of searching the Captain's quarters, the bridge and the chart room, questioning for routing instructions, secret logs, wireless code and mail. My task was not rewarding for *Scientist*'s Captain had done his job well, seeing to it that everything likely to interest us had been ditched before we arrived. My swag was confined, therefore, to odd items such as binoculars, signal flags and a chronometer. Yet as we were so new to it all, Fehler and I took considerably longer to effect our mission than we should have done, the novelty of being on a British ship in such circumstances in itself serving to delay us. There was something inexpressibly strange about searching through cabins where pictures of girl friends and wives, mothers and children, gazed down almost in reproach as one rifled among the personal belongings of those who had so recently and suddenly departed. But war was war, and bloody lucky they were that they were not worse off . . .

Searching the officers' quarters, I was surprised to note how cramped and stuffy they were, for *Scientist* was quite an old ship, and even her Captain's cabin was but half the size of my own quarters on *Atlantis*. The wireless room provided us with another form of interest. Kasch had done his job thoroughly—a direct hit reducing the place to a mass of broken timbers and twisted steel. Yet the operator had had a miraculous escape, and had managed to climb out of the shambles with his only injury a slightly wounded arm.

The sharp smell of the burning jute permeated every quarter of the ship. I emerged on deck to come across a dead Lascar. He lay crumpled on his stomach, his skull blown off, a pool of blood surrounding him. From it little tributaries were slowly trickling into the salt water of the gutter. I looked at him and felt faintly sick. I had, of course, seen corpses before, during anatomy classes, but this, this heap of broken bone and mangled flesh had but a mere twenty minutes earlier been a man in his prime; a man in health, who had died through violence.

No time for soliloquizing now. I glanced at the youngsters of my party who had formed a sort of silent half circle behind me. Their faces were deathly pale. One of them looked as though he was about to vomit. 'All right. All right,' I said, 'Stop gaping.' We moved on.

To make quite sure of sinking *Scientist* we opened her sea cocks as well as planting our charges.

Back on *Atlantis* we experienced yet another aspect of the ship sinking business, namely, the administrative problems of looking after survivors.

Bedding and bed clothes had to be issued; crockery as well. Next we had to 'document' our prisoners, and afterwards interrogate certain of them—an 'intelligence' procedure which we subsequently abandoned finding that it yielded no returns.

Naturally our main interest lay in the reaction of our captives.

Scientist's 'Sparks' provided Surgeon-Commander Reil with his first 'enemy' patient. The radio operator's devotion to duty had been fruitless for The Frog later told me that, although *Scientist*'s first 'Queen' sign had eluded our jamming the signal had passed unnoticed. Such a disappointment not withstanding, 'Sparks' was a very cheerful sort of fellow, and aptly nicknamed by his comrades 'Sunny Jim'.

Scientist's Commander, Captain Windsor, O.B.E., was very bitter about our Raider luck. It appeared that he had been off-duty and asleep at the time of our sighting, and despite express orders to be roused in the event

69

of any other ship being sighted, no one had called him until it was too late. At this stage of the war many merchant sailors were inclined to be derisive of the warnings of surface raiders. One could hardly blame them since only the late-deceased *Graf Spee* had so far attempted the business in a big way, but Windsor, a most conscientious and efficient officer, had felt the blow badly.

The loss of his ship worried him enormously, for he believed that had he been warned *Scientist* would never have fallen into our hands.

We found that the officers and men of our first victims were very good types of the old 'professional' Merchant Navy, but by the time we had settled them in their quarters Fehler and I were so worn out that we had no zest left to celebrate their capture. The prisoner problem had taken us four hours to solve.

Apart from its 'historic' interest, our encounter with *Scientist* was of considerable significance in so far as that it demonstrated that British ships would use their wireless, despite our flag-and-shot-across-the-bows technique. The whole procedure of attack had accordingly to be revised, and after *Scientist* we endeavoured to operate a sort of shock treatment—firing several rounds at once across our opponents' bows. But it didn't help, and as the arm of the Admiralty tightened even more upon the Merchant Service our own measures became progressively tougher. We tried firing straight for the wireless room simultaneously with our declaration, but this tactic too proved a stumer for every ship was now becoming 'raider conscious' and would turn away as soon as it sighted another. Thus we were forced to adopt night tactics, either approaching in the dusk and shelling the enemy at very short range and before he had a chance to use his key, or else overhauling in the dark and attacking at dawn. Once a merchantman stopped, and her radio fell silent our firing also ceased, but in the meantime the punishment was often severe. We could not afford to take chances.

When *Scientist* sank, someone on the bridge gloated, 'That's the stuff. That's how I'd like to see all their bloody old tubs go down.'

But Rogge shook his head. 'I don't agree,' he said 'Let's just look at it as a necessary job. Ships are rather like human beings you know. Each has a life of its own and each dies differently too. Yes, I'm sorry to see them go.'

Such a philosophy would not have been appreciated by the majority of the crew, but it gave me considerable food for thought, for I found that what Rogge said was true.

Each ship died in a different way. Some died gracefully, and some did not. Some struggled painfully for a long while, straining against their fate. Some plunged into the depths with the noise of their breaking echoing over the waters and the flames cascading from their bowels. Some capsized with their keels afoam, like the back of a whale before it dives. And some, like *Scientist,* slid gently down, carrying their pride with them.

CHAPTER SEVEN

DANGER OFF SHORE

A QUIET night . . . a still sea . . . and the beam from a lighthouse slid across the waters dappling the decks of the tall grey ship with radiance and shadow, framing her bridgework in a ghostly pallor, sweeping away on the sea again to continue its unending circuit.

Her seeming innocence a cloak for what promised to be the nastiest and most hazardous of missions, the raider *Atlantis* was ploughing her way towards the shore.

'A hell of a night for the job,' someone grumbled on the bridge. I nodded. A sky of velvet, studded with the stars of the Southern galaxy, spread its dome around us, a dome that, in three directions, merged and blended with the distant sea-line but to the north was broken by the pulse of the lighthouse and the irregular formation of shadows that were neither of the sea nor of the sky. For the first time since leaving Arctic Europe we were peering through the dark at the outline of the land, but it was a land as alien and hostile to us as was our mission to these otherwise tranquil waters. For, slowly though our ship throbbed on, she left a lethal legacy behind her, of mines, nearly one hundred of them. Theirs the only discord to disturb the night's tranquility, they rumbled along the launching rail, flopping into the sea astern, raising a splash of silver amid the frothing wake; the wake that now cut across the golden track the moon was sending over an otherwise unrippled sea.

Down in the mine room Fehler glanced at his watch and at the launching rail, glittering faintly in the low burning light. Another of his steel black charges was on

72

its way out, the 'asparagus' surrounding it when silhouetted briefly at the stern giving him a momentary illusion of some strange primaeval brute of the sea. Another splash . . . and another black spheroid began to trundle past. Young Fehler grinned tightly at the obscene suggestion chalked upon it. 'You've spelt Churchill wrong,' he called. 'There's two L's!"

I did not view the decision to indulge in mine-laying right under British noses with unqualified approval. The sooner we got rid of Fehler's precious toys the better I would like it. I eyed uneasily the inscrutable shore. Come to think of it not even Fehler was terribly keen about the project. There was something unpleasantly impersonal, almost sinister, in the way in which these things struck without warning and regardless of whether one was friend or foe, and for his part there was little interest in an explosion that he could not personally control.

A soft wind carried across the sea the mysterious scent of Africa, laden with fragrance of its spices, and the age-old tang of its swamps and forests. We were by now so close to the Cape that we could see the headlamps of cars, passing along the coastal road, and reflecting their brightness back from the rocks. It was a night of idyllic tranquility and possessed of much beauty.

But with things as they were most of us had little time for its aesthetic appreciation. We were far too busy calculating the dangers that this mile-from-land tactic of Rogge's might bring, and we would have dispensed with the moon and the stars quite cheerfully in exchange for a sullen and overcast sky, and endured quite well the discomforts of a less tell-tale and placid sea. We found ourselves automatically timing to a nicety the emergence of the beam from a series of blinks to its dazzling zenith. The shore seemed tenanted by a host of watching and vigilant eyes, and there were other watchers as well, the men who manned the ships that passed us so peacefully to east and west, ships taking us for one of their unaggressive and worried selves.

It was with a sense of relief that those of us not directly concerned with other tasks, engaged ourselves in engineering an elaborate sideshow for the benefit of the prisoners. They were bright at putting two and two together, these English seamen, so we planned to turn their astuteness to our own account. They would probably have a pretty shrewd idea of what was going on, and in the event of any untoward occurrence—such as their being rescued from the prison ship to which we hoped to transfer them—would lose no time in 'spilling the beans' to British Intelligence. This would be most unfortunate. But how to screen our real activities from these intelligent detectives? I take a modest bow for the somewhat theatrical solution. Instead of the proverbial red herring, I said we would give them a 'Nazi submarine', a 'submarine' created by some elaborate sound effects which would be heard and speculated upon in the prison quarters below.

The idea was popular. First we carried out engine manoeuvres which, to these shrewd observers, would denote the arrival of another craft alongside us. Next we put pilot ladders over the side—the noise of the operation is so easily identifiable! And then, to complete the picture, we sent men up and down the ladders, and put out a call for the doctor. We particularly prided ourselves upon this latter subtlety, judging that it would be overheard by the wounded wireless operator from *Scientist*, who was installed in the sick-bay, and would, we had no doubt, be duly faithfully passed on by him when Captain Windsor came visiting.

Our charade may seem to have made much ado about little, but in actual fact it was in keeping with our role that even in the smallest ways we should create confusion, making every incident a mystery!

From a defensive bluff for the benefit of prisoners who, after all, had but a slender chance of escape, we moved on to yet another aspect of our guessing game. Why not carry the illusion still further, I thought, and leave a deliberate clue or two for the British authorities ashore? For if we could spread the belief that a submarine pack was ready for action in these 'safe' waters repercussions might be major.

We prepared the 'evidence'.

First we obtained a life-buoy and painted boldly on it the inscription U-37, then we overpainted, as though an unsuccessful attempt had been made partially to obliterate the numerals for the sake of security. We had quite a bit of fun with the lifebuoy . . . We kicked it and trampled it, and dirtied it with oil and then, having torn out one of its lifelines, we flung the sorry object into the sea, with the pious prayer that it would ultimately end up on the desk of the Naval Intelligence officers at Durban.

Should it do so we had no doubt that the gentleman concerned would have a sharp enough brain to deduce, in the best Baker Street fashion, precisely what we wanted him to deduce—U-boat pack off the Cape. And maybe mine-laying at that.

Such diversions apart however, we were by no means sorry when the last of our mines had been jettisoned into the sea, nor when, with the breaking of the day, *Atlantis*, well out of sight of the shore again, pursued her course north-eastwards into the vastness of the Indian ocean.

I quote from my diary: '18th May . . . So the blasted mines went off after all! I hear from Cape Town radio news of 'an explosion near Cape Agulhas'.

'22nd May . . . Intercepted message from Admiral Columbo warning all shipping of "a raider disguised as Japanese". So our early sins have found us out! What a shock! Did *City of Exeter* blow the gaff to people too adept in adding two and two together?'

'23rd May . . . *Kashii Maru* now dead! *Atlantis* now respectable cruiser sterned *Abbekerk* flying the Netherlands flag. Nice colour scheme of Jap replaced by drab brown and dull olive. A pity . . .'

'25th May . . . Well, well. After all our security. Propaganda Ministry elatedly announces "Eight (EIGHT!) British merchantmen have been lost on the mines laid by a German raider (!) off Agulhas!" In addition—says Ministry—three ships overdue, three enemy minesweepers lost. Who said our Dr. Goebbels lacked journalistic flair?'

At this stage in our fortunes news of far greater import than the activities of one small ship intruded upon our world, news that held us all to the radio set. The Blitzkrieg had begun. All Germany was on the march. Within a few days of the *Scientist* affair, our Armoured Divisions were smashing their way through the barriers of the west, and now, as our ship throbbed northward into the Indian Ocean, our minds were focused upon the flaming skies above Dunkirk. To the fanfare of the trumpets each High Command communiqué proclaimed it as a major victory, and with England recoiling on herself, and France in chaos before the thrust of our panzers, peace at last, we said, must be in sight. Each day seemed better than the day before. Each edition of the News Digest brought fresh reports of battles won, of cities falling. Being young, and some might say foolish, some of us chafed and fretted at the thought that they were being robbed of glory. The vast majority, however, were more preoccupied with considering how they'd sample the delicious fruits of peace.

'Paris has fallen!' The word was round the ship even before Rogge could announce it over loud speaker system.

The marching songs that now came echoing over our radio found a tremendous response among us, but our reaction had little to do with the Nazi ideology. Most of the crew were not concerned so much with the result of our victories upon the history of Europe, but rather with the result as it concerned them personally. They thought the war was practically over. They rejoiced in the idea that their daily drill, their chores, their crammed existence under the constant threat of destruction, and their severance from their homes and families would soon be over. They had no particular desire to tour the world sinking ships at a certain amount of peril to themselves. They would much rather plant cucumber in their small garden, or breed pigeons, or spend a night at the beerhouse. And now they thought they had abundant reason for rejoicing. We were still not far from the Cape of Good Hope. Wouldn't it be very nice to make a leisurely trip home, with a call at Durban's beaches maybe? and a frolic with a good slip of a girl in Cape Town. . . .

To mark the fall of Paris, Rogge ordered a general issue of one pint of beer per man: 'Why only one pint?' someone queried.

Said Rogge, 'Don't think it's all over yet.'

While maintaining the semblance of God-like reserve expected of his station, Rogge seldom missed anything of significance in the behaviour of the molecules around him, and, as even the slightest discord in the rhythm of our corporate life could touch responsive echoes in him, the spectacle of men pouring beer into the ocean—beer that he, Rogge, had personally bestowed on them—was one that he could scarcely accept as a normal behaviour pattern. There must, he reflected, be Something Wrong.

The seaman, just about to ditch something over the side, jumped guiltily as the duty officer approached, and came to an innocent attention.

'What have you got there?' said the duty officer.

'A bottle, sir.'

'What sort of bottle?'

'A beer bottle, sir.'

'Then what were you going to do with it?'

'Throwing it away, sir.'

"What, the bottle?'

'No, the beer, sir.'

'Why?'

'Because it's hot, sir.'

* * *

77

Rogge called aside the Mess Steward as the officers' party was at its height.

'What's the matter with the men's beer? I'm told it's hot.'

The white-jacketed steward hesitated the merest fraction. 'Well, sir . . . the weather . . .'

'Yet I and the rest of the officers have just enjoyed iced champagne?'

The steward smiled deprecatingly. 'Oh yes, sir. But that's from the WARDROOM refrigerator. We've no space in the others for beer.'

Rogge frowned. 'I see. Officers first.'

'Well, sir . . .'

'No, no,' said Rogge, 'that won't do. If that's the case, then no more iced champagne!'

Needless to say, Rogge's resolution was by no means popular with the wardroom but, by venting our alert displeasure on the unfortunate steward, we managed quite miraculously to ensure that ice-cold beer was available for the next celebration—the surrender of France. So the champagne flowed freely after all.

France had fallen. In a wardroom appropriately gay corks popped and glasses clinked as the healths of even the most distant of relatives and acquaintances were 'prayed for' the easy way. Talk was of home. Soon it would all be over. Soon we'd be going back; this life would seem like a dream long left behind us; this evening a cherished memory, a tale to retell in the years to come. This was the night, we'd say, the night that marked the beginning of the end.

'But what about England?' said someone.

There was a laugh. 'Well, how the devil can England last out on her own?'

'But the Americans? In the old days Roosevelt's pledges would have caused a declaration.'

'America! Now America . . .' said the Admin. Officer, taking a deep breath.

'Oh, my God. Now we're going to have Mein Kampf', I thought, but we were spared a harangue on 'degeneracy' and 'racial purity' by Fehler's proposing, 'Tell you what. Let's have a sweepstake on it—how soon it will end I mean. I prophesy September,' and he drew a ring around the third of the month.

'A month from now,' suggested another. 'I'll give it till Christmas,' said a third.

And so they went on, each officer ringing a date on the calendar while one of us collected the stake money.

Most estimates varied between four weeks and four months.

'And what's yours, Doctor?'

The jolly Reil was unusually thoughtful. 'Since you ask, I suggest July—July NINETEEN-FORTY-FOUR!'

There was a roar of laughter.

'You're bloody hopeful,' remarked Fehler.

The doctor shrugged and turned to me. 'What do you think, Mohr?'

I smiled. 'I suggest about the same as you, Reil. But just to be awkward I'll even go one better—July 1945.'

'You'll be jolly lucky if the cash lasts that long!' quipped an officer after the din had died down.

I never got my 'prize', but it wouldn't have been worth much—not in July 1945; in any case, there was no opportunity to collect it . . .

Four years, five years . . . In these, the days of success, such periods of time seemed beyond the margin of our contemplation, and the doctor and I were classed as the pessimists of the ship, our guesses being considered so absurd that not even the Admin. Officer could really be cross with us. Continuing conscientiously with his task of indoctrinating a class of a dozen volunteer seamen, May 1940 was a silver month for him and June and July as golden as the eagle he so earnestly served.

You don't wage a war with calendars and champagne.

We sighted the Norwegian, *Tirranna*, on 10th June. We approached her on a gradually converging course, and her captain had vowed, 'I just won't let that bloody Dutchman overtake us.'

The race continued for three hours, with *Atlantis*

running almost parallel until four and a half miles away. And then we let our quarry have it . . . '

The Norwegian was rashly game, and scarcely had our first shells fallen around her than she opened fire and began to screech out a warning. It took us thirty salvos to silence that accursed radio and *Tirranna*, our second victim, took heavy punishment.

When I climbed aboard her I found her decks were literally covered in blood; it lay in pools wherever one trod. Five men were dead but there were many wounded. Her captain was suffering badly from shock, and he almost burst into tears as he spoke to me, dazedly repeating 'But Norway made peace with you, to-day'. A novel line of reasoning I thought but one that aroused quite serious reflections on the value of continental victory while the sea remained unconquered, reflections also on the difference between the appearance of our agreement with the Quisling Government and the fact—the presence of Norwegian ships upon the waters, ships bound for ports under British controls, carrying cargoes under British licence, and working for the return of the Norwegian Government in exile.

Tirranna was a valuable prize, modern, spacious and fast. And her cargo was valuable too, consisting of wheat, three thousand tons; of wool, six thousand bales. She carried besides, 178 trucks, 5,500 cases of beer, 300 cases of tobacco, and a mountain of food which included 3,000 cases of canned peaches and 17,000 cases of jam.

We had not tasted fruit for weeks, so some of the peaches we kept for ourselves; but the rest of the cargo we planned to send back to Germany. *Tirranna* was obviously too precious to sink and she was fast enough and Norwegian-looking enough to evade the British on the way back.

But she carried loot more poignant than food or machinery.

To her had been entrusted the mail of the Australian Expeditionary force, the first consignment since the men's departure from Egypt, and there were innumerable evidences of feminine solicitude, food parcels, cigarettes, tins of sweets and at least five thousand pairs of socks, most of them knitted in the finest and softest of wool.

There were scores of thousands of letters. They were written by wives and mothers, by sweethearts and sisters, by fathers and grandparents, by people who, so to speak, had left their loved ones at the station and then gone straight home to pour their hearts out on paper. In one respect all had the same refrain . . . 'Write soon, as soon as you can . . .' 'Look after yourself . . .' while there was a stack of epistles ending in 'I hope you like the birthday cake I'm sending . . .'

Well, war is war . . . and full of bitter ironies for *Tirranna*'s officers told us that officials at Melbourne had briefed them that the Indian Ocean was really quite safe and suggested that the mines off Agulhas were probably a legacy from *Graf Spee* which, of course, had been sunk several months before.

We could not afford to linger too long in unpacking our prize for, although her radio signals had given her position incorrectly, and we had, in any case, succeeded in partially jamming them, the traces of our guilt and her vain struggle were all too evident. So we sent her South, hundreds of miles south—'Put her on ice' in fact, with a small prize crew, and instructions to wait until we rejoined her.

England still fought on, and, by the time we attacked the *City of Bagdad*, one of our number had already forfeited all hope of winning that victory sweepstake.

We opened fire in the early morning of 11th July and the action possessed an element of irony as the ship was a former Hansa vessel taken by the Allies as reparations after the first World War. Her lines were unmistakably German, and I was intrigued to find, on examining her, that much of the engine-room machinery still bore the names of German firms.

We opened fire at less than 3,000 yards after she had refused to stop and sent instead the scream of her radio vibrating through the ether in an attempt to describe us, and the position of our engagement.

Our first salvo tore down the partition between her wireless room and the captain's cabin, wounding the radio operator and silencing the set.

On coming aboard I peered into the wreckage to see her Commander, Captain Armstrong White, stooped over his desk, resolutely ransacking the drawers to ensure that everything likely to be of use to us had been destroyed. The room itself was a shambles, and he was lucky to be alive.

The Captain's back was turned so he did not see me. After watching him for a second I said conversationally, 'A little untidy, sir?'

Not turning, and still engrossed in his task, he replied absentmindedly, 'Yes, I suppose it is.'

'A bloody awful mess, Captain.'

'And a bloody fool thing to say,' he snapped crossly, and turned round to give me a piece of his mind. He was astounded—to put it mildly—when he saw my German uniform, but, in the long run I found that the joke was against me for my call had been made five minutes too late to be of advantage to our cause. There was no doubt that Armstrong White had certainly been thorough in his work, while even the City liner's signals, violently terminated, had not been made in vain. Despite our jamming they had been picked up by an American ship which promptly retransmitted them and sent out the query, 'Who shelled by?'

So this pro-British neutral wanted our description: We swore at her embarrassing proximity and her obvious desire to help, but then, with a flash of inspiration, we too got busy on our radio, using the code sign of the *City of Bagdad*, answering briefly, 'Cancelled. Erroneous . . .' We only hoped they could not tell the difference.

Two memorable incidents are associated in my mind with the sinking of the *City of Bagdad*. One concerns Fehler, who had been sent aboard her to finish her off.

'Where the devil,' said Rogge peering through his

binoculars as the boat carrying the demolition party pulled away from the doomed ship, 'is *Fehler*?'

I took a look myself, but that flaming beard was missing.

'My God, I can't see him either,' I said.

A moment later the explosive charges rumbled through the black hull, and smoke began to belch across the sea. A ghastly thought occurred to me. I could hear that familiar voice saying thoughtfully, after *Scientist*, 'I wonder how it would feel if one were to stay on the ship as it sank.'

And Fehler was mad enough, daring enough, to try anything.

Rogge seemed to read my thoughts.

'If that reckless so-and-so . . .'

Then a figure materialised on the heavily listing deck, climbed with painful slowness to the side and—to our immense relief—threw itself into the water.

Said Fehler later and after a long and not altogether enjoyable chat with Rogge, 'I just wanted to try out the sensation!'

'I hope,' I said severely, 'you enjoyed it!'

The other incident—my somewhat unusual introduction to the *City of Bagdad*'s Captain—had a more lasting influence for from it originated a wary wartime respect that has ripened over the years into a firm peacetime friendship.

To the news bulletins of neutral radio stations, *Atlantis* was indebted for information that not only kept her apace with THIS world but also, on occasion, saved her from a precipitate departure into the next!

It was about the time of the *City of Bagdad* encounter that, listening peacefully to a news digest from San Francisco radio, I heard the announcer's nasal voice laconically remark, 'The Dutch motor vessel *Abberkerk* has been sunk . . .'

Abberkerk. For a moment the full implication didn't dawn. *Abberkerk? . . . Abberkerk? . . .* By God! *That's* US!

Soon, quite near the spot where a 'Dutch' ship called

83

Abberkerk had been doing a lot of German 'business', a neutral 'Swede' appeared. Some of her paint was new, by the smell of it. Her stanchion posts too—two more than possessed by the Dutchman—looked very smart, and not many observers would have suspected that they were but two days old and made of oil drums, sail cloth, and the timer that had once provided a 'Depot Ship's main armament'.

As I checked over the loot carried by our first three victims, I little thought that the next encounter of *Atlantis* would yield only the simple salvage of a child's toy . . .

CHAPTER EIGHT

CHILDREN BENEATH OUR GUNS

As THE boat from the burning liner *Kemmendine* approached *Atlantis*, the little Indian boy in the gunwale wept and prayed in a separate Hell of his own.

'Please God, save me. Please God, save him. Please God don't let him die. Please God don't let me die.'

The dark eyes, filled with misery, were fixed helplessly on a swimming sailor and even when the man eventually closed his fingers on the rowlock and hauled himself aboard, the child still kept on praying. He was still praying when he came aboard *Atlantis*. Indeed it was as if he could never stop.

'Steady now' we said. 'He's all right. You're all right. He's saved. You're saved.'

But the shock that had hit the boy when our shells first found the *Kemmendine* took a long time to wear off. The machinery of his panic activated like a gramophone, only slowly running down and stopping finally when he'd sobbed himself to sleep.

It was on 13th July that we met *Kemmendine*. A liner bound from Cape Town to Rangoon, her passengers included a number of English women and children 'going out' to join husbands and fathers in Burma. There were also Indians, mostly merchants, who, with their families had been evacuated from Gibraltar. Thoughts of danger had been far from them all on that sunlit morning for they were free of the U-boat area and when the crew had removed the black-out from the windows of the dining saloon only a night or two before there had been a lot of good-natured banter about the Captain's over-caution in keeping his gloomy precaution going for so long. Most of the passengers had just finished breakfast when they learned a ship was sighted and with the excitement that comes over ocean travellers at such moments the English broke off their interminable swapping of photographs and stories about home and husbands to troop on to the boat deck and enjoy the diversion of watching the stranger pass. Even the Indians, hitherto busily gossiping about the child that was to be born to one of them, eventually yielded to this distraction. To the passengers of *Kemmendine* the War seemed very, very far away . . .

We heard *Kemmendine*'s transmitter being tuned up. We opened fire at 9.30 a.m. . . .

'Good work, Kasch,' said Rogge.

The liner lay stopped. Her radio was silent. A surrender signal flew from her mast, and smoke was beginning to climb faintly around the dazzling whiteness of her superstructure.

Kasch grinned. It hadn't been bad, he thought. Yet another success for the artillery men. A perfect economy in the use of shells. His very first salvo had been sufficient to do the trick, one shell holing the water-line, another wrecking the radio cabin and for a second his hot and stormy eyes flickered appreciatively at the men who served the guns, pleased that his hard driving had welded them into this compact, nicely shooting machine. Kasch was far more interested in the mathematical satisfactions derived from such encounters than in the physical impact of his theories upon the human element at the shells' receiving end. That his accurate shooting resulted in sparing life was a good thing of course, for less well drilled crews would have created minor massacres. But it was the technical aspect—from the speed with which a gun crew got to work to the spread and fall of their shot—that absorbed him most.

We commenced to close in: some watching curiously the activity on the liner's decks as her boats began to fill; others, including myself, checking over equipment in preparation for boarding. Then the incredible hap-

86

pened, a flash from the gun on *Kemmendine*'s stern . . .
Someone shouting 'She's opened fire!' . . . a crash
and a splash in the sea beside us . . . and our blasphemies were emphasised by a column of water, forming up like an exclamation mark.

I had never seen Rogge really angry before, for hitherto the reserves of force in his large frame had been
held in the check; the result of a self-discipline grown so
effective through the years that we had come to regard
our Captain as imperturbable and unrocked by any
storm.

'Salvos' he ordered, and Kasch's guns obeyed.

We winced as the thunder broke. Rogge would blow
the liner to Hell! Kamenz swung round from the drifting gun smoke, 'Could be a mistake, sir.' Again a hail of
shells and tracers tore into our offending adversary. Kamenz took another look, 'There's only one man on the
gun. Some bloody lunatic who doesn't know what's
what . . .'

Rogge made no answer, but hesitated, then motioned
with his hand:

'Cease fire.'

But he was still furiously angry and indeed he had
every reason to be so. He had ceased firing because Kamenz's interruption had jerked him back to the realisation of the carnage we might create among the crowded
boats, but this consideration only added to his anger.
Above all things Rogge hated useless destruction or
waste, and the gunner's apparently fool-hardy action had
invited both.

As it became apparent that women and children
might have been involved in our retaliation, Rogge's anger reached boiling point.

Women . . . children . . . Mentally I cursed the
war as I swung myself on to *Kemmendine*'s deck, then
shelved the humanities in coping with the practical
problem of searching a ship that was already burning. I
photographed the dining room, the spectacle providing
in itself a little commentary on the wastefulness of war,
and the suddenness with which the civilised and every-

day can be trasformed into a ruinous menace. From the smouldering woodwork came thousands of sparks, dropping like fireflies on to the thickly carpeted floor, and as I focused my camera a freshly starched table-cloth suddenly burst into flame; little tongues of yellow and white blending almost immediately into an embracing sheet of fire. A minute longer, and the blaze was sweeping across the debris of what had but recently been a well-appointed room—while all around me lay a jumble of knives and forks and crockery that our shells had jarred into heaped confusion beside the upturned chairs.

Minutes were precious so I dashed off to the purser's office to seize what documents I could, but scarcely had I begun my search than the companionway became filled with smoke. Black and choking it came rolling past the door, with the crackling fire behind it. With no time to stand on ceremony I left with the work undone, and raced for the deck, my eyes streaming and smarting and the heat clutching at my heels.

Our 'drill' had by now been completely disorganised. There was no chance at all of picking up anything valuable and the boarding party were already hurriedly remustering on the deck.

'Blast the 13th,' shouted Fehler. 'We won't even be able to blow up the bloody ship.' Which reminded us . . .

'Christ,' I said.

'The charges!' finished Fehler.

We had dumped them on the deck when boarding *Kemmendine*. Now to our horror we found them ringed by flames.

'Over the side!' I shouted.

The men's reactions were rapid. Ours equally so. We almost fell into the boat and left in such a hurry that we had no opportunity for collecting any swag, only a child's teddy bear and a rabbit which I had snatched from the side of a cot.

Alongside *Atlantis* the boats of the liner rolled heavily in the swell as our crew peered curiously down at the strange sight of women—yes, women, among the pale and dark faces of the seamen captives. The transfer promised to be a tricky business for the sea was running high, and while a sailor could be left to jump for it, a woman or a child quite obviously could not. Then someone said 'Coal buckets', and our problem was solved. Coal buckets—just the job.

The buckets, five feet high and half as broad, were lowered on ropes over the side, and the children, strapped in them, hoisted to the safety of the deck, much to the apprehension of their mothers but with no hurt to themselves. Then come the turn of the women. They were roped around the waist and pulled on board, an unenviable experience for them, and a rather risky one as its success depended on their leaving the boats at the exact moment when the swell was at its highest. But fortunately this manoeuvre was also unaccompanied by injury, and we were finally able to complete the job by bringing the expectant mother in, lashed in a hammock.

With such a variety of prisoners aboard, our once neat decks were looking more than a little untidy when I got back from my visit to the liner, picking my way through a mixed throng of women and children, Hindus, British seamen and marine guards, the latter with pistols at their belts.

Rogge was not pleased by my account of our misadventures on *Kemmendine*. He always hated sacrificing valuable torpedoes and our failure to sink the ship with our explosive charges meant that torpedoing was now the only course left. It cost us two tin fish to finish the *Kemmendine*. And when the end came she folded in half, her bows and stern forming the sides of an immense agony-shaken V which disappeared in minutes beneath a boiling sea.

Surgeon-Commander Reil was not only a capable doctor, he was an astute psychologist and a humane man as well. That is why when an action was in progress, he preferred to spend his time in the glittering white sick bay, realising the stress imposed upon his patients by the noise of the battle they could not see, while, being besides a calm and prudent medico he took advantage of his vigil to make ready the tools of his trade, for, once a fresh batch of wounded came aboard every moment would be precious. Reil liked his patients, and in general his patients liked him. He hated the guns, and when *Kemmendine* reopened fire he swore at the violence of our return. It was a sore point to him that nobody seemed to have thought of some way of cutting out the incredible vibration of *Atlantis* at such moments, and he was perpetually apprehensive that the jarring might jeopardise the success of the more delicate of his operations.

Now he had a new job on his hands, and as he went towards the wardroom he cursed inwardly the shy pernicketiness of Rogge in wishing it on him. For his task was to be the guide, philosopher and friend to the women and children, and he alone would have the responsibility of their welfare so long as they were aboard *Atlantis*. Brother officers, of course, had not been lacking in envious comments about his appointment, comments that varied in the degrees of their coarseness. But Reil was not consoled. He was far more interested in his purely medical activities, and the captain's firm belief in the discreet tradition that a doctor, in default of a priest, was the only suitable protector for unescorted females, irked him. As he approached the wardroom the dapper doctor nervously adjusted his real bow tie . . .

He pushed open the door. A buzz of conversation met him.

'Absolutely unpardonable!' vehemently exclaimed the plain lady in the corner. 'It's a wonder we weren't all murdered.'

'But madam,' said the embarrassed young officer, who was acting temporarily as host, 'it was really quite . . .

Commander Reil lost the rest of his sentence in the torrent of her denunciations.

'Please, please,' said Reil.

There was a pause in which his new charges turned

90

to regard him. With the exception of the plain lady he noted that the women were extraordinarily calm and self-possessed. But God—the plain lady! When she'd first come on board she had labelled the men of *Atlantis* with every expletive that the vocabulary of a lady would allow. 'Brutes, murders, people who spent their time shooting at innocent children' were but the mildest terms of her abuse, and beneath her invectives even the toughened marine guards winced and wilted.

The young officer looked with relief at Reil. With his most suave of peace-time bedside manners the doctor stepped soothingly towards the lady. Inwardly his mind registered 'self-indulged, rather vulgar, probable tendency to high blood pressure' But outwardly he summarised the situation with a bland 'My apologies, madam. A most distressing time. Now perhaps a little drink . . . ?'

It worked, and Reil, after another reassuring word or two, was at last free to take stock of his other prisoner charges. Among the Europeans was a woman with her 14-year-old daughter. They stood a little apart from the rest, the girl's arm linked nervously through that of her mother's. Reil made himself agreeable. The girl, he learnt, was fresh from a convent school and her mother was desperately anxious about the effect that life among so many war toughened sailors might have upon her.

Reil was introduced to an elderly officer of the *Kemmendine* who spoke with a rich Irish brogue. His name was McGowan, and he was the liner's doctor.

'A good idea that drink of yours,' he said. 'There's nothing better for shock than a drop of the best.'

Reil judged that similar treatment would be acceptable to his opposite number. 'A double?'

'I'll take it neat, thank you!'

But what was the matter with small boy in the corner? He was whimpering forlornly despite all the efforts of the women to console him.

'Where's my little chair?' he kept on asking. 'What have you done with my little chair?'

'What little chair does he mean?' asked Reil.

91

A woman explained that *Kemmendine*'s carpenter had made the lad a chair which he was to have been allowed to take with him when the liner docked at Rangoon. The child had spent the last few days of the journey watching his gift being completed, fascinated by the skill of the kind-hearted carpenter.

'Poor kid,' thought Reil. 'So that was HIS war loss.' Reil fixed another drink for the doctor, and had one himself as well. He felt he needed it.

I found Rogge in his cabin, still angry about the reopening of fire after *Kemmendine*'s surrender.

'A very bad business,' he told me. 'And we'll have to do something about that fool of a gunner. What do we know about his background?'

'Oh, he's young and keen, and very new to the sea,' I said. 'Comes from London they tell me and was a window cleaner in peace time.'

Rogge brightened. 'A window cleaner?'

'Well, so they say.'

Rogge shrugged. 'Oh well. What CAN you expect from a window cleaner?'

Personally, pondering on the fact that some of our best men reservists and volunteers had once driven trams, served on milk rounds, or worked in cement factories, I found myself at a loss to see what a man's peace-time job had to do with his efficiency at sea.

'So no court-martial?'

'Not in the circumstances' said Rogge, absorbed with some papers before him.

Trust Rogge to get out of an embarrassing situation without appearing to lose face.

In actual fact the so-called 'window-cleaner' (for all we really knew his peace-time profession was just as likely to have been that of barrister!) was justified in his action, as we later discovered.

It transpired that our first salvo had burst a steam pipe on *Kemmendine*, making hearing almost impossible and at the same time telephonic communication with the bridge had been severed. He had not realised that his ship had surrendered. And the target was tempting!

To us, who had not seen a child for nearly five months, the presence of the children on *Atlantis* became an event of first-class importance, and the problem of how to keep them amused was eagerly undertaken by some of the family men in our crew. As an initial step we devised the 'kindergarten'. Despite its grand name this consisted basically of a heap of sand piled in a corner of our dummy hatch, until now used as a reserve 'swimming pool'. We drew the sand from our ballast, added a few toys whittled by the crew, and set a few deck chairs around for the mothers so that they could sit and supervise their offspring. Although so simply equipped the spot soon became a great favourite with the youngsters who, when not fooling with 'Ferry'—Rogge's Scottie and *Atlantis*'s mascot—would play there for hours. It grew to be quite a rendezvous for their admirers as well— both German and British alike, although in this, the battle for affection, our rivals emerged victorious, one of them, a quartermaster, completely winning over the children with his fantastic yarns of adventure afloat; yarns in which I gather he invariably featured as the hero!

Robin I particularly remember because of his capacity for getting intrigued by anything mechanical. His interest seemed insatiable, and his favourite spot was beside our practice gun, which he would watch in fascination as the dummy shell was loaded, 'fired', and then rolled down the side into a basket. In our practice races between gun crews he provided an excited audience, and our alert friends, the enemy, quick to see opportunity in the manner in which our crew indulged him, used to employ him as a sort of innocent 'spy', after each exploration, questioning him about local gossip, and pumping him for information about the ship's lay-out.

Two Indian children also became favourites. They were Gopi, a six-year-old boy, and Bati, a girl of seven,

93

who, with the ingenuity of their race, were quick to seize such slender chances for childish amusement as existed on our ship. One day, while awaiting the arrival of the cook, one of them was accidentally struck by a carelessly opened galley door. What confusion! She hollered like hell until Cookie bribed her silence with a bar of soothing chocolate, then Gopi, seeing what balm was to be had for tears, followed suit, and had likewise to be silenced with sweet comfort. The children realised they were on to a good thing, and after this you could always find the pair of them lurking hopefully near the galley door, emitting squeaks of surprise and pain every time it opened. Their duplicity was obviously patent—once they were even caught out howling before the door had actually moved—but so bravely attempted that the cook had not the heart to refuse the consolation for which they clamoured.

The arrival of our 'privileged class' of prisoner considerably complicated the problems of accommodation. We sent certain of the women and children to a cabin to the fo'c'sle, their sole furniture consisting of six bunks, two tables, a couple of benches and a wash basin. It wasn't terribly cheerful, but the best we could manage. Some of the passengers had very little clothing with them for *Kemmendine*'s end had been so abrupt that we were prevented from carrying out our usual clothes collecting task and their make-do-and-mend devices proved ingenious.

From some of our football shirts they cut out and stitched items of underwear, while one lady, still endeavouring to remain fashionably elegant, converted a shirt given to her by one of our officers into a kind of 'evening dress', adding a chic effect by a cummerbund of pink tissue. Fortunately the lady was a very small lady, and the officer a very tall officer!

The girl from the convent school remained very shy and frightened, and no one could get a word out of her, but her mother's fears must, I feel, have been more than a little assuaged because when Reil offered the woman a key to lock their room they returned it saying that they felt sure that they had no need of it.

INDIANS! A storm of protest broke from our injured cooking staff.

'Black bastards in my galley!' swore the chief cook. 'It's impossible. The Old Man must be crazy if he thinks we'll stand for it.'

Overhearing the remark, I put my head round the galley door. 'You'll get used to it,' I said.

Rogge, it was, who'd first seen the possibilities of turning the presence of our captured Indians to advantage. A great lover of curries, he had long criticised the inability of our cooks to produce savoury rice as it should be served, and now, with the arrival of the Asiatics he saw his chance and seized it. 'All right,' he said. 'If our cooks can't do it then the Indian prisoners can.'

It was but a short step from employing Indians in the galley to utilising the services of their co-racialists in other spheres, and while the cook became amiably reconciled to his uncomplaining new assistants, the system worked well in other departments of the ship. For the Orientals made themselves useful in a hundred and one different ways . . .

Of the Indians thirty were employed as oilers and cleaners, while Mohammed, answering the nomenclature of 'Boy' despite his white beard and advanced years, took over our cash and accountancy system. Of the captured Chinese some served as stewards, while others, of coarser fibre, later provided labour squads to handle our loot. The Indians were happy as long as their varied prejudices regarding caste and religion were upheld—they had their own cooks to ensure their food was free of the grease of pigs or cattle. The Chinese were happy as long as their labours yielded a 'percent'. Once, after boarding a ship carrying large quantities of clothing I saw each of the yellow men help himself to about twelve hats, which he proudly carried in a sort of telescopic column on his head.

95

Of our native passengers from *Kemmendine*, one, a very elderly Indian, was so strict that he kept his family of fourteen in purdah, and despite the stifling weather these unfortunate souls never saw the light of day for as long as they were with us.

Most of the Indian merchants had lost practically all their worldly wealth with the sinking of their ship, and they amazed us by their philosophical attitude for, where one would have expected despondency, one received instead a shrug and a laugh. 'Life is the main thing,' observed one. 'We'll get our money back somehow.' He was right. They did. For when only two years ago, I called in at Gibraltar while on my way to Turkey, I found my former prisoner again set up in business and he was doing very-nicely-thank-you. His tiny shop was crammed with Indian chests, silk, and carpets, and our meeting, most cordial, wound up with his request to 'tell any of your friends who might care to call this way'.

Our relations with the European women, to whom we had allotted two of *Kemmendine*'s stewards, were extremely formal and correct, and contrary to the possibly gloomy anticipations of Rogge, the prisoners were soon regarded by our crew as just part of the normal landscape of the ship.

They were courageous, these women, and I can remember only one who showed an antipathy towards Britain and her cause. Yet, strangely enough, we would have thought her to be the last to feel this way. For the lady concerned was no less than the plain lady, the one whose complaints were so frequent and loudly spoken—complaints over trivialities that the rest of our passengers disregarded with a dignified calm—that we'd christened her Devil's Roast.

Devil's Roast was quite a character, we thought, and her grouses eventually more amused us than otherwise. Obviously a well-indulged type. Her special complaint was that the bartender on *Kemmendine* had left his post after the first salvo. 'Would you believe it,' she said.

'Leaving the bar at a time like that! Worse still, the fool locked it!'

Certainly the lady was somewhat partial to her 'drop', and our looted Scotch provided a frequent panacea to her wounded susceptibilities.

Once when the Scotch 'ran dry', after a party in the prisoners' quarters, the 'D.R.' stepped smoothly to the rescue. 'Oddly enough,' she said, 'I happen to have a bottle in my quarters.'

We exchanged a smile. But how to get the stuff? We couldn't very well pop into the women's quarters ourselves—not with Rogge's hawk-like vigilance all round us—and female prisoners couldn't be allowed to roam through the ship at will. So we allotted her an escort armed according to the book, with regulation pistol and two hand grenades! We watched the procession depart, the escort very correct, though slightly bewildered, the plain lady, purposeful, nose in air.

When they returned a few minutes later, we noticed the bottle was not quite full, and the guard, I thought, looked unusually sheepish. We decided to ask no questions . . .

It was only after our *Kemmendine* guests had left *Atlantis* that a discordant note crept in to the picture we had formed of a hot-tempered amusingly domineering woman, who called a spade a spade and stood-no-damned-nonsense-from-anyone! Examining mail prized from another of our captures, I found an intelligence report from British agents in Burma—a report on our captive's husband! He was, I read, under suspicion of spying for the Japanese. Judging the husband by my impressions of the lady, I laughed the thing off as a cheering example that it was not only in Germany where unpopular utterances were penalised by the snoopers and pryers. But Rogge was rather thoughtful. He had received a letter from the lady that, in thanking him for the way in which she had been treated aboard, hinted mysteriously that she was Irish and not English and had thought it tactless to mention this fact before the others. 'Now WHY?' puzzled Rogge.

Our perplexity soon vanished in the problems of the day, but when we eventually got back to Germany we were astounded to find that the Satanic Joint was broadcasting for Joyce; and forthermore, had written in German an anti-British book.

I wonder how she is faring today?

August 2nd, and *Atlantis* lay stopped undergoing a thorough engine overhaul and repaint.

For six weeks we had kept *Tirranna* 'on ice', waiting for us in the quiet south, and when we rejoined her we had been told, 'We haven't sighted even the tip of a masthead since you left.'

This reassuring report persuaded Rogge that this was as good an area of the sea as any in which to carry out the work we had hitherto postponed. Then once it was completed we would send *Tirranna* home, using her as a convenient ship to carry the women and children and other passengers whose presence would be a handicap to the new wave of attacks he planned.

We set to work and soon the ship was surrounded by a complicated tower of scaffolding festooned by pots of paint. With the painters perched like buzzards on the masts, or hanging like bats from the rigging; with working parties curing the steel with mercury ointment and paint; with acetylene lamps burning into metal and the staccato hammering of rivets, the whole ship throbbed with the activity of a construction yard, and Kuehn, our second in command, found ample scope for the voice and scowl that had earned this former bo'sun the tough soubriquet of 'Captain Bligh', however gold his heart.

Our mid-ocean refit had followed much hard work and heartbreak in removing such of *Tirranna*'s loot as would be handy to our ship; and the transference of over one hundred tons of diesel oil had entailed a particularly tricky operation; the oil pipes being heaved in by ropes and *Atlantis*, towed slowly by her prize, staggering and plunging through the heaviest of seas, a heavy anchor chair shackled to the towing line to prevent it from tightening and snapping. By the time our 'unpacking' had ended only our medicos felt pleased with themselves, both of them having secured in the most remarkable fashion, something for 'the profession' out of the general pickings.

For a long time our junior doctor—Reil's deputy—had been bemoaning his inability to catch up with his medical studies, and he was still complaining when he and I first took a boat over to our victim. Thousands of pieces of printed matter from her extensive mail had been read and ditched by our prize crew, and the water around her was covered with specks of white pulp. Then I noticed drifting on the oily swell, and almost scraping the side of our launch, a beautifully bound book. In idle curiosity I put my hand over the side, and picked it up. I looked at the title, then passed it over to the doctor.

'More your line of reading than mine!' I said.

Sprung glanced at it sourly, then 'Oh my God,' he said, 'A miracle!'

The book was no less than a treatise on the latest techniques of war surgery.

Sprung was jubilant, lucky again! A drill, used by a radio amateur, aboard *Tirranna*, caught his questioning eye. 'So delicate,' he said. 'So finely balanced.'

'What?' I joked. 'Is the junior genius about to build his own radio set?'

'Skull trepanning,' he murmured absently, and tapping the drill with his finger added, 'With this little gadget I can repair anybody's brainbox.'

I privately hoped that whatever injuries I might ever sustain would be confined to some other region of my body, but the drill came up to Sprung's expectations. All too soon he had to attend to a British prisoner, with a splinter in the brain, and the amateur's tool extracted it. Said Sprung, the sweat running down his face, 'It may not be up to their Harley Street specification, but the result is the same. The patient will live.'

The weather for our refit was initially favourable, a period of calm seas and clear skies, but on 2nd August, it started to rain, an event of importance for, as a result of the mists that accompanied it, a fifth victim came waltzing into our arms.

Pfeilsticker ran so fast to his post of duty that he scarcely had any breath left to call up the gun.

The stranger had swept out of the rain squall only a few hundred yards away and *Atlantis*, with her crazy mass of scaffolding, lay like a sitting duck in the rising sea. Even Rogge's imperturbability was temporary shaken as the klaxons sent out their urgent, unexpected summons.

For a minute the ship was completely confused, the men dropping paint buckets, sliding down from the masts or hauling themselves up like cats from the dinghy by the stern. They came to the guns in overalls, or stripped to the waist, with sweat, paint and oil intermingled, while one unfortunate sailor all alone in a dinghy came rowing frantically after us as we started the engines, terrified at being left behind in the event of our departure.

'Oh, you bloody fool,' said Pfeilsticker, as someone running past him trod upon his feet, then he blushed as he picked up the telephone, swearing not usually being his habit.

'Captain Bligh' was swearing too. But there was no novelty in that.

Then, once again, the machine took charge of us all, and once again, well drilled sailors in a warship, we waited for our opponent's full appearance.

A cruiser? Anything but. By an extraordinary coincidence the newcomer was the Norwegian *Talleyrand*, sister ship to *Tirranna*. She came bouncing out of the rain storm noticing nothing except the familiar shape of her sister.

We opened fire within four minutes of our first alarm, and *Talleyrand*, taken completely by surprise, surrendered without bloodshed.

* * *

100

Our preparations for *Tirranna*'s journey were now almost complete, but the departure of the ship would, we realised, present us with the necessity of communicating with Berlin by radio, for unless we identified our prize and announced her course our submarines might attack her on the long track home.

But how to avoid betraying our position to the British? In the end Rogge arranged that we should travel a thousand miles to the south before sending our signal, and then get out at speed; stabbing into the northern reaches of the Indian Ocean, hopeful that, unless they bumped into us on the way, the D/F of our pursuers would lead them only to an empty waste . . .

We said goodbye to *Tirranna* on 4th August. She carried all the women and children, all men over fifty, her own crew and that of *Talleyrand*, some of the Indians, and a fifteen-year-old cadet.

The setting for our parting was ironically gay. As *Tirranna* moved away the passengers of *Kemmendine* were standing on the deck, waving and singing. They were all in good spirits, and as they sang the British prisoners still abroad *Atlantis* started to cheer and picked up the refrain.

I did not realise it then, but this tune was to make a lasting impression on my mind, and I have never heard it since without being strangely moved. For none of us had any premonition of the fate that was so shortly to overtake *Tirranna* and the youngest of those aboard her. As we watched *Tirranna* moving away the words of the song the passengers were so lightheartedly singing floated back across the water. The song was 'Goodbye Sally . . .'

CHAPTER NINE

DEADLY ENCOUNTERS

As WE passed through the multi-hued waters of the Indian Ocean the business of killing became once more the dominant motive in our lives, all else faded with the unreality of a dream, or passed as the flotsam that dwindled, ever more remote, on the fringe of our shimmering, racing wake . . .

Scientist, Tirranna, City of Bagdad, Talleyrand, and *Kemmendine* and the mines around the Cape . . . all these were recent events as we made ready to close upon *King City* in the stormy August night. Yet, to speak honestly, they seemed far closer to me when I sat down to write the preceding chapter than they did within days of their actual occurrence. It was always the 'next' that was important. Never the 'last'. Hunted, as well as the hunter (nearly thirty British armed merchant cruisers were now scouring the Seven Seas), we had no time to indulge in reveries on the past. Looking back could do no good.

We sighted *King City* on 24th August off Madagascar. It was an encounter which caused bitterness among our British prisoners; an encounter which didn't leave us with the pleasantest of taste in our mouths.

We shelled *King City* when we need not have done so. We shelled her not knowing she was a harmless merchantman. Ane we killed six of her crew, among them four apprentices, barely more than lads. Yet such is war and all its filthy complications, that I do not see how, unless we were clairvoyant, we could have avoided this tragedy of which a British prisoner afterwards wrote, 'This was the most pitiful story of any ship.'

King City was the first to be sighted by our look-outs at night, and her misfortunes began when we noticed that, in seas where merchantmen ran furtively and on erratic courses to reach their goal, *she* lay stopped and silent. Naturally, we were suspicious.

I came to the bridge, my eyes still dazzled by the transition from the brightness of my cabin to the murky blackness of the night: a starless night, and rain falling thinly like a mist into the unquiet sea.

'What price the tropics now?' grumbled the officer of the watch as he huddled his neck yet deeper into the collar of his greatcoat.

I squeezed in beside him, squinting vaguely to port. It was certainly chilly. A beast of a night.

'Rum looking job,' said the officer of the watch. 'God knows what she's up to.'

Through the night glasses I discerned a humped grey shadow taking shape out of the blackness. A ship all right. But what sort of a ship? The funnel seemed almost flush against the square built bridge, but I could not make out the usual mast of a merchantman. Another squint, and then a squall obliterated her. I became aware of Rogge at my side. He said 'We're turning on an opposite course. I'm going to increase speed to maximum, and we'll go in for a closer look.'

We started to turn. Then someone said, 'There she is again,' and the murk lifted and we could see the stranger more clearly. This time she was moving, although at low speed. We watched her until a few minutes longer, and then, quite unexpectedly, she stopped again. Had she seen us? She must have done. We felt sure of that, terribly sure at the time.

'Come on. Make up your minds,' grumbled the signals officer. 'If you're an innocent merchantman, then why the devil don't you do what your precious Admiralty tells you and turn away!'

'Unless of course,' remarked one of us dryly, 'our innocent merchantman happens to be a Q Ship not looking for subs. Just looking for us . . .'

A Q Ship? Could be. We knew the British AMC's

were prowling after us. Maybe they'd taken a leaf out of our book, disguised their guns, assumed sheep's clothing?

As we considered the prospect the ship ahead restarted her engines and again commenced her leisurely, enigmatic crawl. We followed suit, tailing along for nearly an hour, sailing on a course practically parallel with that of our victim, waiting tensely, on tip-toe with readiness for action, expecting at any moment to see the yellow and scarlet blaze of her guns flare outwards from the dark. Yet still she continued her course, still showing no signs of interest in our identity.

'Cool customer,' commented the officer who'd advanced the Q ship theory. 'Playing us at our own game, eh?'

And even the taciturnity of Kamenz was broken by the simple phrase. 'Queer, I must admit. Yes, very queer.'

Kasch stood beside Rogge, two dark shapes against the binnacle's low light.

'We'll wait for the dawn. If they'll let us,' decided Rogge, 'Then we'll go in. Two rounds first, just in case we're mistaken. But if not, give 'em the rest in a bunch!'

'Thank God for that' I thought. 'At least we'll get it over with.'

I was dog-tired and the bridge held small comfort. I wanted to get my head down and had almost ceased to care about the outcome.

Dawn's first light, and with the paling sky the crash of our 5.9's in thunderous salute. Split second only from our Battle Ensign's breaking the shells hit home. Devastatingly home. Direct hits, both of them. And as the target trembled a tower of blossoming smoke . . . A pause . . . just long enough for a man to call upon his Maker, and then the flames swept up, soaring amidships, setting her bridge ablaze.

We waited for the come-back. It never came. Our shells had struck with the effect of a match thrown into a pool of petrol, flinging the flames savagely through the ship, with a force that was uncontrollable. And against this man-made Hades we saw her armament—a puny anti-submarine gun, a weapon common to merchantmen, unmanned and with its barrel pointing uselessly towards the stern. The decks we thought were camouflage for six-inchers, were revealed in all their innocence, as jagged and scarred and empty as a discarded sardine tim.

'Away boat.'

Ours now the job to give what help we could. The sea was running very high. As for a moment I steadied myself against the rail a qualm assailed me. A second's fault in timing you damned fool, I reminded myself, and you'll be faced with a twelve foot drop as the waves fall beneath the boat. Men have been smashed to pulp against the sides of their ships . . . boats have been capsized by the avalanche of the waters . . . Shut up you damn fool and concentrate . . .

With a scream from the davits and a roar from the ocean we hit the surface. It dropped like a lift carrying our boat with it, then sodden with sea and salt we rose again to strike out unsteadily for the inferno on our beam. Not for the first time nor the last, had we good reason to be grateful for *Tirranna*'s loot. We'd taken her whalers with us, and splendid sea boats they were; cruiser sterns, you could steer them by tiller. They were just the job for a night like this.

Kross, the helmsman, echoed my thoughts. 'Lucky we're not in our motor launch now,' he shouted. I bawled back my agreement for bitter experience had proved our regulation naval launches of little use in really rough seas. But the waves dropped our boat again, and Kross, uncomprehending, his face drenched with spray, spluttered, 'I said, sir, it's lucky . . .' The rest was lost in the thunder of the waters.

Our adversary was horrible to behold. Across the flames fast-spreading backcloth moved minute shadows—the shapes of men struggling to lower the boats, desperate to escape. A float went over the side. I saw it flop into the water, and at once become surrounded by the heads of men as the swimmers struggled towards it. The heat could be felt three hundred yards away as up from our victim shot a myriad sparks, showering into drifting wreckage, spattering boats now packed with desperately rowing men.

'A bloody miracle,' I said when later I discovered that only the victims of our salvo had failed to make *Atlantis* from the inferno of their ship and the wilderness of the dawn. Very pluckily the crew had brought their wounded with them, and eventually we were able to locate and save them all. A miracle indeed.

I took photographs when the rescue work was over, and our guns had again opened fire, this time to put an end to *King City*'s agony. Nothing seemed to go right that infernal dawn. We were over two hundred yards from the target, yet our shell splinters came whistling back across the waters making us duck. *King City* had been carrying 5,000 tons of coal from Cardiff to Singapore, and vast inky masses of it shifted and rolled and rumbled in her battered holds, before pouring, like volcanic lava, through the gaping voids in her hull. We watched in silence as towers of black smoke pillared into the sombre sky, while the waters, now strangely calm, still reflected the blood red of the fire.

When her final moment came *King City* expired like a sea monster in mortal pain. As the water lashed the red hot iron of her hull a white steam surrounded her, a terrible hissing swept across the sea, and turning on to her belly she terminated the proceedings with an uncanny screech of agony, leaving for minutes after her passing a swirl of water, bubbling, steaming and seething above her grave.

We returned to *Atlantis* in a somewhat subdued frame of mind, Kross, whose normal post when not my helmsman was at the ship's ice plant, being more than usually quiet. One of the most polite men in the ship, you would not have recognised on first acquaintance the skill and cunning that had made him a master of small boat manoeuvres or guessed at the quiet courage

106

and strong compassion that lay beneath his surface suavity. He was gloomy now. And I was gloomy too. We had witnessed the barbaric poetry of war and we had not liked what we had seen.

'Well,' said Rogge, a little later. 'Now we know the reason for the Englishman's odd behaviour.'

And it was so simple. So tragically simple. She had never even seen us until it was too late!

Gradually we learnt the full story. When, at long last, our presence had become known, *King City*'s first mate had rushed for a torch to signal to us. Too late! Our gun flaps shot up and our shells hit home . . .

'But why did you stop and start, then stop and start again?' I asked.

'God Almighty,' said the exhausted seaman. 'Don't say you didn't KNOW!'

King City, it transpired, had stopped in the first place because one of the ventilators on the furnace room had broken down. They had managed to repair it—hence their getting under way—but then it had given once again.

It was a tragic episode, and next day we noticed a definite coolness in the behaviour of our British prisoners.

One of them said accusingly to me, 'You were too blasted trigger-happy in *King City*'s case. She never had a chance. You shot a sitting duck, and your very first shell killed four apprentices, asleep in their bunks. Another is dead now and there's a bloke in the sick bay who's got his stomach ripped out. He's married. He was aching to get home to the little son he's never had a chance of seeing. Nice sort of war isn't it, don't you think?' And he turned away.

For a moment I felt really angry. Wasn't the business bad enough without having its details rubbed home? I half moved to follow him to explain, or try to, the combination of coincidences that had led to this sordid encounter. I thought better of it. It really wasn't worth while.

For how the devil were we to know? How the devil

does anyone KNOW? If our target had proved to be other than she was it was we who would have been doing the swimming—and the dying. If we were hasty, well, hesitation might have meant the end of us all.

At the same time, as we observed to each other in the wardroom, we wished we had never met the ill-fated ship—a reflection that was, of course, a luxury in wartime.

The *Athelking* incident, following within a fortnight the *King City* tragedy, was also marked by misunderstanding.

Very alert, her Captain had ordered his gun to be trimmed when we were still eleven nautical miles away. When we did nothing, and showed no sign of changing course—we were steaming across her bows—the gun crew stood down, but on our ordering maximum rcvs and coming into the attack, our fire was promptly and vigorously returned.

At this, of all times, our electric rudder circuit had to break down, and we circled helplessly, banging away erratically till we managed at last to steer from aft. *Athelking* surrendered shortly afterwards, hoisting the signal 'W'. (I need a doctor.)

Reil was about to climb into the boat when our signaller suddenly warned us, 'Ship has resumed sending, sir!'

A sharp order, and we re-opened fire, but ceased almost at once as our signaller's voice was heard again—'Mistake! Mistake! It's another ship!'

The O.Q.Q. was, in fact, a signal from the s.s. *Benarty*, which, unknown to us at the time, was almost within earshot of our guns. She had intercepted and re-transmitted *Athelking*'s original message, and hers was the 'voice' heard over our radio.

Athelking, even after receiving her death blow, still contrived to haunt us, her bows jutting from the waves like an accusing finger, until finally, we had to dispose of her by riddling her bow tanks with machine-gun bullets.

* * *

'Well, even an ocean raider must rest sometime,' said Rogge, his square shoulders bent over the chart.

So far, *Atlantis* had more than done her duty. A score of eight merchantmen totalling nearly 60,000 tons was not bad. Not bad at all. Especially, we reflected, as the actual period of operation had only really begun since the meeting with *Scientist*. The sturdy old Hansa liner had certainly given the Royal Navy something to think about; started quite a hue and cry in these hitherto tranquil waters. From the ebb and flow of enemy radio signals, from the documents *Atlantis* had captured, it was obvious that the enemy was experiencing all the inconveniences and waste of sudden re-routings, cancellation of sailings, and late arrivals of urgent cargoes.

'Think like your opposite number.' That was Rogge's maxim, and that was why a huge wall plan of the Indian Ocean bearing the words 'Admiral Colombo' now decorated the wardroom.

Picturing himself as installed in the hub of Royal Navy Intelligence in Ceylon, Rogge had marked upon the map what he deemed would be a reasonable British assumption of *Atlantis*'s movements by connecting our first three operations, *Scientist*, the *City* and *Tirranna*. An intelligent calculator of our intentions would, he presumed, have estimated that we were bound for Australia. In point of fact another raider, a few weeks earlier, had commenced to operate off New Zealand in June, and this had perfected our alibi. The intention was to confuse the enemy regarding the identities of our raiders, and Rogge chuckled as he wondered if the little side-show of the 'submarine buoys' had come off. If it had, then there would be yet more bewilderment. For, so far, none of our U-boats had operated far south of the equator.

'Put yourself in the enemy's skin,' was his advice. 'Think the way he thinks. He's got to look for you somewhere, and the more energy he uses up in looking for you, the better it will be.'

By now the black dots on the chart that marked British warship movements—supplied to us by Berlin—were clustering around our hunting area once more, and having quite successfully set the Indian Ocean aflame, Rogge decided it was time for a rest while the fire brigade exhausted their energies among the ruins.

So while *Atlantis* was on her way to the little used waters of the south and travelling slowly across the so-called Australian Trade route, did we come unexpectedly across the *Commissaire Ramel*, a murky silhouette and proceeding without lights.

'Ship sending signals. Medium and short wave as well.'

The Frog's voice was immediately followed by the shouted command, *'Feuererlaubnis!'* (Shoot!)

Into the dark screamed the multi-coloured ribbon of the tracers, steaming into our adversary amidships to silence the instruments that betrayed us. A pyrotechnical bridge curved between *Atlantis* and her prey, and then, like some miniature atomic explosion smoke mushroomed from the stranger, and the red and yellow flames began their now familiar drunken dance.

As in *King City*'s case the destruction progressed with terrifying speed. As we watched a pin-head of light shot out from the temporary darkness of the stern. Our signallers spelt out the words 'send a boat', and then the lamp's blinking was lost completely in the dazzling glare of the flames.

Into the whaler we went, the seas pouring round us high and steep. A terrible glow had arisen from the *Commissaire*, but the valleys of the waters had sides so sheer and shifting that only in rare and reeling intervals could our stinging salt-lashed eyes catch sight of her. Her boats had separated in the mind and we had to shut off our engines at intervals and drift in an attempt to catch the direction from which the men's voices, feeble against the wind, cried out for help. Fortunately the British had fitted emergency lights to the Mae Wests of their crews, and this helped us enormously. But it was the most macabre affair we ever witnessed. Now and then, staggering into view to disappear, and reappear,

110

we caught a glimpse of the torches being used by the officers from *Commissaire*'s boats, a succession of tiny sparkles on the foaming white ridges of the waves.

'What's that?' shouted Kross.

I looked to starboard where an object was tossed from a wave crest to fall into the trough. Could be wreckage; could be . . . ?

It was a small raft with a youngster clinging to it for dear life. We drove towards him, and reached out to help him over the side. But he made no effort.

'Come on, curse you,' I shouted. 'Don't be a fool.'

For a second I had a glimpse of the white, hysterical face of a boy who cried something at us before our boat tilted and we momentarily lost him from view.

Finally we had to drag him aboard. Just a cabin boy of fifteen, but he fought us all the way, shouting 'Don't kill me. Don't kill me!'

At first I thought it was a plain case of hysteria. Who wouldn't feel hysterical in a sea like this? Only later did we realise that the boy had genuinely believed that we had only saved him for torturing. This was the first time we encountered the fruits of the propaganda that was being directed at our activities.

Our rescue work continued for three or four hours. We were drenched to the skin and icy cold. We were battered by the seas like dice within a cup.

Still afloat, our adversary was by now red hot. Through her port holes the glare of the hell within gave her the illusionary appearance of a passenger liner, her lights ablaze in the long dead days of peace. But the only music that echoed across the water was the crackle of the flames, and the noise of the breaking going on inside her; these sounds alone we heard above the moaning of the wind.

Commissaire's sinking was in the Wagnerian tradition established by *King City*—a monumental mass of glowing scarlet iron hitting the ocean with a terrifying roar, followed shortly by a blackness so intense that we felt like men suddenly struck blind. One moment the flames bathed the sky with blood; the next darkness, and a cold, wet wind blowing all around us with nothing else to be heard save the slap of the sea against our hull, the wail of the winds around our rigging . . .

The men from the *Commissaire* came aboard *Atlantis*. They were a motley crew. The Captain, a 64-year-old Scot, had been brought from retirement in Australia to command the ship. Of the remaining sixty-two, fourteen were French, nine were Negroes, and the rest Australian or British, but very few, so far as we could see, were professional seamen.

'Why are you in the merchant navy?' I asked one of them, a smoke-grimed, hard-bitten Australian.

'Oh,' said he. 'I JUST JOINED FOR THE FUN OF IT!'

CHAPTER TEN

THE SINKING OF THE 'TIRRANNA'

It was 22nd September 1940.

Able Seamen Seeger picked up a pencil and drew a thick black line across the calendar. Eliminating in a sure and heavy stroke the remaining eight days of September, he wrote firmly above the 22nd just one word—HOME! Then, whistling, he wandered to the deck.

Seeger had every reason to be happy. Originally, when the Old Man had detailed him to make up one of the small prize crew to take *Tirranna* home, he had had more than a misgiving or two. All very nice in a way, he thought, but running through the British blockade on a 10,000 mile excursion in a ship where fourteen guards were supposed to cope with 300 prisoners wasn't everybody's cup of tea.

Yet considering everything, especially considering that ever-so-lovely French coastline—just three miles away, just 5,000 or so tantalising yards, a mere three-quarters of an hour's 'walk', if you took it easy—well, considering everything, they'd done very nicely thank you. They were home; or pretty nearly so. The cheery Seeger went on whistling. He was whistling 'Tipperary'. An odd sort of tune you might think for a fighter for the Reich to favour, but catchy, and indeed bringing back to him for a moment the memories of *Atlantis*, and how the prisoners from *Kemmendine* had told him they'd been singing this tune and bashing out 'Mademoiselle from Armentieres' on the liner's piano only the day before they'd been caught.

Funny how some tunes cling. His father used to whis-

113

tle 'Tipperary' to him when he was a kid; he'd brought it home after the First Lot. What were the English words again? 'It's a long way to go . . .'

Old Lieutenant Mundt peered down at the French fishing boats, now lying by *Tirranna*'s black and travel-soiled hull, and at the men who were listening to his faltering French with such blank incomprehension; men who had now become almost as symbolic to him as the dove that alighted upon Noah's Ark.

He could hardly believe it. The desperate run was over and the tension that had so steadily built up as the prize had neared the 'bottleneck' had collapsed like one of the Met. Officer's balloons when hit by the bullet of a practical joker.

In a quarter of an hour, he, Mundt, would be ashore; treading the cobbled pavements; seeing the sun glittering on the *pavé*; hearing the sounds of wheels and women's voices; feasting his eyes upon green shutters and grey houses. His was the task of reporting to the local Naval Authority the arrival of the prize, and fixing arrangements for her reception. He was still a little breathless at the thought that they'd beaten the blockade. Maybe a decoration or two? And perhaps there would be a band to play them in?

'*Mais je ne comprends pas . . . ?*'

The words and the sight of the swarthy leatherlike face of the French skipper brought Mundt abruptly back to earth again, and once more he started to cope with the complicated business of making himself understood to a bunch of idiots who didn't seem to know their own language.

Aware that—owing to the native's insistence on dialect—the original awe of his crew for his linguistic abilities was wearing a little thin, he demanded very slowly, distinctly and painstakingly, emphasising each syllable as carefully as one might to a backward child, that he be given passage forthwith to the shore. It was an exhausting process, and when the deal was eventually concluded he felt quite hot and somewhat flustered.

Once in the boat he tried to engage his hosts in conversation, but they were silent, sullen almost. They regarded him with a certain phlegmatic indifference that made him feel uncomfortable, and by the time he had set foot on the jetty he found that he had shed much of his original exuberance. He looked around, rather futilely, for Somebody-in-Charge, and a sense of anti-climax overcame him. *Atlantis* had been a world on her own, with *Tirranna* a projection of that world. To his bewilderment Mundt now experienced the first effects of his long divorce from the shore; a feeling of loss; an odd detachment from the people he now saw around him; an odd self-consciousness as the result of an unfamiliar setting. No. There would be no brass band. He knew that within the first few minutes.

He had a devil of a job getting through on the telephone to Naval H.Q. Whoever-it-was he spoke to seemed almost irritated at being interrupted in whatever-it-was he was doing and Mundt began to feel somehow apologetic for bothering him. Then he spoke to someone else, someone who seemed to treat the arrival of this laden-prize from halfway across the world with about as much enthusiasm as a lock-keeper disturbed from his Sunday dinner to arrange passage for a dinghy.

Tirranna was to wait where she was. Owing to enemy minelaying she wouldn't possibly enter the Gironde without a sweeper escort. She would be met the following morning.

'Tomorrow morning? Mundt was astounded. 'But that's twelve hours away!'

'Well, what's twelve hours to you?' said the voice, joviality creeping in.

'But what about enemy submarines?' Mundt protested.

The voice laughed. 'Don't worry, Lieutenant. There are no submarines in this area.'

As Mundt stepped out into the blazing sunshine he was possessed with a feeling of disquiet. He tried to shake it off. Group West, he told himself, knew best of

115

course. Besides, a ship didn't make a journey like *Tirranna*'s to be pipped at the post . . .

The English passengers on *Tirranna* viewed the coast of France with a pleasure not quite so unalloyed as that of their captors. Nevertheless, some of them privately admitted it was a relief in a way. After the necessarily roughish accommodation of *Atlantis, Tirranna* had seemed almost luxurious. She had sufficient space for her 95 white prisoners and 179 Indians, and for the civilians she had provided comfortable cabins, room to breathe, and service of stewards. Not that you could feel you were on a pleasure cruise however much you tried; not when you realised that your official destination was a prison camp!

At first the optimists had looked forward to meeting a British warship. But when, only two days after leaving *Atlantis, Tirranna* had had a narrow squeak with a British cruiser, a few of the passengers were almost grateful for the miss. They'd been told that *Tirranna* wouldn't make a fight of it—not with such a cargo and with so small a crew—but you never knew, and a few shells sent to stop her in her traces would hardly have earmarked Germans only for their prey. Then new apprehensions began to arise. The approaches to the German-held ports were heavily patrolled by British submarines, craft that of necessity could not hope to discriminate in their choice of victims, or have the time or means to fidget about survivors. On the whole, therefore, it was with mixed emotions that the prisoners had first sighted the blue coast of Spain rising swiftly up to starboard, and now that they were in enemy territory, so to speak, they decided to accept the inevitable and make the best of things. At any rate, they agreed, they'd got the children safely through all the hazards of the sea.

As Mundt returned from the shore he noticed two or three of the kids larking around the rails. What, he wondered, would the future hold for them? Well, one thing about it, the monotony of an internment camp would not affect them as adversely as their elders. Astonishing, he reflected, how children, the world over, seemed possessed of a defensive resilience, an infinite capacity for creating pleasure in their land-of-make-believe.

Seeger could literally FEEL the curiosity of the seamen prisoners, when, instead of immediately entering the Gironde, *Tirranna* commenced instead to cruise slowly up the coast.

'What the hell are we waiting for?' he heard someone say.

Said someone else, a weather-beaten Norwegian, 'Some monkey business ashore, no doubt.'

Seeger, who knew the reason, kept his mouth shut but the buzz soon got around notwithstanding, as such things do. The Royal Air Force had dropped mines in the river, rendering it unsafe for navigation. But there was no need for alarm. No need at all. In the morning *Tirranna* would be met by the minesweepers that would escort her in.

'So we've yet another night at sea after all,' said one of the English, his cheerfulness reflecting his pride in the R.A.F.'s alterations to the schedule.

'We ought to celebrate,' said another. But he said it with a sardonic emphasis for he was an old, old sailor, who had spent many years at sea.

Mundt had the fidgets. The longer *Tirranna* was kept waiting the less he liked it. Just where the devil were those minesweepers? The night had passed, the dawn had passed. It was now nearly lunch time. And still they hadn't turned up. He found himself nervously looking seaward.

Seeger still whistled (Tipperary), but rather more absentmindedly than usual. What the hell were they fussing around for? Why didn't they just bash straight in?

Another hour passed, and another. Lunch came and went. Some of the smallest children had been tucked up for their afternoon nap. A few of the women were resting in deck chairs, the sun on their faces, and in their minds thoughts of home and curiosity as to what fate this alien shore would bring.

'Don't worry, Lieutenant. There are no submarines in this area.'

The torpedoes struck . . . One . . . two . . . three!

For a second after the crash there was a silence of horror and surprise. Then hell broke loose.

The hitherto level deck swung to a crazy angle, one rail sliding towards the water, the other rearing high against the sky. Mundt picked himself up as the alarm bells hammered, women screamed, and 300 people rushed clumsily for life. Semi-dazed, he blinked at the chaos, focusing finally on a civilian passenger sliding down the slope towards the sea.

'Not that way,' he shouted. 'If she goes down quick she'll turn on top of you!'

Seeger took the tough way, the sailors' way, an upward climb to the rail silhouetted against the blue sky, and was just about to lever himself over when he noticed the Englishwoman. She stood clutching the rail, her gaze fixed upon the clouds. Postponing his impulse to get out quick, Seeger hollered at her, but she took no notice, and just stood there staring, her mind seemingly far from the frenziedly splashing multitude below.

'For God's sake, jump!' Seeger shouted.

The woman made no answer.

'Jump!' screamed Seeger. 'She's going down.'

Then, blaspheming against the impulse that stopped him from saving his own skin first, he hauled himself, slithering, hand over hand along the rail, to reach her side.

'Come on. We'll go together' he panted. 'There's plenty to give you a helping hand down there.'

The woman half turned. Her face was still, and set. Her thoughts he realised, were thousands of miles away. She just hadn't got a clue. For shock had paralysed all thought, all fear. Seeger tried to wrench her hands from the rail, to knock them forcibly free. Impossible. The slender hands seemed frozen to the iron.

118

The ship gave a sudden lurch. He cracked his fist down on her wrist. 'Damn you, jump,' he almost wept. Another lurch, and his thinking stopped. He found himself in the water striking out blindly to get away from the downward suck of the swirling waters.

'Don't worry, Lieutenant . . .'

Back in the Gironde a flotilla of minesweepers had been waiting for hours the order to sail, waiting with steam up. The men were ready, the officers impatient, and all that they wanted was the word to go. But they didn't get it, not until it was too late; not until a few minutes of *Tirranna's* receiving her death blow; for someone had blundered. So, instead of bringing triumphantly to port a fine prize and a valuable cargo the sweepers' task was finally the melancholy one of searching for survivors among the wreckage. And the word had come too late for them even to be effective in this sphere of action, an aircraft of the German Air Force being the first to reach the scene followed speedily by a destroyer.

On entering the blockade area the passengers had been warned to remain dressed at all times of the day and night, and instructed to keep their life jackets in constant readiness. These precautions resulted in the majority being saved, but the toll was still tragically high, for such was the speed of the disaster that the children had little chance.

Robin, Sally and their mother—all three were lost. Nine of the Indian children also went down, and among them was the baby, the baby born to the mother from *Kemmendine* we had brought aboard *Atlantis* in a hammock.

When the *Tirranna* plunged, Mundt had trod water, bawling to others to do the same; mindful that after a ship's sudden sinking a stream of debris often shot to the surface with the speed of a torpedo, killing or maiming those who floated on their backs. Now, rescued, three cameos of disaster still flickered in front of his confused brain.

The kid the sailors were trying to fix up with a life-jacket . . .

The English girl, crying bitterly because she was looking for her mother, and crying in vain because she had lost her spectacles and was so short-sighted that she could only see a few yards ahead of her. She was alone on a float when they found her and they didn't like to tell her that the spectacles would have made no difference . . .

And old Dr. McGowan, McGowan of *Kemmendine*, who had become within minutes the most vital and important man of all. His consulting room and operating theatre a wave-lashed raft, he'd gone about the business of saving life with the sangfroid of an eminent surgeon receiving from rubber-wheeled trolleys a relay of patients on operating day in a city hospital.

When Mundt, who had also done his best in the work of rescue, finally reached the shore, he was mumbling something about 'No submarines . . . not in THIS area, Lieutenant.' And then he'd started to laugh, the laugh of hysteria.

It was some weeks before we of *Atlantis* heard the story of *Tirranna's* end. The news horrified us all, prisoners and captors alike. The loss of women and children disturbed us considerably, particularly the cook. I noted, without comment, that he became particularly edgy whenever that galley door swung unexpectedly open.

But we were not to know that the tragic coincidence that had beset *Tirranna* had meanwhile led to our being labelled as Nazi thugs of the lowest calibre; worse still, murderers, men who had massacred innocent men and children while they lay helpless in their lifeboats.

This rumour, which we only heard after the war was over, had its origin in our forgetfulness.

We always endeavoured to make sure on sinking an enemy ship that lifeboats, and other flotsam likely to give away the scene of our encounter, were destroyed. When we'd removed *Kemmendine's* passengers and crew to *Atlantis* we therefore decided to sink the boats

120

by machine-gun fire, thus providing gun practice for our crew as well as destroying the evidence. Unfortunately two of the boats remained afloat, and drifted out to sea.

When a British ship found them the salvagers formed their own grim conclusions as to the fate of the occupants. One could hardly blame them. Empty, bullet-ridden and bloodstained (the blood, incidentally, came from a wounded seaman successfully treated in our ship's hospital), the boats seemed all too obviously the evidence of atrocity. Two and two were put together, and, as *Tirranna's* unfortunate end had meant delay in news filtering out as to the fate of *Kemmendine's* passengers, the answer made a somewhat sinister five.*

* British prisoners, interviewed by me, have confirmed the validity of this story. The rumours, although never encouraged by any responsible official source, were undoubtedly widespread at the time of which Mohr speaks, and caused pain and anguish to more than one relative.   A.V.S.

CHAPTER ELEVEN

GUESTS OF THE FUHRER

THE BRITISH sailor sat calmly near the pilot ladder of the stricken ship. Except for one pitiable shred of tissue, his leg had been completely severed. A tourniquet had been improvised to block the downpour of his blood. Now, ashen faced, he looked at us, as we looked at him, both parties silent.

Another survivor came forward. 'Your first shell . . .' he said.

Slowly the British sailor grinned at us, cigarette gripped with the firmness of pain from the corner of his tightened lips. 'Hey, chum,' he said. 'What about my leg?—shall I take it along with me?'

This bloody joke at his own expense became a major topic among our crew, and the respect regarding the tough British attitude 'when in a hole' skyrocketed. But the more sober ones among us added a few reflections of our own on behalf of the moral qualities of a foe, whom, so far, they had had little occasion to fathom . . . Opportunities of getting to know that British point of view were, however, to be abundant in the months ahead.

On leaving Germany, *Atlantis* was occupied by a crew of 347. By May, we had taken 76 prisoners. In June we took 99 more. By mid-July we were carrying 327. And even after transferring most of these, owing to new conquests, we were nearly 'house full' again in September, with 293. Throughout our cruise we were to house, in all 1,283 'guests' from the ships we encountered.

The orders of High Command were explicit. The

credo of the Führer was that there must be no contact with our enemies bar that essential for effecting compliance with our orders. Prisoners were to be kept in confinement with only brief periods for exercise. Contact between German and Briton was in other words on the level prevailing in a prison camp—which may have sounded reasonable enough to some of the people back home, but was anything but reasonable when considered in relationship to the daily circumstances of our lives, for, as we argued, our raider had none of the amenities even of a prison camp. Barbed wire fever was common enough ashore. How much more so would it be in the narrow, confined spaces of a ship, a ship, moreover, that would be fighting actions with the prisoners aboard her?

Rogge gave the problem considerable thought bearing in mind the physical and mental stresses of men crammed beneath decks in tropical weather, beset by fears when they heard the guns cracking above them, and existing in conditions that were unhealthy to say the least. He resolved to modify the regulations as circumstances warranted allowing as much latitude as was consistent with security.

In gereral the Prisoner Problem placed us in a peculiar dilemma. On the one hand it was abhorrent to us to turn crews adrift in isolated waters. On the other we could not choose well frequented areas because of the risk to ourselves. In any case boats were not the 'secure placcs' ordained by international law. Yet each ship we sank brought fresh survivors—to crowd our prison quarters. In the end we decided to have as many as we could; accepting a security risk by allowing the prisoners as much time as possible on deck, even as much as eight to twelve hours a day.

The prisoners certainly needed all the fresh air we could give them. Their quarters, for obvious reasons, were on a lower deck than that of the crew. Although, as their numbers increased, we shipped our Asiatics into the mine-room aft to make room, conditions for the Europeans were very grim, and it is difficult to describe adequately the discomfort of men so crowded, and in a temperature that was always above 30 degrees Centigrade. Despite special ventilators the place was like an oven, and a London captive once complained to me, 'It stinks like the bloody Black Hole with all the bodies in it.' An apt description . . . !

The worst moments for the prisoners undoubtedly arose when we engaged other ships, for although we took pains to promise them that they would be given an equal opportunity of escaping should we emerge the vanquished, they knew that their get-away might be difficult. I remember when I reminded some prisoners, 'Well, we're all in the same boat . . .' a seaman summed up their plight in the terse phrase, 'Yes, mate. And it will best suit us if the bloody thing sticks its keel up!"

On another occasion a captive grumbled during one of our 'reassuring' addresses, 'Why not cut an escape hatch in the bottom and give us the key?'

Well. It couldn't be helped. But we did not envy the lot of the men below. Bad enough for us . . . but for them . . . By day, the indefatigable Captain Windsor used to walk around the decks comfortingly assuring any one of us who cared to listen, 'Can't last for ever you know. Wait till you meet that cruiser!'

But we knew, despite the brave face that Windsor, and not only Windsor, tried to put upon it, that our prisoners must have endured the tortures of waiting, and the apprehensions of such a meeting, to a degree that made our own misgivings seem trivial by comparison. What a terrible dilemma! To know that the guns of their own people were the enemies from whom they had the worst to fear; to know, when under guard, that the enquiring friend might also serve in the role of executioner.

During our early actions the prisoners knew nothing of the type of ship we were engaging, or how the battle was faring. Their sleep would be shattered by the urgent klaxons, preceding the crash of the upward rush of our gun flaps and the much-hated clatter of the ammunition hoists travelling through the steel-encased shaft that passed right through their quarters. Then the guns themselves would open up, ear-splitting in this echoing box of a hold, the impact ripping like an electric shock along the hot steel deck, and the spent shell cases rattling like castanets in a crazy dance above.

Once, and once only, was I in the prisoners' quarters when an alarm was in progress. It was purely a practice warning but it gave me a vivid idea of how they must feel when the real thing was under way. And here, amid the crush of two hundred men, in this cramped and gloomy space full of a sickly odour, where laundry, dancing askew on the pitiable strings between the bunks, brushed damply against one's face, I resolved to attempt at least something to alleviate the fears arising at such moments.

From this time onwards we made broadcasts to the prisoners before an action, informing them that we were about to attack, that the target was a merchantman, and that it would soon be over. We also repeated our assurance that, should the enemy not be what he seemed, they would have an equal chance with the rest of us. A peculiar type of comfort? Maybe . . . to those who have not endured cooped-up captivity under fire. But at such moments I believe that even the most indomitable of our 'guests'—men who literally prayed for *Atlantis*'s ending—experienced the longing for survival that comes to every man, for, however strong the spirit the inner self, even unacknowledged, is there to play the tempter!

My own diary records a conversation with the indomitable Captain Windsor that accurately sums up a different outlook on the 'situation' prevailing between captor and captives on our much-hunted ship: I talked with Windsor *re* the hottest places on earth. I suggested Aden; Saigon.

He: 'You don't know the hottest yet.'

I: 'Where's that?'

H: 'Hell.'

Slightly annoyed, I emphasized: 'Then we'll both go there together!'

Such barbed shafts were common between British and German in conversations that were often, otherwise, quite cordial. For, much though each side might respect the individuals on the other, neither was stupid enough to forget that for the duration we were still enemies by virtue of the war that was responsible for our meeting.

As the days went by, the bizarre quality of our association was further emphasised by the manner in which enemies would mix on speaking terms during uneventful days, only to part again beneath war's discipline as the command 'Shoot!' prefaced the arrival of fresh faces, fresh voices, as from our latest victim, came the now familiar staggering procession of the pale-faced, bleeding, sometimes hysterical wounded.

And what strange contrasts we witnessed! Rogge encouraged contact between the respective crews. British prisoners attended our boxing contests and later, they, too, became contestants. Allied officers got together to form that astonishing burlesque 'The Broadway Bar'. Actually the Norwegians were the senior partners in this the brain-child of two passengers, both of whom were employees of a whaling company, though the British soon acquired an 'interest'. The chain of membership consisted of Norwegian officers' buttons slung on a string and the 'bar' was a bunk on which rested either some very indifferent whisky—loot which we sold generously at 1/6d. to 2/- a bottle, because we did not like it ourselves—or battered mugs of cold tea in lieu of . . . This retreat they regarded as holy ground, and, to foster still further the illusion of civilised club life, they introduced a set of rules governing the behaviour of members. The club committee condescended sufficiently to accept German officers as 'guests' but their proviso binding on host and visitor alike was that there should be no political discussions. So for a while we would forget the war, talk of ourselves, the films we had seen, and the gardens back home, the books we had read, and the adventures we had experienced in the days that now seemed centuries ago. But, inevitably, the King Charles's Head that we had sought so well meaningly to avoid, would appear before us, and *with the blood still* on it! Talk of home brought thoughts of relatives. Thoughts of relatives brought reminders of the dangers that they, too, were encountering. Start to think about those, and one was on a bitter theme indeed . . . the cause of the war . . . the allocation of war guilt . . . whose country right or wrong? Automatically the voices would rise, and prejudices become inflamed as each man answered in his own way—his country's way . . .

'All jolly interesting. Now let's talk about SEX.'

The remark drawled through the heated argument between two of our officers and their British opposite numbers, the sort of argument that was really beginning to have an edge to it. The speaker was one of our senior British guests, Captain Armstrong White, whose ship, the *City of Bagdad*, you may recall, had been the third of our victims. 'Let's talk about sex . . .' In trying days this phrase became the stock recipe for assuaging tempers strained by the times and the tropics into breaches of good manners. But such interchanges of courtesy in our everyday relationships by no means precluded the sharpest practices regarding the broader issue . . . The Issue . . . the all-embracing argument that had flung us into this precarious proximity. Some examples come particularly vividly to mind as I look back at the 'manoeuvring' that went on behind our cordial façade . . .

The amiable Armstrong White—piercing furtively together a list of our sinkings, the names of men transferred, the arrivals and departures of supply ships, and other valuable data that subsequently proved of great assistance to British Intelligence . . .

The indefatigable Windsor—building himself a sextant, and obtaining by no means inaccurate estimates of our course . . .

Captain Smith, of *Zamzam*, transferred to *Dresden*— helping monocled Dr. Hunter, to plot her track . . .

The 'simple' sailors—creating a peephole through which they could spy upon the 'goings on' in our seaplane hold . . .

And those equally 'simple' men, who casually dropped tiny pieces of paper into the water, and made innumerable calculations regarding our knottage and bearing . . .

All these things come back, as much a part of the *Atlantis* saga as any of the deeds of our own men when the guns eventually wrote her doom, as apparently motiveless at times as the wanderings of our ship backwards and forwards across the oceans, yet, activated as she was by the sombre, automatic, and invisible control of the spirit of war that had now become as casual and accepted a part of our daily life as eating or drinking.

We used the trappings of neutrality to mask our ruthless guns—Dr. Hunter used a screen of children for his sun shooting experiments. We read, examined, and pieced together every scrap of captured correspondence, sending any important extracts to Intelligence in Berlin. Our prisoners, for their main source of information, relied upon any unguarded, friendly confidences they might glean from our crew.

I remember the day when our doctor threw a birthday party for a certain British captain, which resulted in the English sea dog 'drinking to forget' so abundantly that he ended up, immovably asleep, in the doctor's bed, while the doctor himself lay prostrate on a divan. Equally, I remember how, with the aid of such opportunities for contact, an English artist was able to piece together from hearsay, a remarkably accurate plan of our ship's layout, being incorrect only in one major detail, namely, that he credited us with one eight-inch gun. So, in plot and counterplot, yet, and in courtesies too, passed our days.

Of course, some friction was bound to arise between captive and captor, although there was so little ugliness that I still marvel at it all. In General Regulations for Prisoners, I, myself, caused some misunderstanding by my choice of wording in Regulation Six. It began: 'The

Command likes to ease conditions by giving as many liberties as possible, such as time on deck, washing facilities, etc.' 'In return,' I added, 'We like to hear a friendly Good Morning when the Commander or the acquainted officers pass the deck; consideration by moving out of their way, and co-operation by keeping deck and quarters clean and tidy.'

It was that 'Good Morning' that did it. What did we mean, asked the officer? Were his men to be *ordered* to say Good Morning and stand up whenever a German officer appeared? If so, we could expect trouble. I explained that we had simply made the request because of the rudeness of a small number of the crew members who, once they'd found we were not quite the sheer brutes they'd expected, had been becoming extremely obstructive. We were, I said, trying to behave as decently as the exigencies of war would allow, and we expected our prisoners to appreciate this. What would the officer have thought if, when visiting quarters on his own ship, he had to pick his way over the outstretched legs of lounging seamen? This explanation, conceded the officer 'seemed reasonable', and we did not have any subsequent difficulties in this direction!

Only once did we have to take disciplinary action against a prisoner, and this arose because of his insolence to a British officer. Right from the start we had the alternatives of either degrading the British officers by taking over complete control of the prisoners themselves or supporting their authority, and, within the limits of security, leaving to them the everyday administration of affairs. We chose the latter course. As far as possible crews messed together according to their ship. Their officers were responsible for transmitting our routine orders, and, as a result, were still in positions of comparative authority, and even allowed to retain their stewards. Generally, thanks to the bonds of national loyalties, the crews stuck close to their officers, but there was always, of course, the minority of 'sea lawyers', those vocal malcontents that are of no use to any ship. To people of this kidney our arrival just meant that their officers no longer had the right to control them, and that they 'could do as they damned well pleased . . .'

On the occasion of which I write, a seaman refused to obey an order from his captain, who, feeling very awkward—the man had taken full advantage of his position—was about to do the job himself when one of our people intervened. The seaman was later brought before me!

'Why did you refuse to obey orders, and insult your captain?'

He answered: 'I'm not his f—g servant, we're all the same now. He's no better than me. No one can force me to fetch his be—property.'

We sent that man to the cooler until he should change his mind. Said Rogge, with brutal frankness, when the miserable fellow's captain pleaded for him, 'YOU say it's a petty, trivial thing, but I'm not concerned about YOU. I'm concerned with discipline. If other men see this fellow getting away with disobedience—whatever the cause—they'll try the same thing themselves. Then our people will catch the idea. Such examples are contagious.'

The seaman found the cooler not to his liking, and changed his mind within a matter of hours.

A far harsher punishment was imposed by court-martial for another offence involving our prisoners, but this time a German sailor was the culprit. Just after his ship was taken an English officer asked what had happened to his binoculars, which were of great sentimental value. I told him they had been taken off safely, and that although we could obviously not allow him to have them during the cruise, they would be labelled as his personal property, and stored. But when we checked we couldn't find them. Inquiries were made, and we instituted a thorough search. One day a note was found in a companionway. Addressed to me it read: 'You will never find the binoculars. I have thrown them over the side.' We had an awful feeling that this was probably

130

true, but we still endeavoured to find the culprit. Eventually we narrowed down our list of 'suspects' to about five men. I asked them to copy the note. One of the men made two mistakes in spelling—though quite an educated seaman. We realised they were deliberate so we arrested him. He confessed and was sentenced to three months' imprisonment.

The British officer came along to ask for a lighter sentence and when he found we would not change our minds, he protested, 'I'd never have mentioned the confounded thing had I thought he would be punished so severely.'

Rogge, so reasonable to those who had served faithfully and well, coldly shrugged. 'No alternative. If I let one off, there'd be no holding the others.'

The man was shipped to Somaliland by the first available boat to serve his sentence. Said Rogge, 'A thief is no use to me.'

As officer-in-charge of the prisoners I received constant complaints about the food, and in a diary confiscated from one prisoner I found the following sardonic commentary on the *Atlantis* cuisine:

'Then we have some absolutely lousy concoction such as a vile dish of spinach, resembling a sloppy mess of that fine mossy kind of seaweed, or green slime in a swamp. And it tastes as bad, or worse than it looks . . .'

No. Our fare was by no means popular, although our prisoners, on their return to England, were fair enough to concede that in the main we shared and shared alike—a fact that considerably gratified us when we read about it in a captured copy of the *Daily Telegraph*. The biggest grouse concerned the bread. We were not only used to black bread but considered it far more nutritious than white, providing a roughage absent from our otherwise scant diet. On weekdays, apart from Wednesday's curry, we had a one-course meal of either peas, beans, lentils or noodles, accompanied by a minute portion of blood sausage (again most unpopular with the English). For a 'treat' on Sundays we had dried potato chips (not to be confused with the palatable fried chips), a meagre portion of tinned vegetables and tinned meat, or as a change a goulash.

I was amazed to read a report from one prisoner that the 'perpetual' sauerkraut was the worst ordeal of all. Sauerkraut was a delicacy and far too precious to dole out so lavishly. But the British didn't appreciate it and doubtless the remembrance of a dish or so remained extraordinarily vivid. For breakfast we drank ersatz cofee—the 'Nigger's Sweat'—and ate a hunk of bread and marg, and with it sometimes a spoonful of jam. The supper menu was equally comprehensive!

The worst privation was the lact of water. Every man, whether German, British, Norwegian or native, received on average a quart a day for washing and drinking alike. All taps were locked, and water was issued only by the pump master. We drew it twice daily, after breakfast and after tea, and it was a strange sight to see an eager queue of prisoners and captors alike waiting for the daily dole; so many thousand miles from London and Berlin yet following for this simple necessity, the slavish queue custom of the shore.

Nothing must be wasted. Tea left over from one meal must be drunk during the day. Surplus food must not be hoarded, but returned after each meal. A notice headed 'General Regulations for Prisoners' spotlights, I feel, the manner of our economies.

'Fetch only necessary quantities of food; if this proves insufficient ask for more. Food which has not been eaten because it has not been liked, or for other reasons, MUST UNDER NO CIRCUMSTANCES be thrown into waste bins, or the pig food tins, but returned to the galley. Return of food will not entail cutting down of rations. Throwing away food will. Waste of drinking water, tea, coffee, will entail cutting down rations.'

All in the same boat . . .

How, seeing the plight of our victims, could we adhere to, without deviation, the strict letter of regulations? How could we remain entirely aloof, and detached from men whom one encountered each day sprawled under lifeboats in the shadow of the funnel, snatching wherever opportunity offered, scant cover from the punishing, strength-sapping sun? Our common sweat tended to remove many of the traditional barriers established between prisoner and captor; in fact as we sometimes argued amongst ourselves, were we not all in some way or other captives of the hardest master of them all—the sea?

Meanwhile, however correct our relationship with the English, we kept ourselves alert against surprise.

Captain Hill, of the *Mandasor*, described us, after his release, as 'nice chaps, but . . .' a remark that serves also to sum up our attitude on *Atlantis* towards Hill and his friends—people whom it was pleasant to talk to, but dangerous, in wartime, to trust too far . . .

CHAPTER TWELVE

HELL SHIP

'PLUTARCH' THEY called her, but that was back in 1912, on the day when she slid down the slipway, gleaming and new, a 5,000 tonner, built for the tramping trade of the bright and prosperous mercantile empire of Britain.

Durmitor the Yugoslavs renamed her, at a re-christening ceremony some twenty years later; after she'd borne the storms of a war and the doldrums of a shipping slump; on the day when, somewhat tarnished and her engines worn a bit, she was sold by Britain to foreign masters.

But in 1940, late 1940, *Plutarch* called *Durmitor* got a name of a different sort; the name by which she was to be known the best, the unflattering title of Hell Ship!

We'd caught her on 22nd October, a rusty veteran whose appearance had not improved either with age or change of flag, a tramp of tramps, her stack and super-structure soiled by the coal she used so profusely, her plimsoll line invisible owing to her cargo's weight.

Yet in this floating flat-iron lay our only hope of relieving *Atlantis* of the bulk of the prisoners who now so crowded the ship and presented so many problems both of the immediate and the future.

It was bad for us to have so many mouths to feed, it was bad for the prisoners cramped in quarters that had not become barely endurable. And most of all it was bad for our plans—the presence of these hundreds pre-saging obvious complications for the next stage or our mission, a new series of attacks on the approaches of the Gulf of Bengal.

We had hoped that *Commissaire Ramel,* met so unexpectedly, could have been taken intact in which case the prisoner problem would have been rapidly resolved as she was the 'right size' for the number we intended to tranship—about 300.

But it was not to be. *Commissaire*'s spectacular end had served only to aggrevate our problem by giving us yet another crew to care for and we could now afford to wait no longer.

'*Durmitor* is hardly the sort of ship that you yourself would have chosen for the trip,' I said, 'We're not exactly pleased about it either. But we can't find anything better; so it's up to you to make the best of it. It's not going to be a picnic, but if you co-operate with Lieutenant Dehnel, you'll find conditions will be easier.'

The prisoners clustered in front of me, some serious, as though considering the practical problems of the route ahead; some grinning, openly sarcastic, and one or two, on the fringes, muttering to each other out of the corners of their mouths. I looked at the officers, some of them very old acquaintances by now, men whom one had talked to, or men with whom one had had the odd drink, men who . . . 'Yes, nice chaps but . . .' I thought, 'and there are nearly 300 of them against only fourteen of ours.'

So I added, 'I must emphasise, however, that any attempt at resistance will be crushed. Don't think you can ever get the upper hand, it isn't worth your while to try. *Durmitor*, I must remind you, has time bombs fixed to her bottom. In the event of serious trouble the ship will immediately be sunk.'

The British did not seem unduly dismayed by this threat, nor even particularly perturbed at leaving *Atlantis* for the barnacled old tub that was to carry them to Italian captivity. Our farewells were cordial enough, and as regards *Durmitor* the prisoners went a-jumping, believing, as I have since heard, that there might be a chance yet of securing their freedom. Man is born to optimism.

* * *

Dehnel stroked his short, carefully trimmed imperial, his hefty frame vibrating energy and confidence as the prisoners filed aboard his first command. He was not oblivious to the difficulties ahead, but he was confident of handling those difficulties. Dehnel liked handling difficulties. There was a slight swagger in his step as he walked to the rails of the bridge.

Durmitor's journey was scheduled to last about 19 days, so the prisoners, to keep them quiet, had been told 'about a fortnight'. While, as a further expedient to keep the peace, he, Dehnel, would repeatedly refer to signals allegedly received from *Atlantis*—thus inducing the state of mind where his charges would feel that the raider was 'just around the corner' and that rebellion would bring speedy reprisal. Not that Dehnel, at this stage, was unduly perturbed about his prisoners' reactions. If the journey could be kept amicable so much the better, but if not, and if all one's little dodges failed, then of course there was still another way of securing compliance.

A machine gun had been mounted on the bridge and trained upon the forepart of the ship, where the prisoners were cooped up behind a barrier of wire. Now, as the sentry shouted for silence among the jostling three hundred, Dehnel said, 'Gentlemen, I've something to demonstrate.' His wave of the hand was followed immediately by a racket of a machine-gun fire; a spread of bullets lashing into the water ahead.

Was the 'demonstration' really a success? Some of the prize crew—regarding the deliberately non-committal faces of the prisoners—had their doubts, but at least, they thought, we've given them the hint if they care to take it.

The first tribulation of the prisoners of *Durmitor* arose from the nature of her cargo.

Salt . . . They began to hate the name of the stuff, the smell of it, the taste of it and most of all the feel of it.

The only accommodation available for the Europeans was in Number One and Two holds, 'accommodation' provided by tons of salt being jettisoned over the side until there was just sufficient space left for the men to stretch out, a hundred per hold.

Salt . . . It formed the bed they lay on, rough, however hard they'd worked with spade and hands to smooth it, cold even through tarpaulins we had given them for mattresses, and hard to the bones, however tough their efforts to carve out niches and 'tailor' them to fit aching hips.

Salt . . . Bringing discomfort to chafing skins and cuts, clogging their clothes, stinking in their nostrils.

Salt . . . And beneath it all a honeycomb of holes, a secret city of vermin, a place of rats, lean rats that came scurrying out at nights, to run across the faces of the men, and becoming progressively bolder, took to nibbling at the dead skin upon their feet.

Yes, salt was the worst enemy of all, or so it seemed to the prisoners during the first few days of their journey, but it would have taken more than even this discomfort to earn for *Durmitor* her subsequent title. It was down in the bunkers of the ship that the real devil lay, a devil that was to transform a meagre diet into a near-starvation diet, a devil that was to stretch fifteen days of anticipated grimness into twenty-nine days of hell . . .

Someone had been doing a bit of private business during the earlier part of *Durmitor*'s cruise. Someone had been fiddling with the coal supply. Someone had given short weight!

The news hit Dehnel like a blow on the teeth. Before being assigned to her task it had been estimated that the ship possessed only the narrowest margin over the bare minimum of fuel that would be necessary to take her to Mogadishu and Dehnel had been warned to go steady to avoid waste. But now the entire set-up had been overturned. There was no margin. No margin at all. The figures produced by Yugoslavs' chief engineer had

137

turned out to be mistaken, hopelessly mistaken, and Dehnel now realised with horror that *Durmitor* had only the slimmest of chances of reaching the shore.

Rations were scarce enough, even for the period of time originally envisaged, for, to be candid, we had supplied our prize with a lower scale than that prevailing on *Atlantis*. We had had to think of our future and this decision—which was reasonable enough at the time we made it—began to show grimmer implications for the more Dehnel succeeded in conserving his fuel supply the longer *Durmitor* would be at sea and the longer at sea the further he'd have to stretch the ration.

Dehnel scowled as he thought of the unpleasant prospects ahead. It would be a far longer trip than planned and prospects of a safe arrival seemed, to say the least, to be remote. But one thing was sure. He was a loyal officer and believed in what he was fighting for. It was his duty to save his ship and bring her to the destination ordered. His duty he determined to do his utmost to fulfil, however painful the conquences.

He reduced speed—to five and a half knots.

Rain squalls had been expected when *Durmitor* left us. Seven days had gone by and still they hadn't come. On the Hell Ship, baking beneath the full force of a tropical sun, the water tank supplies grew less and less.

Dehnel issues the order . . One cup per man per day.

Desperate in the heat, some of the men began, furtively, to tap the steam pipe lines, sucking down the warm and rusty water, inviting illness in the days ahead. Not a guard intervened. There were too few of them to discipline the everyday activities of the prisoners, and, as the crisis grew, they concentrated more and more upon the major problem of holding the crazy ship against rebellion.

The rains came, and the men thronged the deck shouting and chattering, collecting the precious drops in every implement they could find; letting water flow upon their sweating bodies; lifting parched lips towards the downpour. But the rain brought a curse to accompany its blessing; the water, soaking throught the hatches on to the salt beneath, and turning the surface into a slush, introducing to those who had been unable to make hammocks for themselves the horrors of rheumatism and running sores.

Rumours spread among the prisoners as the days passed by . . . The German crew were living on the fat of the land . . . bacon and coffee, fresh fruit maybe . . . Dehnel met a deputation . . . Invited them to see for themselves the state of the stores . . . But still the hatred grew, smouldering resentfully as the men looked aft to the black machine-guns shimmering in the sun's fierce rays, while the sight of the white-capped officer on the bridge became to them a symbol of the reason for all their misery and their sufferings, the epitome of all they fought and hated.

On 11th November both British and German participated in commemorating the dead of World War One. Dehnel made an Armistice Day address. A rifle shot announced the start of the two minutes' silence. Another shot terminated it.

Then life, or maybe existence, continued as usual, with the ship in the doldrums, crawling at three knots now, through an evil, sticky, almost motionless sea.

MacLeod, the Second Officer of *Kemmendine*, had occupied himself usefully during captivity, manufacturing a sextant out of scraps of wood, and making calculations that now proved conclusively to the prisoners that *Durmitor* was not intending to make for Madagascar to land them in neutral territory, but was continuing instead towards Somaliland . . .

The truth about *Durmitor*'s course could be no longer concealed; neither could the truth about her shortage of fuel. The stench of burning paint had begun to hang over her, sickening the exhausted men. At first one or two of them thought the ship was on fire, until they realised that it was yet another product of Dehnel's ingenuity. With little more than coal dust left in the bunkers he was manufacturing cakes of fuel out of paint and ashes!

Dehnel tried hard . . . odd bits of tarpaulin were roped together and hoisted to the crosstrees in an effort to utilise the wind. The ship's furniture was hurled into the furnaces. *Durmitor* staggered slowly on and for a brief space the sweating, harassed lieutenant—looking very different now from the spruce Dehnel who had assumed command—thought his prize would make Mogadishu after all.

But the bad luck of *Durmitor* persisted. An intercepted wireless message revealed that British cruisers were now shelling the town. He would have to turn away and run for safety somewhere else.

The hatch covers went into the fire . . . The aft derricks were cut down . . . The deck planks came up. And the ship struggled on.

Durmitor reached the tiny settlement of Warsheik on 22nd November. The journey of eighteen days had stretched into twenty-nine!

Dehnel, who possessed no proper sea charts of the area, began signalling to the shore for a pilot, but Warsheik was coy, no answer came from the cluster of white houses around the quay, no one appeared on the glistening distant beach.

By 4 p.m. Dehnel's patience was exhausted. He would bring *Durmitor* in on his own. Five minutes later and she had climaxed the voyage by running on to a coral reef.

So this was Somaliland—and glory by the truckload! Eight truckloads to be exact, and carrying not only the Allied prisoners but an infuriated, protesting Dehnel, and his bewildered prize crew as well! ALL had been captured by the victorious Italians, ALL were driven down to Mogadishu and paraded in triumph; ALL were used to bolster the town's shaky and sagging morale. A Roman victory!

It was many hours before Dehnel had explained himself and he and the Yugoslavs had managed to rejoin the ill-starred tramp, now refloated and anchored. Yet still he had his troubles . . .

When he tried to take her out she ran aground again, and when he got her off and sailed at last into Mogadishu the Italians, far from being glad to see him, requested him to go away. 'Your presence,' they said. 'may provoke another British bombardment.'

It was with intense relief therefore that he eventually sailed his charge to Kisimayu, and with even greater relief that he washed his hands of her and prepared to rejoin *Atlantis*.

As for *Durmitor* herself? She was finally captured by the advancing British; restored in due process of time, to Yugoslavia; survives to this day—Fehler having seen her quite recently in the blue, untroubled waters of the Mediterranean. The adventures of *Durmitor* involved factors on which I do not feel competent to dwell. But from the maze of complaints made by British prisoners at the time, and the counter claim of Dehnel that they could have helped him do much to improve their lot, only three points stand out as undebatable:

That the cruise evolved into an astonishing feat of seamanship by Dehnel, operating in very adverse circumstances; that, however aggressive his manner, the trouble never reached the stage where blood was shed; and, lastly, that it was a voyage of extraordinary hardship, a voyage worthy of a Hell Ship.

The plight of the European prisoners in the Italian prison camp was even worse than that they had endured on *Durmitor*. Medical facilities were completely primitive. Four men died of the dysentery they had contracted during the voyage, ninety-seven of the remainder went ill—many of them with a fever that also claimed as victim the camp's second-in-command and even after their release their trials were by no means over.

From a cutting from an Australian newspaper of the time I read, 'But one of the bitterest grouches some seamen seemed to nurture was about the manner of their reception in British East Africa after their release. The Royal Navy had an organisation to deal with its rescued captives; so had the Army. Merchant seamen were like unwanted children left on a doorstep.'

The struggle with officialdom unites the nations! At the time when the British cruisers were barring the path of *Durmitor* to Mogadishu, we on *Atlantis* were listening with considerable annoyance to a 'pep' broadcast from our Propaganda Ministry; a broadcast deriding 'the yellow and incapable attitude of the British Navy which had not been able to find and destroy a single German raider!'

CHAPTER THIRTEEN

THAT DARTMOUTH LOOK

IN THE oppressive tropical night a Norwegian tanker lay
stopped on the long slow swell of the Indian Ocean. Her
crew, rifles in hand, stood alerted and silent, peering
out into the blackness from which a launch was now
approaching, a launch occupied it seemed by but one
immaculately turned out officer of the Royal Navy and
two ratings.

The launch drew alongside. For a few moments it
rode beside the steep black hull, the officer peering up
at the ship; the men on the ship peering down at him.
Then, as the swell carried the launch high, he grabbed
at the lower chain rail and a second later stood upon the
deck. His left hand ripped open the Royal Navy tunic;
his right hand knocked the badge with the fouled anchor flying from his brow . . . Another move and a
German Navy cap was jammed upon his head, even as
the pistol came from his holster, and he said, 'I am an
officer of the German Navy. You are my prisoners!'

It was our Flying Officer (on 10th November, 1940),
who had first sighted the *Ole Jacob* in the course of his
wide and sweeping circle to the north. It was Rogge
who'd planned the ruse to spare us the use of our guns,
to save the tanker from a conflagration, and win for us
a valuable prize, and it was I who performed the excursion into dramatics that led to my becoming a 'Lieutenant, Royal Navy'—a metamorphosis ungazetted and unguessed at by the Admiralty, and as temporary as that
of *Atlantis* in the role of the British auxiliary cruiser
Antenor.

It happened like this . . .

When the seaplane brought us the glad tidings of a tanker we pondered on how to take our quarry intact. *Ole Jacob* was too valuable a prize to destroy totally; a problem considerably complicated by the consideration that even one shell would sent her up in smoke—and if no shells, then how were we to take her?

Said Rogge: 'Quite simple. You, Mohr, will be granted a British commission; so will the ship! We will take *Ole Jacob* by surprise and at pistol point.'

At this stage of the war we were receiving daily intelligence reports from Berlin revealing the names of British armed merchant cruisers and their area of operation. This information was not the produce of secret agents, but the result of some very clever work on the part of our Admirality Cipher Service—busy unscrambling British Naval messages and assiduously circulating the contents to the raider fleet. Although by no means fool-proof—the mechanics of decoding took considerable time, and our information regarding the exact deployment of the enemy was often two or three weeks out of date—the Berlin reports provided us with a basis on which to assess, at least, the ocean in which our opposite numbers were operating. Hence we adopted the title of *Antenor* as being a ship whose presence in these waters would probably be known to the Norwegian skipper.

In the smooth, breathless dark of an Indian Ocean night, the tanker, caught up with at last, loomed hugely on the sealine as I came out of my cabin—the perfect product of Dartmouth, or so I hoped, for I had not a few qualms about my appearance for this expedition. Althought at first I'd felt satisfied with the 'Englishness' of my rig, subsequent glances at the mirror left me pondering as to whether I'd really only succeed in making myself look like just what I was—a German in disguise! The more I looked, the more I feared; even the British webbing that I'd donned in lieu of my leather gun belt seemed to proclaim an aggressively Germanic appearance. And that cap began to worry me enormously. Just how did the fashionable in the Royal Navy angle their headgear? Should one still adopt the Beatty touch? But perhaps I was over anxious, for while Kamenz grunted sarcastically, 'That shouldn't fool anyone,' Rogge just grinned, looked me over, and said, 'You'll do.'

Our heavy naval searchlights began to blink . . . British armed merchant cruiser, *Antenor*. What ship?'

A pause, and then, somewhat hesitantly; 'Norwegian tanker, *Ole Jacob*.' Another pause, and another signal, a coy, 'Please do not follow.'

'Stop,' we commanded. 'Stop.'

But *Ole Jacob* seemed as shy as an elderly spinster accosted by a stranger in the moonlit park.

She: 'Why do you ask me to stop?'

We: 'British armed merchant cruiser . . .'

But the old lady was taking no chances. She needed more reassurance than this. From her wireless room came the squeal of Q.Q.Q., the signal that all of us so loathed and feared; yet we did not fire. Instead, with the authority becoming a Royal Naval Ship, we told her, 'Don't use wireless,' adding that she must stop immediately as we wished to interview the Captain.

The lamp blinked on, and we grinned at each other as her radio signals ceased, visualising the indignation of the tanker men . . . 'This bloody suspicious naval vessel wasting our time when we're in such a hurry . . .' Fidgeting and fussing about our papers when there's all those raiders to be looked for!'

For a few minutes more the exchange of signals continued, and then, compliant at last, the tanker went off the air, commencing to diminish speed until she waited, hove to, on the still sea.

I got into the launch. Beside me were the two ratings and to all intents and purposes she was otherwise empty. But concealed under a huge tarpaulin lay seven more of our comrades clutching tommy-guns, pistols and hand grenades.

'Good luck, sir' said someone, and we were away. We could almost FEEL the doubting suspicion emanating from the silent tanker. Never, I reflected, had a ship seemed quite so high above me; never had a ship seemed so uninviting and charged with hostility. As we neared her we saw some of *Ole Jacob*'s crew mustered in a business-like fashion around a gun; others, we were uneasily aware, were crouching low against the rails. And no one said a word. The silence was ominous, hostile. I didn't like it. They seemed too suspicious. Instinctively my right hand began to slide towards the butt of my pistol. I checked the impulse. If they were going to be nasty I'd need more than pistol-play to get me out of this!

We came alongside, and a gruff voice behind the light demanded, 'ARE you British?'

Our answer was lost in the scraping of our bows against *Ole Jacob*'s hull. I looked desperately for the pilot ladder. There wasn't one! Things looked bad. A group of officers now clustered amidships; we caught the outline of the objects they were holding—rifles! For seconds we lay there without a helping hand or a welcoming word, the silence broken only by the swell lifting us up and carrying us for a minute that seemed like an hour. This mustn't last! As the seas rose I jumped for the lower chain rail, grabbed hold, and pulled myself up. And there I stood, facing this unwelcome crowd on whose brows a sullen mistrust was evident.

I quote from my diary:

'Now or never! Before I'm unmasked I'll break the tension myself. In a trice my insignia is revealed and once again, as so often in war, surprise has robbed an opponent of initiative. I reach for a rifle and throw it over the side. I point to the boat, out of which come clambering my men. As the first supporting tommy-gun glints beside me I run along the deck, taking the steps of the stairs leading to the bridge in bounds. At the top I encounter the Captain. He has seen all. Before I regain my breath he says "I give up!" '

This extract, written only a day or two after the adventure, provides an accurate reflection of the excitement I experienced AFTER the event. At that time I had little opportunity for enjoyment, or even for undue qualms. It had certainly been touch and go. A violent reaction from the first man whose rifle I grabbed might have precipitated a hail of fire which would have meant THE END for the boarding party, for myself—and the Norwegians as well!

But there was *no* violent reaction; we had taken our prize intact, and without bloodshed, and it was quite a while—after all I was fourteen years younger at the time—before the perspiration began to gather on my brow and my knees began to feel unaccountably weak. After the crew's surrender we examined our catch. *Ole Jacob* was not, after all, carrying the precious fuel oil we had expected, her cargo consisting instead of several thousand tons of aviation spirit. Very nice I thought to be able to deny the enemy such a windfall, but it wasn't much good to us. However, such problems were not mine to worry about, and we forthwith proceeded with yet another deception, designed this time to allay the suspicions of those who might be hunting us following *Ole Jacob*'s initial squeal. Despite our ruse her signals had, in fact, gone out to Colombo, so we used her own radio, with its distinctive key, to cancel the message and inform the British that we were now proceeding after a false alarm. This device was to have a most amusing sequel, for it not only satisfied the enemy, but, the best joke of all, deceived our masters in Berlin; so much so that they sent us a communique stating that ships in the Indian Ocean were now so nervous of our activities that a Norwegian tanker had panicked when confronted by a British AMC, though later cancelling her call for help!

The *Ole Jacob* incident provided us, in retrospect at least, with an adventure that was in welcome contrast to the general grimness of our mission, unaccompanied as it was by loss of life, and incurring no damage save hurt feeling. But, to clear up misconceptions regarding our tactics, I had better explain that to fly a flag other than one's own—or 'sail under false colours'—is accepted under International Law as a perfectly legitimate ruse

147

of war, with the one proviso that no open act of hostility takes place until the disguise is dropped.

The ruse is as equally permissible when flying one's opponent's naval ensign as it is when wearing the flag of a neutral merchantman. Similarly, the proviso applies not only to the ship but to the individual—hence my care to divest myself of my British 'trappings' and show German insignia before I pulled my pistol; hence also our creation of that special tube from which our Battle Ensign could break only a second before our guns opened fire.

A rather nice distinction? An emphasis upon the letter rather than the spirit of the law? All distinctions in law are of necessity finely drawn, and we did at least observe the letter.

About this time, and by a similar device, though in less tense circumstances, we captured another Norwegian tanker, the *Teddy;* switching on our glaring searchlights at only 600 yards. 'Stop at once. What ship?'

She: 'What do you want?'

We: 'I want to search you.'

She: 'O.K.'

After a while a vaguely uneasy 'Can we go now?' was followed by 'No. Wait for my boat.'

She: 'What ship?'

We: 'H.M.S. *Antenor.*'

Teddy, however, helped even the score a little by giving us a most embarrassing farewell; in fact by the time she was through with us our faces were far redder than those of her captured officers . . .

Having taken her crew aboard *Atlantis* we sent the zealous Fehler to finish off the job by sinking *Teddy* with explosive charges. Unhappily, his enthusiasm got the better of him and his 'pets'—a larger type than usual—exploded with such dramatic effect that she erupted in a smoke cloud which was visible for scores of miles; a tell-tale column of black to act as guide for the questing British: a sort of marine volcano that forced us to flee from the spot like men who had inadvertently

148

tripped over the burglar alarm while trying to crack the safe.

I was probably the only man aboard who welcomed this unexpected display, for it enabled me to snatch a breath-taking ciné shot of the sinking—a shot which ironically enough was later to be used in the film version of *The Cruel Sea*. I received no felicitations for the masterpiece. My permission was not asked, nor was a reproduction fee paid—this particular piece of 'confiscated enemy property' being conveniently housed in the archives of the British Admiralty! I am happy to say, however, that the same ruse that provided Mr. Monsarrat with his picture of a tanker tragedy also prevented any of the horrific results portrayed in *The Cruel Sea*. There were no casualties on *Teddy*.

That Dartmouth look had its Conway counterpart. In our wanderings we occasionally posed as a British merchantman—destroying the two surf boats which we had originally carried for use in the Pacific, but which looked out of place on a Britisher, and building ourselves instead a convincing-looking dummy gun aft with a platform that was exactly similar to the ones we had noticed on our victims.

Captain Windsor, who once said that HE would not have been fooled by our changing silhouettes providing, of course, that he had first been notified of our original description, sowed the seeds of unhappiness in Rogge's brain; seeds which were to germinate during the long period of our voyage. Never could we find out exactly WHY Captain Windsor would not have been fooled, but probably he was basing his comment on the fact that Clyde-built ships had much lower cross-beams than ours, and British ships, at that time, did not go in for modern Meyer bow and cruiser stern. Their bridges were not so high and their decks were less flush, and their funnels were more square, but despite such differences we found that a little bit of make-up—such as putting one's sailors into British tin hats and wearing British-type respirators—often went a long, long way.

In the business of deception, radio itself became a vital weapon both to the hunter and the hunted, and, as demonstrated in *Ole Jacob* and other incidents, it, too, could be made to wear false colours.

In World War One an operational build-up could readily be detected by changes in the rate of flow of wireless messages, and both London and Berlin had now learned to put this lesson to good account. Our own methods—back at the Admiralty—sought to provide a constant stream of signals at the same level and tempo all the time whatever the emergency. Accordingly more than ninety per cent of the groups sent could be mere 'fillers', such as a long article from the *Voelkischer Beobachter,* or purely advertising matter, namely, 'Young lady required by young gentleman, etc.' A code sign in the first group immediately indicated to our operator at the receiving end that they were redundant, and thus saved him wasting his time in transcription. Similarly, we had taught our naval operators to develop a uniform style of sending, to avoid any significant variations of the tempo, or provide any clue as to the identity of the sender. This uniformity, however, contained certain drawbacks, which became evident when we wished to send signals which purported to come from sources other than German. So, to meet such emergencies we used two former German Merchant Navy operators whom we had brought with us from Kiel. These men took over the key whenever we radioed Mauritius or Colombo. They were positively forbidden to develop a naval technique and encouraged instead to persevere in their highly individualist merchant navy style . . .

It was the morning after our *Ole Jacob* success . . . it was 11th November . . . it was the anniversary of the Day of Armistice . . . but our thoughts were far from peaceful and our gaze was focused on the shimmering distance; on a huge column of funnel smoke announcing the approach of a V.I.P. victim, the reopening of tragedy after an interval too lighthearted to last . . .

CHAPTER FOURTEEN

TOP SECRET

AUTOMEDON'S SMOKE hovered right in our path, saving us even the necessity of changing course. In a few hours we were so close that if we'd waited much longer we would have had to have made a deviation in order to avoid collision.

'If she used her radio now,' I thought, 'it will be suicide.'

But within seconds of our warning shot we heard again those R.R.R.'s. It was brave . . . it was futile . . . yes, it was suicide . . .

'*Feuerlaubnis!*' And into the elderly steamer with her long antique stack poured the shells : . .

I'd seen some of them looking pretty bad, but *Automedon* was the worst of the lot. My first impression as I swung over her side was one of astonishment, incredulity even, at the degree of havoc our shells had wreaked. *Automedon* rolled, and as she rolled a mass of broken hawsers and ropes rolled with her; jagged splinters of steel and rope sliding around my feet, and the escaping stream of her broken pipes breaking an otherwise uncanny silence. Her funnel was as full of holes as a colander, her stanchion posts were riddled with shell splinters and the disintegrated timber of her wireless cabin lay like a heap of wood shavings, smouldering dully on the shattered deck.

One of the boarding party whistled through his teeth. Beyond that we were very quiet, hardly a word was spoken. Part of the accommodation deck had collapsed, and a gap as wide as a barn door yawned in front of the bridge, its edges serrated like a tin prised open with a bayonet. Sandbags, hurled from the machine gun posts by the blast of the shells, lay ripped and crumpled, spilling their contents on to a tangled mess of torn aerials and life-jackets, of shattered floats and broken planks— all just part of the bric-a-brac that the impact of our salvoes had heaped in an extraordinary wild confusion.

But the worst moment was to come when I managed to climb the companion ladder to the bridge, reaching over gaps from which the rungs had been ripped away like straws, dodging the razor-sharp edges of the buckled steel plate, and the trap of the sagging electric cables. For, as I hauled myself up to the charthouse, I saw the dead. Every one of *Automedon*'s six officers had been killed. They had died instantaneously as the result of a direct hit on the centre of the bridge . . .

We got to work on the strong room and were amazed to find that this ancient ship had been entrusted with fifteen bags of secret mail, including one hundredweight of decoding tables, Fleet orders, gunnery instructions, and (so-called) Naval Intelligence reports. What the devil were the British about, sending such material by a slow old tub like *Automedon*, I puzzled. Surely a warship would have been a worthier repository? We could not understand it.

But only after I'd spent an hour with an axe in breaking down the lock of *Automedon*'s massive safe—to find nothing but a box with a few shillings in cash—did we discover the prize find of our cruise. It was contained in the chartroom, within a few feet of where the officers had fallen, and I realized then the full and tragic irony of the situation.

The six had given everything for their Cause, and yet the very totality of their sacrifice, had defeated the object for which it was made. Into *Automedon*'s keeping had been entrusted Top Secret documents, documents that her crew was unaware even existed, while the officers, although realising their importance, had been killed before they had had a chance to order their destruction or stretch out a hand to do the job themselves.

Our prize was just a long, narrow envelope enclosed in a green bag, a bag equipped with brass eyelets to let the water in to facilitate its sinking. The bag was marked 'Highly Confidential . . . To Be Destroyed.' And the envelope was addressed to 'The C.-in-C., Far East . . . To Be Opened Personally.'

'Excellent, Mohr,' said Rogge. 'Quite excellent.'

The contents of the envelope were spread in front of him and as the sun, streaming through the gap between the chintz curtains of the stateroom, fell upon the highly polished table and glittered along the cut grass of the heavy ashtray, *Automedon* and the grisly memories of the bridge seemed very far away. We were elated by the nature of our capture. The documents had been drawn up by no less an authority than the Planning Division of the War Cabinet and contained the latest appreciation of the military strength of the Empire in the Far East. There were details regarding the deployment and equipment of Royal Air Force Units; there were details of naval strengths; there was an assessment of the role of Australia and New Zealand; and, most piquant of all, a long paragraph regarding the possibility of Japan entering the war, a paragraph accompanied by copious notes on the fortifications of Singapore.

'Excellent. Quite excellent!' . . . And now to use the documents to German advantage.

Said Rogge, 'We must make the most of this, and here's the way we'll do it . . .'

We needed diesel oil. *Ole Jacob*, our recent capture, carried aviation spirit. The neutral Japs had diesel oil. The neutral Japs needed aviation fuel. And now, to overcome any political coyness——not that we anticipated any—we had this priceless report as well.

Rogge called Kamenz. 'I've got a new job for you,' he said. 'You're to take *Ole Jacob* on a journey to the north. You're to help us do a spot of diplomatic horse trading.'

In the crowded harbour of Yokohama the crew of the freighter watched idly the trim Norwegian tanker come slowly in from the sea. She dropped anchor and soon, after the customary formalities, crowded tenders commenced to leave the ship, bound for the shore.

Well, well, the envious watchers complained. The crew of the Norwegian certainly did not waste any time in getting in a spot of leave. Not like some . . . !

They were surprised, therefore, when the ship weighed anchor again within only a few hours of her arrival, but it wasn't until much later, when the liberty men came aboard from the wharfside bars and the hot spots of the city, that they heard the full story. The Norwegian was the long lost *Ole Jacob*, and a prisoner of the Germans, she had just put in to dump her former crew under the beach before running the gauntlet of the sea—Destination Unknown.

Ole Jacob had, however, left something else behind apart from two freed crews for the Norwegian Consul and an envelope of documents for the German Naval Attaché; she had landed one of *Atlantis*'s officers and he, like the documents, was for transmission to Berlin. A slightly more difficult process you might think—delivering this stocky, florid, determined fellow, to a Germany beset by a ring of foes—than popping the envelope into a diplomatic bag? On the contrary. The journey of Kamenz, suddenly recalled to Reich for a Top Secret conference, was one that was quite smoothly expedited.

It was all so simple . . . First the neutral Japanese arranged his transport to Vladivostok, and next the neutral Russians—so soon to be Britain's Allies—answered our Admiralty's request for aid by giving him full facilities for travelling home by the safe route, the land route, the trans-Siberian railway. As simple as that.

Kamenz enjoyed every minute of it. A most interesting journey, he told us later, and one by modes of transport far more congenial than that employed to bring him back. For when our globe-trotting navigator eventually rejoined *Atlantis* it was after a 16,000 mile journey by submarines—Germans being no longer *persona grata* with the Kommisars and Operation Barbarossa being now in full swing.

Some neutral merchant ships did carry war supplies. But on board the *Atlantis*, "Industrial machinery for the Philippines" was really a deadly 5-9 gun!

Admiral Bernhard Rogge, commander of the auxiliary cruiser—and armed merchant raider—*Atlantis*, with six of his officers.

April 17, 1941. German sailors on *Atlantis*'s deck watching the *Zamzam* sink. Of the 202 passengers aboard, 138 were American citizens. This led to an international incident.

Rogge encouraged rivalry between the German crew and their English and American captives. A boxing match appealed to both.

A captured Norwegian tanker is utilized to refuel the *Atlantis* and other German ships.

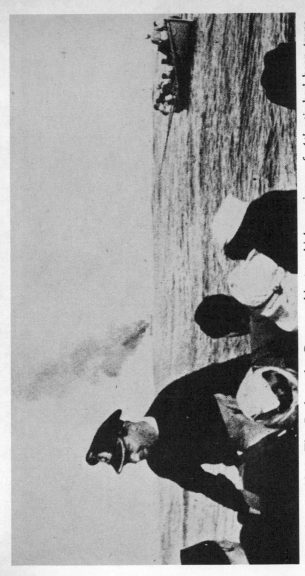

December 1, 1941. The *Python*—the German ship to which survivors of *Atlantis* had been transferred—blazes in the distance. It, too, was sunk, leaving the men adrift once again.

December 8, 1941. The survivors are taken aboard a Nazi U-boat to be returned home . . . and America has just declared war on Germany.

After three weeks, all survivors are again transferred, this time to Italian ships. Upon finally landing in St. Nazaire, Ulrich Mohr says farewell to two of the Italian officers.

Meanwhile, just about the time that Kamenz was making himself comfortable in a Soviet railway carriage, another interesting example of political and economic expediency was being demonstrated in the remote South Carolines. There *Atlantis* lay placidly refuelling with diesel oil and in the Marianas the aviation spirit of *Ole Jacob* was handed over to the Japanese in exchange.

Said Rogge, 'A replica in miniature of Roosevelt's policy towards Britain.'

Observed a young officer cheerfully, 'Yes, they are interprising fellows, these Japanese. Now I remember reading in a book about the last war that at Tsing-tau . . .'

Tsingtau! There was a disapproving silence. Some people, quite obviously, had a habit of always saying the wrong thing at the wrong time.

Adversity is said to find queer bedfellows. Success provided others, equally as strange for the Germany of 1940.

Komet, fifth and last of so-called First Wave, was now emerging on the seaways of the Pacific. Yet I wonder how many people realise the manner in which this raider—later to sink the 18,000-ton *Rangitane*—contrived to evade the Royal net to get there?

Komet got out from Germany by a back door, sailing in Russian territorial waters and under the escort of Russian ice breakers through the freezing Bering Sea. Her journey was an extraordinary one. Presumably, due to British diplomatic pressure, the Red Navy changed its mind when the raider had only reached half way, and sent instructions ordering her return. Her commander refused, and although (after a farewell vodka party), the Red ice breakers were withdrawn, he persisted in pursuing the cruise, this even despite the fact that he possessed no sea charts of the area concerned and faced a hazardous 700-mile journey through pack ice.

Komet seemed to surround herself with an aura of

'diplomatic incident', and on one occasion camouflaged herself as a Jap so outrageously, while sheltering in the midst of four Japanese ships, that the Captain of one of them, a Japanese Naval tanker, was even moved to lodge a protest! Later, off the island of Nauru, she distinguished herself by first sending Christmas greetings by signal lamp, then issuing a warning to get to safety at once before opening fire on the phosphate works. It was a spectacular little bombardment, but unfortunately had a bad effect on the Eastern end of the Axis, for the phosphate works were controlled by Japanese!

'Neutrality', we simple sailors found, covered a multitude of sins. It could also create a multitude of embarrassments.

Until we'd met *Automedon* our most profitable 'Intelligence' catch was the 6,000 ton *Benarty*, which, in duitfully retransmitting *Athelking*'s warning signal had not only caused us to re-open fire on *Athelking*, but had signed her own death warrant. For, when we discovered that *Athelking* was not to blame and that another ship was responsible for sending we started a search . . .

It was obvious from the circumstances leading to our mistake, and the strength at which the signals had been received in our radio room, that the culprit was close at hand. But finding her was one thing; catching her, we agreed, was quite another. Obviously no fool, and quite aware of the danger she had incurred in performing her duty, she was running before us, sending our R for Raider every minute. It really seemed as though the *Atlantis* luck was out, for darkness would have fallen long before we could get her in the range of our guns, and with her evasive career we would not be able to engage her before the morning, by which time she would be far too near the shore either for our comfort or our safety.

Rogge pondered on her description. 'Mostly a native crew, I suppose?' he mused.

'It's customary, sir,' I said. But what the devil did the colour of their skins matter?

156

Rogge turned to Bulla, the seaplane pilot. 'Could you manoeuvre sufficiently to fire down a ship's funnel?' he asked.

'Oh yes', said Bulla. 'Barring accidents, sir.'

'Good,' said Rogge, ignoring the accidents. 'A chance for the Arado to win some glory. If we can't take the Englishman by shells, we'll take him by panic. We'll scare the coloured boys up on deck. Flush 'em out!'

The plan worked. For, as the seaplane dived almost vertically over *Benarty*'s stack, the gunner poured in a long burst . . . straight down the shaft. The effect was dramatic, and as the Arado ran in for a second attack, *Benarty*'s decks became thronged with a mob of Chinese and Lascars, terrified out of their wits and intent only upon escape; a panic-stricken stampede that the English officers were quite unable to control. Her furnace rooms destroyed, soon *Benarty* lay stopped, ours for the taking.

Our new capture carried a very valuable war cargo including 1,000 tons of lead, 100 tons of zinc, and 400 tons of wolfram. The latter was a commodity worth almost as much to Germany as its weight in gold, but it was packed in such small bags that we had no time to transfer more than a very limited quanity for the hue and cry was now really clamorous and the ether alive with signals.

However, said Rogge, we had succeeded in denying the stuff to our enemies, and that in itself was a victory.

Unlike the doctor who took as prize some hundreds of orientally-manufactured cheroots, and literally forced himself to become acclimatised to their use by accepting physical sickness—my main interest in our capture lay in the mess of official correspondence she carried. Much of this was most useful to us, while from that which was not, I was able to deduce, to my surprise and pleasure, that the British were as afflicted as ourselves by the Red Tape warriors of the shore; literally every sore foot of the elephant cow Bha Mang was reported to London Head Office, while a document relating to the issue of a thermometer by Naval Stores, Rangoon, evidently necessitated twenty-three copies!

Our capture of *Benarty* was a classic of its kind, the sort of action in which, in later years, one's passing success is not marred by memories of the dead; the sort of action that one has normally only one chance in a million of implementing, let alone bringing to fruition.

But for the destruction of *Automedon* the Japanese presented Rogge with an elaborate Samurai sword, though its delivery was a little delayed. It was made eighteen months after the carnage and the shells . . . a few weeks after the collapse of Singapore.

CHAPTER FIFTEEN

LAND HO!

'LAND HO! *Land ho!'*

Out of the wrack and the murk she staggered, tossed like a grey ghost ship through a black and angry sea. With the gale behind her and her diesels straining, the raider *Atlantis* had reached the Islands of Despair.

'Land ho!' The shout from the crossbeams was hurled back by the wind as the dull morning broke around us, and our crew came crowding to the rails. A long, dark stretch of reefs spread before us, expanding in every direction as the first pale light fell upon them from the east. The clouds hung heavily and low, occasionally shifting and parting to reveal the black conical tops of a gigantic mountain range. The spray broke over us, unerringly finding the cracks and crevices in our defensive clothing, chipping our frozen cheeks, and spilling into our sea boots until our feet were swollen and numbed, as if we'd been paddling in an icy pool. But we were too excited to care about the weather for every eye was turned towards the shore—the first land we had seen since our mine-laying off the Cape, the first land we would tread since leaving our Fatherland behind us . . .

It was Rogge's decision that had brought us running from the seas of perpetual sunshine to this tip of desolate Antarctica and the black and white bleakness of the Kerguelens.

We needed water and we needed it badly. Nine months had passed since our break-out from Germany and our tanks were now dangerously low. Ordinarily our distilling plant could help, but it worked on coal and we needed all the coal we had as ballast to maintain the steadiness of the ship.

Water, water everywhere, yet in the entire twenty-eight million square miles of the Indian Ocean, not a drop to drink! What was to be done? Rogge, the navigation officer and myself pored over our extensive collection of handbooks and charts. Prince Edward Island was barred to us owing to its frequent fogs and inaccessibility. New Amsterdam and St. Paul were equally unacceptable for precisely the reverse reason. Both were in the main shipping lanes, and we had no desire to be surprised by an inquisitive British cruiser. Finally we fixed on the remote Kerguelen Islands. Fifty degrees south, and in an area seldom used by merchant ships, the Kerguelens had countless bays and fjords where we could lurk in hidden anchorage, and, although the scene of Norwegian whaling and sealing expeditions in the past, it was probable that by now they were uninhabited. Also we could be assured that, thanks largely to the German survey ship, *Gazelle*, they were comparatively well charted.

So, in early December, on the first Sunday of Advent, on the hottest and most humid of Indian afternoons, we turned our bows southwards, the sea line shimmering in the haze, the vast dome of blue above untouched by any cloud. The sun fell vertically upon sweating, naked shoulders, and upon *Atlantis* performing her duty as listlessly as the rest of us, with none of her old fight evident. For this was an area of calms where no wind disturbed the mirror of the sea—a distorting mirror that alternately foreshortened and lengthened the image of our ship, reflecting her only in grotesque, indecent caricature. There was no resistance to her bows, no liveliness from the ancient enemy around her keel. When the mirror clouded, it was not from any apparent pressure from the wind, but from some composition of the sea itself, dulling over with a surface more like thick oil than water, heavy and unhealthy against the oven of the hull. This, then, was the

160

setting when Rogge, after prayer service, talked to the crew of the voyage ahead. His words found great favour among us. We were to see and feel the land again and breathe into our lungs the exhilarating tang of clean, cold, fresh air.

Fresh air! As our prow cleft its path ever further to the south, the temperature began to fall. Each day was colder than the one before, and soon the tropical summer was quite forgotten as we headed into deepest winter. Leather jerkins and overcoats, some of them the loot of former encounters, now transformed the appearance of us all and, as the weather changed the seascape altered with it. Rain squalls, great dark towers of them, loomed slowly above winking jagged lines of wavetops, lines as tooth-edged and pointed as the seas of a Silly Symphony. The wind, more and more westerly, freshened every hour, first a gentle stirring, then a light breeze and lastly a distant booming that swelled into a violent crescendo of sound, a mad concerto in which the reeling ship herself became an instrument adding her own voice to the discord of the waters.

And so we came to the Roaring Forties, that site of storms enjoyed (vicariously) by all schoolboys, and remembered romantically, or viciously, by the men of the brave old days of sail. It did not take us long to decide that anything we had ever read or heard about this quarter of the world was true. The winds of the earth seemed to howl around our masts and rigging as though seeking to snatch the entire ship into the catastrophic swell. Hourly the sea grew darker and the sky heavier. Clouds of doom seemed to rush up at unbelievable speed, and our ship bucketed from giant crests into abysmal troughs. Fresh injured were received every day by our sick bay.

Time after time I experienced for myself the vicissitudes of the old salts of the wind-jammers. I was lifted out of my bunk, hurled across the cabin, stunned by my wardrobe, then tossed back across the floor to hit my bunk again as *Atlantis* leaped and rolled and fell. The drawers shot out from my chests and wardrobe like

161

shells from a cannon, spilling their contents in inextricable tangles until the place resembled a haberdashery store after a blitz and it was a common sight in this sea of violence, to see coats—and heavy sea coats at that—streaming out, seemingly at right angles from the hooks on which they were hung.

For the crew's benefit I prepared a daily serial thriller on the ship's blackboard. Its theme: Facts About The Kerguelens. To my dismay the facts were anything but cheering. The islands owed their name to an optimist, the French Count Yves Joseph de Kerguélen–Trémarec. Commanding the frigate *Fortune*, he believed he had discovered Australia and was so excited that he never went ashore, rushed straight back to France to collect a full-scale expedition. In the Bastille, when the costly Bourbon project had failed, he thought up a different name for his discovery—the Land of Despair.

The next visitor, however, was more fortunate. He was Captain Cook, and from 1776 to 1873 whalers and sealers plied their trade there, using the island as a bleak rendezvous on voyages that lasted up to three years. But apart from such enterprises and transitory visitations from warships of all nations, the islands, because of their inhospitable hinterland, remained unexplored and without a permanent residence on them until a M. Bossiere, apparently abundantly provided with money but possessed of little common sense, rented large tracts of the island territory from the French Government in order to raise sheep. Years later, he returned precipitately to France, his mission a complete failure; himself ruined in health and pocket.

Such then was the 'paradise' to which we came, a shore swept by ice-cold waters, with fog and mist around us and our ship grumbling and protesting in every plank.

It was nine in the morning when Action Stations sounded throughout the ship. Desolation or no, we were taking few chances, and our guns were trained against the shore line. Gradually the low ridge formed into a black, forbidding, tumbled mass of rocks, its gloomy coat flecked only by the varying greys of the strata; the occasional vivid green of clinging moss. But, as we watched what had been merely a pin-head on a map two weeks before become transformed into the reality of gloomy peak and monotonous plain, our spirits soared and our hearts rejoiced. Even the grim islands appeared to fall in with our mood for, in the lea of the hills, the wind dropped, the waters smoothed, and we reached a sudden tranquility.

A flurry of orders. The clang of the engine-room bell, and into the water with a steep rush and thundering splash went our anchor for the first time in more than 250 days!

Ahead was the bottle-neck entrance to the concealed anchorage where we aimed to lie, a hide-out known as Gazellehafen, after the survey ship. To the starboard jutted a low cape. We knew that in the outer bay there had once been a settlement devoted to whaling and sealing, and Rogge wondered whether the British might not have reoccupied it as a wartime radio and observations post. Accordingly I was placed in charge of a landing party to reconnoitre over the cape. If there should be a British radio station I was to capture it—attacking by surprise so as not to give our enemy the chance of telling the outer world about us. We wore civilian clothes, we posed as harmless fishermen and we travelled—for the sake of verisimilitude—in a captured Norwegian whaler. Under the planks of the boat we placed our sub-machine guns, readily accessible but not visible from the shore. Beneath our thick jackets we carried pistols and potato masher grenades. And we reckoned that our disguise would enable us to get close enough to our enemies to open up and overwhelm them in a rush.

A 'good luck' sign from Rogge, and we were on our way, through water that was now of the tranquility (but not of the temperature and colour) of a Pacific lagoon.

Carefully we eyed the shore, straining to probe the grey stones, the slabs of granite, and the slowly rising hillside. Quite suddenly the Q.M. grabbed my shoulder

163

and hissed in my ear: 'Something moving on the beach!' There was no going back. We switched on our engine and raced towards the shore, ready for the challenge and the slamming flurry of shots that would announce the spread of the war to its furthest latitude yet. But nothing happened . . . Then, as we rounded the Cape, we saw a small open valley, with four or five huts at the foot of a rising hill. The huts stood clear against the rocks and the sky, the paint peeling from decaying wood, the light thrown back upon us from the windows. There was an incongruous verandah on one of them: it looked, for all the world, as though a Swiss chalet had been transferred to Antarctica. Then the man in our prow saw a figure that, wandering uncertainly by the water's edge and watching our approach, was obviously the physical manifestation of that 'something on the beach'. He reached for a tommy-gun, training the tip of the glittering barrel upon the target as it moved backwards and forwards between huts and shore. Still nothing happened . . . 'Sounds crazy' said the Q.M., 'but whoever that fellow is, I'd say he was drunk. Or mad.'

We stared, more intently. The tension broke . . . The 'drunkard', the 'madman', was caught in the light so that he was recognisable to us as—a very fine specimen of sea lion! Furtively we returned our tommy guns to the bottom of the boat. Then we reached the shore. Reached the shore? What an understatement! We jumped, and we RAN. We breathed in the smell of the land. All our restraint seemed to disappear as we felt the rocks under our feet instead of the persistent shifting of the deck and it was several minutes before we recovered sufficiently to continue on our errand. First, we searched the sheds at the water's edge. They reeked of whale oil and in one we found a kettle full of the stuff—solidified down the years. But stronger than all the smells around us was the smell of the earth itself; the rapturously welcome odour of the soil in the nostrils of men who for so long had known only the tang of the sea. Even the broken and rusted hinges of the dragging, decaying doors seemed to us to possess a homely and nostalgic significance, for these were the things of the land, reminding us of the garden sheds we had left so far behind us, of the odd jobs at home that would have to wait for our return . . .

In extended file we moved along a narrow path that led to the houses beyond. A small brook babbled beside us; short clumps of sparse brown grass were scattered among the stones. Around us the mountains rose slowly to the clouds. Ahead of us the house with the verandah assumed in size—compared with the huts we had just left—the dimensions of a small hotel. We kicked open the door and saw a long room furnished with a stove, a table, two chairs, and an old-fashioned lamp hanging from the ceiling. Next, in this remote nineteenth-century hermitage, we were astounded to be confronted by pictures of scantily-clad girls winking salaciously and invitingly from a calendar of 1936! A date was ringed, 8th November. We found from the title printed upon it, that the calendar was a bequest from a French ship chandler in Tamatave, a main port of Madagascar. We examined, with critical interest, a blonde who was toasting us in Pernod Fils—and proceeded to search adjacent cupboards, but alas the bottles we discovered were all empty, their labels providing an additional proof of the nationality of the island's visitors. Less tantalising to thirsty men but probably possessed of far more scientific interest, was a half loaf of bread that, owing to the peculiarities of the climate, was still, though hard, fit to eat. An odd commentary on ancient reports we had read of rats and mice being prolific in that wilderness! Through the windows we could see a number of trim wire fences—erect monuments to the folly of poor M. Bossiere, and enclosing a place where sheep once bleated hungrily and vainly for sustenance.

We invaded the 'bedroom'. There, ahead of us, was a gigantic old-fashioned bedstead, complete with brass knobs. Lonely M. Bossiere! Then, we were intrigued by the fact that another bedstead stood beside it while, to add to the mystery we discovered bottles of musty jams, rusty tins of fruit and in the tool-shed a crate of dynamite! We wondered why M. Bossiere should have left so hurriedly, and could only conclude that the ship which took him away must have arrived so unexpectedly and left so rapidly, that it allowed him little time for packing. In a nearby pigsty we discovered another strange phenomenon arising from the island's climate. Two dead pigs lay there—mummified. For a few minutes more we continued with our probe and then reported over our portable radio transmitter: 'Settlement uninhabited. No trace of British.' Almost immediately we were ordered to return to *Atlantis.*

Aboard once more, while the landing party was being besieged by their comrades with eager questions about their extraordinary adventure—'just a morning's walk'—I went with Rogge to his cabin where he told us our main problem was how to bring a ship the size of Atlantis into the haven, which, hitherto, had never accommodated a vessel anything like as large. Our present anchorage was linked with Gazellehafen by a large bottle-necked channel some five hundred feet wide. It was decided that we should send in boats to make soundings and lay buoys as markers. The report of the boats' crews returning to the ship seemed highly satisfactory. The water was sixty feet deep in most places, and they had marked a channel one hundred feet wide. Said Rogge: 'We will go in with the tide tomorrow morning.'

We did—and ran into real trouble, trouble that made it seem as though our cruise would be over for good . . .

CHAPTER SIXTEEN

ON THE ROCKS

A RESOUNDING crash and the noise of breaking . . . a shuddering, shaking the ship's whole length . . . a recoil that sent our feet aslither; and *Atlantis* jarred to a staggering stop.

Our ship had struck! She had hit a rock, and she had hit it when right in the centre of the channel that we had marked as 'safe'.

When we'd weighed anchor that morning all the auguries seemed set to favour us. A leaden sky, but a quiet sea, and a passage clearly marked along the channel which led to the inner harbour. Nothing, surely, could be simpler . . .

Atlantis entered the channel mouth travelling very slowly through the hill-shadowed waters, and keeping well within the twin row of buoys that our sounding party had planted. The engine-room telegraph rang as the ship developed a slight drift to port, and Rogge, as a precautionary measure, ordered 'Half ahead' to get action on the rudder. A moment later and the rock had found us . . .

For a split second the significance of the punch that sent *Atlantis* reeling did not register. I just swayed, not comprehending. What the hell? I thought. And then perception cleared as a seaman's voice called out, 'Christ! We've hit something', and someone else shouted, 'A rock. We're on a rock.'

Our first reaction was automatic. 'Hard astern,' and we reversed in an attempt to pull off. But there was no response; only a sound that cut straight across the engines' quiver; a grinding and rasping that set teeth and

167

nerves on edge; a strange and rather terrifying noise—the snarl of the rock biting deeper, ever deeper, into the keel.

Rogge to Engine Room: 'Any water coming in?'

Kielhorn: 'No sir.'

Then a few minutes later the report, 'The drinking water in the forrard tank tastes salt.'

So one at least of our worst fears was now confirmed. The salt was the salt of the sea, pouring into the fresh water tanks in the double bottom between the inner and outer shell of our ship. And the rock that had done the damage was holding us fast.

We tried, of course, all the accepted formulas for coping with such uncomfortable occasions. We reversed engines. We ordered 'Full force astern'. But without effect; indeed it seemed our labours were only making matters worse, for we were now horribly aware that the rock was scraping more menacingly against our steel, each movement louder than the one before, sharper and more rasping.

We sent down a diver. He reported, 'An enormous hole. We're held fast—skewered!'

An apt description. A granite needle, five or six feet wide, had cut up into *Atlantis*, driving her paravane boom ten feet back into the ship, smashing the forepeak and the outer shell.

'Hopeless,' said the diver. 'Quite hopeless.'

A chill passed through us all. A lead thrown out from the port side of her bows showed sixty feet of water. On the starboard it was the same. The rock had hooked right into the steel entrails of our ship. But Rogge refused to take the diver's report as final. He must see for himself, he said, and he insisted upon going down in person although he had never dived before. Nothing else would satisfy him and when he returned it was with the typically optimistic comment, 'Bad. Yes. But not so bad as it might have been. We'll save her yet.'

Anchors were switched from fore to aft, Rogge planning to exert the utmost pull by revving at top speed

168

and at the same time hoisting in the anchor chain with both capstans. But it didn't budge an inch.

'All right,' said Rogge. 'We'll try something else.' He called for tide reports, ordering a tide master to be established ashore so that we could synchronise our effort with the water's peak. Meanwhile he kept us busy shifting all the weight we could into the stern, and, with only a few days to Christmas, we found ourselves slaving in sleet and snow to empty the forepart of our ship, a job of almost unmentionable discomfort.

Men stumbled, cursing as their raw hands scraped the cold metal of our 5.9 shells, each of them weighing over a hundred pounds, and each passed by means of a human chain of aching dog-tired seamen. Next we got to work on the sand ballast, baling it laboriously, a bucketful at a time, before hoisting it up the companionway, and carrying it along the deck. Yet still Rogge found jobs for the exhausted men to do. Cables, ropes and equipment from the bos'ns stores, had now to be dragged aft, and the air was thick with oaths and blasphemies as the working parties manhandled the stuff, toiling until they were ready to drop with the strain. By the time we had moved everything that had to be moved some of the youngsters had to be goaded to their tasks, driven to it with the language and methods of the 'grand old days of sail.'

The task was done. The tide was high. We tried our luck. But all in vain. Again we tried. And still the rock remained firmly embedded in our keel, its grip unyielding. We were bitter in our disappointment, but our leader, still undaunted, ruthlessly drove us on. This time we pumped water into the mine compartment, imposing yet another heavy weight upon the scales that were now our ship, but though we blocked every outlet on our well deck until over 3,000 tons of water were weighing us back, we still could not budge from that accursed rock.

A conference of officers. One of us suggested that we jettison our fuel forrard. But the Captain would not agree. It would entail, he said, the loss of thousands of tons of diesel oil and might put us out of the war for good. What else, then, was to be done?

Dynamite! It was Fehler, of course, who put forward the suggestion. 'Let's try and blow up the rock from below?'

We didn't care very much for Fehler's idea. It might, we reflected, do more damage to the ship than the rock! One or two propositions of a less spectacular nature were then advanced, but we broke up the sitting without any decision being reached, except to try everything we'd tried before all over again in the morning.

On the bridge, a few hours later, I stared dismally into the black of our enforced 'anchorage' considering afresh the alternatives that lay before us. Each was equally uninviting. Either we spent the rest of the war attempting to sustain a rudimentary existence on the Kerguelens, or we spent it behind barbed wire as P.O.W.'s. Of course there was always the possibility that we might be picked up by a brother raider, but the prospect brought no comfort for I winced at the thought of the humiliation that such a 'rescue' would mean for Rogge, realising that never before had I admired our Commander quite so much as now. He had borne his vile luck so well, driving every one of us hard, but himself the hardest of all; a man who was unfaltering, a commander unflustered, full of knowledge, radiating a dogged confidence, and using every card in the pack to fight his destiny.

A faint tingling upon my cheek . . . a sensation different from the general numbness of the cold . . . a moist touch . . . repeated again, and accompanied by a distant whisper that was distinct from the monotonous rhythm of the sea. A wind was springing up, a wind that was soon to transform itself into a howling, tearing gale. But meanwhile, through the hitherto motionless ship beneath me swelled a vibration of action, a tremor of movement that reached from the planks beneath my feet to the focus of my rather sluggish brain, striking a note of alarm, and yet, at the same time, stimulating a new and exciting idea. A new sound was disturbing the ex-

170

isting pattern. The rock was grating and grinding but with a different sound from usual, and the shudder it sent through the deck was different too. At last I recognised what was happening. The wind, now beginning to unleash its full fury, was pushing *Atlantis* to starboard, and our ship was swinging on the rock like a door upon its hinges . . .

In one way this was a portent full of menace—for the granite, by persistent friction might well enlarge the gash in the hull, and yet, in another way, here might be our one chance of escape . . .

I blew the windpipe, activating the whistle over Rogge's bed, rousing him from his brief snatch of sleep after the ardours of the day. Through the speaking tube I explained the new development. 'Good,' he replied, 'I'll be right up,' and soon I was aware of him at my side, a reassuring presence, though almost invisible in the blackness of the night.

We had turned almost ninety degrees beneath the impact of the storm. Now we took a hand in turning the bullying weather to our account, hauling in our stern anchor chain to bring the stern through the wind. In this we succeeded, though this time we were being pushed, as we wanted, in the opposite direction. The bows strained high. With a sound of tearing the ship swung slowly over and then—a louder noise, a sudden lurch, and with a rending crack she slid free.

Free! But how long would our freedom last? There we were, in a ship with only one screw; a ship drifting, side on in an inlet little wider than her hull was long; damaged, battered by the gale, and with us, her guides, unable to see the shore except as a dim dark mass against a slightly paler sky. There were so many things to think about. Astern, an anchor with a cable that had to be parted; other anchors to take in, imminently threatening, that razor-edged needle of granite waiting to pierce and probe anew should we wander off to port.

Despite the bitter cold I found myself sweating profusely, the moisture running down my body from head to toe while Rogge transmitted his orders. For 'eyes' we

171

relied on two men, stationed with the lead lines fore and aft, their anxious voices singing out through the gale the result of their surroundings. 'Ten fathoms! Eight fathoms! Six fathoms! Full ahead engines.' The telegraph rang continuously as, in our desperate effort to avoid fresh disaster, we struggled to turn against the wind. In less than four hours I transmitted over two hundred orders to the engine-room before we managed to escape the trap and head back into the open bay. As our anchors roared down and I heard myself whisper a prayer of thankfulness, a black shape topped the ladder to the bridge. A cool, unconcerned voice queried casually, 'All's well?' It was the officer who was due to relieve me. So exhausted by the battle of the preceding days—three nerve-racking days—he had, like most of the off-duty crew, slept solidly through our final crisis!

At breakfast there was some subdued rejoicing; subdued because we all of us knew that there were still many problems to face; first, and foremost, being just how, in this wilderness, to repair the hole torn by the rock. Also the general sense of depression that shadowed these islands now seemed to have enveloped us all. We had a premonition of tragedy to come. And we were not mistaken.

CHAPTER SEVENTEEN

A GRAVE IN THE SOUTH

IN THE storm battered desolation of the Kerguelens lies
the most southerly German soldier's grave . . .

In winter, encased by the blue and glittering ice; in
summer, sodden by rain and mist, its cross commemo-
rates the first of our company to die—by the name
Herrman, by rank, Leading Seaman; a man with a wife
and children at home to feed, who 'fell for the Führer'
on the day before Christmas.*

That fatal Christmas Eve found Herrman busy on the
funnel, swinging on an improvised rope platform
around its rim, and doubtless thinking as he worked of
the festivities to come, and of the people back home. He
was still very young, and life was sweet . . . It was a
mischance in a thousand that the rope which held him
should have come into contact with the diesel exhaust;
and another, even greater mischance, that the diesel
should have been started up in the course of an engine
inspection. In a second the strands had severed and the
youngster had been sent hurtling to his death upon the
deck below . . .

This tragedy cast its gloom upon us all. Alive, to the
men who messed with him, Herrman had been a willing
and cheerful comrade; to the rest of us he was just one
man among 347, all equally as good. In the muster
book it had been HERRMAN, Matr. Ob. Gefr—just that,
and no more—and yet within minutes, he had become

* Herrman's parents, living in Silesia and suffering the
same fate as others there, were expelled and not heard of
again.   A.S.V.

173

the most important person of all our company, invested by death with a dignity that life denied; a figure possessed of eternal mystery and worthy of all honour!

We formed a funeral party from among his peers; we built him a cross of *Atlantis* oak; we swathed him in all the glory of our red and our white and our black; and we brought him reverently ashore, in his pitiful lonely splendour to the accompaniment of a howling, icy gale. The Commander, bare-headed and in full dress uniform, delivered the funeral address. The salute of the firing party re-echoed thinly among the hills and as a sudden gust shook the Naval Ensign back from the coffin lid, I experienced an almost overwhelming and quite irrational sense of loss—The Song of the Dead Soldiers acquiring in a second a new and personal significance. *Ich hatt einen Kameraden!*

Sentimentalism? I was later relieved to find that such thoughts were not confined to me alone, for used though we were by now to the aspect of death, the symbolism of this remote and windswept grave, containing the first of our own family to die, had touched us all.

Icht hatt einen Kameraden . . . one last salute . . . a bustle among the man's mess-mates, piling stones around the cross . . . a shouted order . . . and we were on our way back to the ship—and the problems of the ship; problems which were by no means inconsiderable, and demanded all our practical attention.

First and most pressing need was to get *Atlantis* into the inner haven, and we were much relieved when this was achieved, our entry this time being unaccompanied by any dramatic turn of events. Next, while undergoing the laborious process of repair we had to protect our ship from unwelcome visitors, and in this respect Kasch proved himself a genius, arranging things so neatly that we were soon almost hoping for a British cruiser to come sniffing along our tracks!

A series of numbers were marked on the cliff face, each number representing a square on our artillery charts. Then we 'sighted' our guns on the cliffs, making careful calculations of range and angle. Kasch was nothing if not thorough! Wind, temperature, air pressure—all the vital factors were recorded; and signallers and gunners were posted on the ridge—equipped with instruments of calibrated glass that would enable them to warn us immediately as to the 'square' in which an enemy appeared.

In short we were very snug—knowing we could see without being seen, and enabled to pour our shells into a foe without him even knowing from where they came. Silhouetted against the sea he would be a 'sitting target'—and destroyed as such.

The next problem was less speedily solved. How to repair our ship?

The hole in her bottom measured six feet by eighteen, and as the hull's steel plates had been forced back at right angles, it looked for all the world, said the divers, like a great barn door! Well, there was nothing we could do about THAT in this Godforsaken wilderness, except, of course, to test the strength of the frames that formed the skeleton of the ship.

The skill and pluck of the two crew members who in peace-time, were engaged in the building trade, now solved the difficulty of patching the leak in the forepeak. Both of them volunteers, they were lowered into the compartment, laden with bags of concrete, sand, and tiles. Then—after a huge luncheon basket had been added—the man-hole cover was closed on top of them and compressed air blown in to push the water out, thus making the leak dry and accessible! For two days the men remained in this self-selected prison until the concrete had hardened, and the leak, well shored up, could withhold the pressure of the water outside. A job well done . . .

Problems . . . More problems . . . Would we EVER come to an end of them?

We sent down divers equipped with the latest model underwater blowlamps to remove the torn and jagged steel flukes that stuck out around the paravane shaft. But the blowlamps would not work, try as we might!

175

This was a staggering shock, for how otherwise were we to carve out these solid, misshapen chunks of steel? 'Only one thing for it,' said Rogge. 'The divers will have to attach cables to the stuff. Then we must haul with the anchor winches until it breaks beneath the strain.'

Never was there a slower and more tedious job. The divers were obliged to spend days in the icy water, laboriously drilling holes in the plates by hand; fixing shackles into holes; then attaching steel cables to the shackles; until finally, very, very gently, the cables were hauled in by the winches and bit by bit, the metal broken. By the time their task was over, these unfortunate men—hitherto suspected of 'exaggerating' the damage with a view to spinning out our stay in the islands—were in a state of near collapse from strain, cold and over-work.

For job Number Three—a close inspection of the inner part of the double bottom cells—we had the perfect instrument in a chief engineer who was never happy unless he was tackling something 'unusual', or, preferably, 'impossible'! He liked to hear things summed up in this way because he could then prove that to him they were quite feasible—indeed simple—and thus, as a result, achieve credit over the 'deck officers'. Kielhorn was chubby, a practical Bavarian with a great love of beer, and an equal love of a job from which he could emerge covered in oil from head to foot.

At the time of our holing, hundreds of tons of sand ballast had rested on top of the man-hole leading to the cells between the inner and outer shells of our hull. Most of this had been moved when we lightened ship in our effort to break free of the rock, but much still remained and had to be shifted pailwise. More curses from the overtaxed crew; more hard labour until its steel gleaming through the yellow, the bottom showed up, and eventually also the ring of screws which marked the man-hole cover. So far, so good. But the man-hole which would enable the engineer to reach the bottom also admitted the sea—the vast pressure of water piled up outside. A job completely after Kielhorn's

176

heart! 'We will build a caisson over this man-hole cover,' he said. 'We shall then be able to gain access quite easily!'

For two days Hold Number One was a bustle of mysterious technical activity, echoing the hissing of blow lamps and the thud of hammers. Every few hours the extent of the remaining oxygen supply was reported to our Captain—who hated to see the precious stuff go. But, otherwise, our well meant enquiries would be met only by impatient, important, knowledgeable grunts and shrugs. Experts were at work! But when at last we were permitted to view the fruits of the labours, we were speechless with admiration. A magnificent job. There it was, a beautiful new structure forty feet down; a sort of dog's kennel of steel built over the man-hole, with an identical man-hole on top, a complicated retreat possessing a system of telephones and airpipes; and a chief engineer eager to go in and see the worst for himself. The chief and his companion, a giant whose lisp had acquired him the nickname of 'Thweizentnerund thehn Pfund' crawled happily through the webframing, looking out to where a few fish looked back at them 'in astonishment' (they said) from beyond the leak. All the time through the telephone they were reporting what they saw—'A lot of frames bent . . .' 'Garboard plate missing . . .' 'Structure itself seems solid enough . . .' and then the cheery reassurance 'It will be all right . . .' In this they were correct, and later experience showed us that the leak did not impair either our seaworthiness or our speed.

Preceding such hectic labours, Christmas Day passed for us, on *Atlantis*, in a manner where serious reflection lay heavily behind the facade of jollity; reflection accentuated, especially among his mess-mates, by the sadness of Herrman's passing however cheerful we tried to be and we tried as best we could.

Fehler, the organising genius, turned from his detonators to the design and manufacture of Christmas decorations, building a Christmas tree of broomsticks, with bits of rope bound round with wire and sprayed with green paint to form effective 'leaves'. Rogge played Santa Claus and the loot from our victims' 'gift parcels' of shoes, pencils, cigarettes and chocolate was wrapped and presented to the crew.

When the Captain—replendent in gold braid and glittering white shirt, black bow-tie and best jacket— entered the deck, the seamen piously opened up with the refrain—'I come down from high in heaven.' A shock to Rogge's religious susceptibilities, but borne in good part, and we ate and talked that night at the same tables as the men who had served, and were to serve so devotedly throughout the hazards of our cruise. Our gathering had an air of nostalgia, which was intensified by the news of the start of the bombing back at home, and I remember particularly, bearded Signalman Winter, normally the jolliest man in the mess, sitting sadly beside a picture of his wife and three children.

At this party—at which nine hundred pints of punch were drunk!—we had opportunities, normally denied us, of hearing the views of our crew, and it became evident to us that the 'glamour' of the cruise was wearing exceedingly thin. It was plain that most of the reservists, despite their loyalty to Ship and Commander—(on THAT we knew we could always depend)—were extremely 'fed up', the married ones being anxious only to get home again, though the unmarried were not necessarily adverse to 'sitting-out' the war in the Kerguelens. It was an 'illuminating' dinner table and later, as our evening hymn echoed over the dark waters, I pondered over the confidences it had evoked. In the end I decided there was not much to worry about. They were all good fellows. We, officers too, were becoming increasingly depressed at the prospects of a war which seemed now as though it was going to drag on for ever, but our misgivings did not affect our fundamental loyalties to stand beside our own and it was the same with them. Whatever they thought of the politicians, or the roles those gentlemen had selected for them, they would continue to work as a team. Yet working for what . . . ?

What destiny was it that designed men to hunt and kill each other across the waters of a world so much bigger and mightier than themselves? . . . But such philosophising was out of place in the Kerguelens, for even while the thoughts formed the need arose to face and cope with the phenomena that had bestowed upon them the title of 'The Land of A Thousand Gales'.

Double bridge watch was enforced, and we dropped our second anchor as a precaution, although, despite the ever growing fury of the blast, there was as yet no sea. The deck was covered in snow; the stars blinded by clouds; and as the men off-duty started to sing of the Holy Child, the eyes of their comrades were alert for the signal that would start the blaze of our guns into the murk, the punch of our shells on a slim grey hull— (carol singing aboard her too, no doubt!)—approaching the dark and menace-laden shore.

A somewhat thoughtful Christmas . . .

In our entire stay in the Kerguelens the most that the average seaman enjoyed of the land he had so eagerly anticipated was a two hours' walk. So intense was our labour that, except for the very few, there was small chance of further exploration, and in this respect both I, and the men of my landing parties, were fortunate above our deserts. A waterfall had been located on a mountain side and we were detailed to find ways and means of 'tapping' the clear glacial water for the ship. A congenial assignment, though prefaced by a warning from Rogge before we left, 'For God's sake, Mohr, don't let Fehler use too much of his precious dynamite on it . . . !'

This water-carrying was no haphazard affair. We discovered that, to tap the tempting fall we would have to build a pipe line, one thousand two hundred yards long; a pipeline moreover carried down an almost precipitous slope, across a flat shore, and through the water of our anchorage . . . We overcame our problems by utilising every yard of our fire pipes and oil pipes, and in two days the *Atlantis* water tanks were the richer by 1,000 tons of the cleanest and coldest and most refreshing liquid we would ever drink. But the operation had been a very nicely balanced business—so much so that, at the finish we had but thirty yards of pipeline to spare.

To us—the lucky ones—came more adventures. Detailed to make a general reconnaissance of the land beyond our hillbound haven, I was able to take a hunting party into the interior—discovering and exploring a waterway that passed through black peaks and treacherous swamps for many miles; making a magical excursion to the perpetual accompaniment of the rushing waters of mountain burns, which dashed their sheer white waters into the streams, creating among us with their music a nostalgia for the German South.

The lure of the mountains had captivated the Bavarians of our party and, despite my urging them on to the vital task of collecting food, their eyes had persisted in wandering wistfully to the glittering spread of the glaciers of Mount Ross . . . towering almost 6,000 feet above us. Eventually we compromised by offering them a climb on a mountain more readily accessible, but I did not realise until too late that I, as officer-in-charge, would necessarily be expected to accompany them. What mountain goats those Bavarian seamen were! They made every crack and crevice in their highway up the sheer rock face, and I was exhausted by the time I weakly succeeded in joining them at the top. Was it worth it? I gazed down upon a landscape possessed of a naked brutality that I had never witnessed before and never encountered since. The surface of the valleys seemed polished beneath the fitful rays of the sun—worn flat through an ice-age of grinding glaciers and the persistent punishment of the winds, and as I looked towards the anchorage, our ship appeared as harmless as a toy. Bleak? Barren? Yes, but enticing enough for us, we who had not seen the beauty of peak or plain for so long, and who, moreover, could expect to see none again for many a wearying month. Having silently drunk our fill of its delights we now turned our thoughts to our bodily needs and the purpose of our expedition. We had the water; now we needed to supplement our food. But with what? In this land where no flowers blossomed, and no tree grew to relieve the monotony of the black and white of glaciers and granite; where animal and bird-life were practically extinct, we expected our search would be difficult. The Kerguelens, it seemed however, had but one obvious suggestion to offer—cabbage!

This stumpy, stunted vegetable was practically the extent of the island's verdure, apart from moss and minute grass, but it grew in fair abundance. We collected a good quantity for sampling by the crew. Eaten raw it was quite good, but when cooked it had the most atrocious smell, leaving the whole ship stinking like a thousand privies!

At this stage we had few guests aboard *Atlantis*, one being kept confined to his 'prison quarters' during our entire stay on the islands, Rogge wisely deciding that it would be too great a security risk both to ourselves and to other ships of our Navy, to let him realise where we were, and appreciate the advantages of such a haven. He was, nevertheless, given like the rest of us the cabbage dish, and nothing of course could disguise the all too pointed distinctive reek of the cooking. I often wondered what he made of it, and whether our 'security measures' proved so secure after all.

Hunting for what scant 'game' we might discover, we one day surprised a mob of rabbits that somehow—whatever the naturalists and geographers might say about it—managed miraculously to survive in this so-called lifeless waste.

Rabbits! Rabbit-stew! Thirty men with service rifles, we eyed our prey with some compassion, then mouths watering, thought of our dinners—and fired. After the fusillade had ceased we advanced to collect the corpses of the massacre . . . But not one single rabbit could we mark upon our butts. All had escaped! The fast shooting sailors of the German Navy, put to shame, went somewhat sheepishly back to their boats, while Brer Rabbit lay low, and showed nothing; not even the tip of his bushy tail slid across the blue steel of our sights.

Fehler, however, had rather better luck. We'd jibbed at his optimism when he brought his hunting rifle aboard at Bremen, but now he had succeeded in bagging some duck. This proved most acceptable, for although we afterwards managed to get the odd rabbit or two, we began to tire of a menu which consisted mainly of Kerguelen cabbage and rabbit curry—or, as a change, Kerguelen rabbit and curried cabbage! We also managed to locate mussels to supplement our diet, and many happy hours were spent in collecting them.

Some of our activities were childish enough . . . The doctor—to the annoyance of his steed—rode a sea lion; and we, after photographing some penguins, managed to capture one, though here our purpose was 'political' rather than practical. In the tropic heat, and now in the antarctic cold, our Captain had ordained that no officer be 'improperly dressed'. Whether we liked it or not, and whatever the circumstances, we must, when on duty, wear the neat, black bow-tie that is the hall-mark of the German naval officer. So we decorated our penguin, and presented him to the Captain with the regulation tie meticulously around his throat. Rogge thanked us profusely—but ignored the hint!

On another occasion we experimented for hours with the dynamite we had discovered in the deserted sheds, firing hundreds of rounds into it and ducking after every shot behind the largest boulders—but our desire of a Big Bang did not materialise.

Ferry's experiences of the islands were confined to one unhappy incident that rendered him deliriously glad to be back aboard the ship again. Bounding ashore, the little Scottie sniffed enthusiastically at every strange smell and unfamiliar scent, frisking and rolling over and over on the beach and giving vent to his feelings in the most ecstatic barks and yelps. But his pleasures lasted for only two minutes. A flock of seagulls swept in upon him, attacking this danger to their peace so ferociously that Ferry had to be saved by the bos'n and carried un-

182

der protective escort to the sea and back to his master Rogge.

Meanwhile, our seaplane was busy in the skies above our remote retreat and not only did its crew make routine patrols seaward to ward against any surprise approach from the enemy, but they also established themselves in the roles of geographers and aerial surveyors. Their reconnaissance revealed that the glaciers came from the slopes of Mount Ross, and not from a mountain range in the south-west as less well equipped explorers had hitherto asserted. Many other inaccuracies also came to light, and so, in between other tasks, we made a new survey of the area for the sake of less belligerent visitors in the years ahead.

Notwithstanding such diversions, however, I was glad when the repairs were finally completed and the anchors came up once more. Slowly we began to nose our way through the ill-fated channel, cautiously edging toward the bay. A few hours later and *Atlantis* was driving her course through the open sea again—the shoreline, and the white roof of the clouds above it, dropping behind her stern, dwindling once more into a long, black, mysterious ridge upon the water, but holding now the body of our comrade and the cross that bears his name.

To work again . . . Within a few days we were once more beneath the relentless blaze of the tropical sun. By the end of January we were operating in the neighborhood of the Seychelles, to the north-east of Madagascar—stalking the British freighter *Mandasor*, and obtaining a 'kill made possible only by our seaplane's daring . . .'

CHAPTER EIGHTEEN

WHERE WOLVES FOREGATHER

THROUGH THE periscope of U-43 the steamer on the sea line was British—unmistakably so.

'Fire One . . . ! Fire Two . . . ! Fire Three . . .' Three tracks of white carved across the water . . . a dull explosion . . . a crumpling of the target in the centre of the crosswires of the eye-piece through which the U-boatman was watching, and the Unterseebooten had achieved yet another success. U-43 was well satisfied.

How could she know that the ship she had just sunk was commanded by a German officer, manned by a German crew; that she had just returned from one of the most hazardous and daring adventures in naval history, and that her cargo was vital to the Reich . . . ?

Yes. The *Speybank* was a ship that I shall not readily forget—not only because of the terrible nature of her end, but also because of the remarkable escapes she had while employed in our service. It was less than a week after sinking the *Mandasor,* that we first encountered her, a 5,000-ton British freighter, which we captured, putting a prize crew aboard, and using her for a number of weeks as an auxiliary to *Atlantis* for reconnaissance work. We had put her under the command of Lieutenant Schneidewind—formerly first mate on the *Tannenfels,* a German vessel on the run from Italian Somaliland—whom Rogge had requisitioned and trained aboard *Atlantis,* much against the wishes of the man's previous Captain.

Speybank—in our service, re-christened the *Doggerbank*—was with us until March when we sent her back to home waters to be refitted for further service with the German Navy. She reached Bordeaux in May, and, undergoing alterations for several months, was installed with a provisional mine-hold. Early in 1943, commanded as before by Lieutenant Schneidewind, she again put to sea with instructions to lay mines off Cape Town.

But she was destined for trouble right at the start, for, running almost at once into an unusually violent gale, she was so battered that the mines broke loose from their moorings in the hold, and rolled dangerously about until the crew, although with considerable difficulty, and at grave risk to themselves, managed to round them up and resecure them. She reached the Cape, without further mishap, but here she was approached and challenged by enemy aircraft. She gave her name as *Levanbank*, stating that she was on her way from New York to Cape Town. The aircraft turned away. The explanation had been accepted!

Schneidewind certainly lived up to Rogge's high estimate of his character. This cool young man brought his ship so close to the shore at Table Bay that he was often caught in the glare of the British searchlights, yet quietly, steadily continuing with the business in hand, he succeeded in laying half of his command's cargo within less than a mile from the watchers on the land. At this stage the rest of the mines were lying exposed and ready upon her decks, and it was, therefore, with some apprehension—to use the sort of understatement Schneidewind would have employed—that *Speybank*'s crew sighted the approach of a British cruiser of the Birmingham Class. But again she escaped. The cruiser, which was under a mile away, focused a searchlight beam on her, but the ray was directed low in the water, and the tell-tale mine-strewn decks remained obscured.

The cruiser: 'What ship?'

Schneidewind: *'Levanbank*. On the way to Durban. Goodnight.'

To which the cruiser replied: 'Wish the crew a good voyage and the Captain a good night.'

185

Gratefully the *Speybank* again proceeded, only to be chased, and challenged when disposing of the rest of her ware off Cape Agualhas, by a British armed merchant cruiser carrying hundreds of soldiers who could clearly be seen upon her decks. This time *Speybank* successfully passed herself off as the *Inverbank*.

But soon her luck changed, for good. After making a second voyage to Yokohama—(during which she met our brother raider, *Thor,* commanded by Captain Gumprich)—she headed for home, packed with strategic war material; a week ahead of schedule. It was this alteration of programme that caused her end, an end not only ironic but exceedingly tragic—only one man of her crew being rescued. All the others who had managed to crowd into the one available boat perished miserably after a long time drifting on the open sea. Some shot themselves. Others jumped over the side. And some gasped out their end where they lay—demented by thirst.

But, back in January before this tragedy occurred, and when *Speybank* was yet with us, the main interest of Rogge and myself lay in a top secret message, creating an excitement unlike anything yet received from our remote Admiralty. The pocket battleship, *Scheer*—whose first sortie had resulted in the famous *Jervis Bay* action—was 'out' again; in fact, she was almost next door, and we were once more to set our eyes upon a 'regular' German warship and talk again to compatriots drawn from outside our own little circle. At present only Rogge and myself knew the keenly awaited rendezvous and it seemed a pity, we said, that we couldn't symbolise the occasion by some dramatic coup. They say the wish is father to the thought. In this case it was father to the deed as well . . .

For, on 2nd February, we sighted the fast Norwegian tanker, *Ketty Brovig*. A tanker! And just in time when we, and *Scheer,* and the Italians operating from Somaliland, were so desperately in need of fuel. We decided to attack at night. Rogge was anxious for a complete sur-

186

prise. By this time, in an attempt to save unnecessary bloodshed, we had arranged an elaborate system of floodlighting whereby, as soon as the command was given our ship stood out in bold relief, a sign in English on her sides: STOP. DON'T USE WIRELESS.

We knew, of course, that the Admiralty had so rigidly defined the obligations of ships' masters that, whatever the odds, they had to send a Raider signal—or at least make the attempt. But, in *Ketty Brovig*'s case, we felt we had an adequate excuse for adopting the risks of the more humane approach—for one single registering hit could precipitate a volcano of gushing and burning fuel, making her an oven in which her crew would roast, and leaving us with but a husk as a trophy.

'Don't fire into her,' commanded Rogge. 'Rely on the sign and a shot to frighten.'

'On lights!' In a second our deck, hitherto silent and black beneath the night, was as bright as the Sportsplatz on the evening of an International Rally.

'No. 1 Gun, Fire . . . !' Almost simultaneously there came the crash of the firing mechanism, the crack of the gun, the whine of a shell—and then a scream of rage from the artillery officer.

'You bloody lunatic! You've hit the funnel!'

From *Ketty Brovig* rose a cloud of steam. She stopped with commendable promptness. For a second we waited anxiously for the first flicker of the inferno to come, but for some inexplicable reason she remained intact.

'Away boat!' As I gave the command I found myself, not for the first time, regretting the occupation war had brought me. A fine job this, I thought, as we approached the stricken tanker—to go aboard a ship where even a carelessly thrown match might cause disaster; to try to save a ship that our damn fool had made a death-trap. But similar misgivings as to *Ketty Brovig*'s insecurity were more than manifest on the other side, for, as we neared her a succession of splashes in the water bore witness to the efficiency with which her Chinese crew were dropping over the side.

As I stumbled aboard the tanker, groping my way towards the bridge, a Chinese appeared from out of the shadows. 'What's the name of the ship?' I asked him.

When he saw me the Oriental's slant eyes almost rounded in fright. With a squeal of terror he fled for the rails and flung himself straight over into the sea. Good heavens! I thought. What kind of a Mephistophelian monster did I look? I shrugged, somewhat amused. Oh well. I'd have to find out the name of the ship for myself. Flashlight in hand I went to search for the wireless room, where the call sign, pinned on the wall, gave me the answer I sought. But what cargo was the *Ketty Brovig* carrying? Was she full, or empty? Like a burglar I ransacked the captain's cabin. Eventually I found her cargo manifest. Better, even, than we'd hoped—4,500 tons of diesel oil; 6,000 tons of other fuel.

Returning to *Atlantis,* together with stray Chinese whom we picked up from the water on the way, we decided that somehow our prize must be saved. Fehler and I, therefore, were now directed to coax, rather forcibly, the reluctant Orientals back to their duty, and once back aboard *Ketty Brovig* a fantastic council of war took place. Sitting around a table in a darkness relieved only by the light of my torch, Fehler and I, together with her Norwegian Captain, and the chief engineer, discussed our difficulties. These were formidable, for, thanks to our confounded shell, there was little pressure in her boilers. We suggested running fresh water in.

The Norwegian chief shook his head. 'Can't,' he said, 'We haven't any hand pumps.'

'Then how the devil do you get up steam in harbour?'

'It has to be supplied by the shore.'

'Most peculiar'—we were speechless.

But the chief just grinned. 'You'll find,' he said, 'that this is a most peculiar ship.'

This proved to be an understatement, for although we tried out various ideas, there seemed to be simply no way of baling water into the boilers from *Ketty Brovig*'s strangely constructed tanks. The first problem was how to prevent what little steam there remained from escaping. One of our men, wrapped around with blankets, volunteered to climb into the bone-searing cloud to get at the main valve and turn it off. Another stood ready to take his place should he fail, and die. But our volunteer got back safely, though almost collapsing on the deck as, proof of his success, the hissing stopped and a sudden silence fell over the ship. So far, so good, yet the situation as a whole still looked far from promising.

We debated whether to fill one of her boilers with sea water, but this would have meant a very short duration of their working life, and no fuel pumps were operating. But now, fortunately, our engineers came to the rescue with one of their typically ambitious ideas. They measured the main steam pipe, and that night in the workshop of *Atlantis* they made a metal jacket to fit the burst. By dawn the pipe was plugged. Now we had to raise steam. But how? Fehler, delightedly taking over command of the tanker, ordered the ship's furniture to be chopped up for firewood, and *Ketty Brovig*'s first revolutions were made possible by the power engendered by desks, drawers and tables!

This done I rejoined *Atlantis,* and we, with the three other ships astern—*Tannenfels, Speybank* and *Ketty Brovig*—proceeded to our rendezvous.

Our 'appointment' with *Scheer* was still, of course, unknown to the crew, and the sudden shout of 'Mast in sight!' brought a twinkle to Rogge's eyes as from our signaller came the rather faltering information that he was afraid it was a warship! 'Action Stations' had been sounded as the usual precaution, and now, while Rogge and I exchanged a sly smile, we could literally FEEL the interrogatives of the crew—What the devil? Why were we going straight for a warship? Was the captain bent on suicide? We kept our comrades cruelly in suspense until barely a minute or so before the look-outs reported the treble turret, fore and aft, that meant 'one of ours'.

For her part *Scheer*'s crew was almost equally as surprised . . . instead of one ship, as expected, they sighted four! We proudly paraded our prizes, and then, after exchanging the usual courtesies between men-of-war we came up to starboard of our big sister feeling rather scruffy and mercantile in comparison with her impeccable rig. Rough seas were running—extremely rough, for a Force Eleven gale now whipped across the ocean—*Scheer* sent us a commiseratory note saying 'she quite understood we would not be able to board her until the weather improved.' But Rogge would have none of this and promptly replied, 'Nevertheless I shall come!' He was confident our Norwegian whalers would show up the naval pinnaces, but in any case we would board *Scheer*—even if we had to swim for it!

We were not put to such desperate measures, however, and after some tricky manoeuvring—the sea was as high as a house—our party managed to board the pocket battleship. I found the going anything but good and our boat plunged deep into the water as I steadied myself on the propeller guard before clambering to the deck, the infernal ship choosing this time, of all times, to drop in!

They gave us quite a good party, but so heavy grew the sea—(quite apart from the hospitality)—that when the moment came for return I found myself marooned aboard her, Rogge, in a critical second, having just been able to jump for the boat, and leaving me behind with no further opportunity of return. So there I was for the night, with not unwelcome change of scenery; my only worry the fear that *Atlantis*, by some strange mischance, might suddenly have to separate, leaving me permanently stranded.

But all was well, and we proceeded for 300 miles to the south without mishap to calmer waters where we were able to exchange more leisured pleasantries. Selected petty officers and seamen from *Atlantis* were invited to visit *Scheer*, where they enjoyed the moral fillip of strutting and swanking to their hearts' content—very much the veterans and the awe of crew who had themselves been 'a mere three months at sea'.

Both ships exchanged gifts—their scale being lavish because they hadn't cost anything! From our own loot, we provided every man on *Scheer* with a fountain pen. In later years we somewhat regretted our generosity for we were amused to find that *Scheer,* in her battle history, had claimed the capture of these trophies herself!

In return we received from *Scheer* a gift that subsequently caused us acute embarrassment. Before meeting us she had captured the English refrigerated ship *Duquesa,* with a cargo of millions of eggs—literally millions. On to us *Scheer* gratefully loaded 150,000. For fourteen days every crew member, and every prisoner—none of whom had seen an egg for months—ate (we estimated) no less than between six to a dozen eggs per day. We had eggs boiled, eggs scrambled or eggs fried; we had omelettes; we swallowed 'Scotch oysters'. But when we eventually ran out of ideas we still had on our hands tens of thousands of eggs that were beginning to make their presence unbearable. No man was sorry when the order finally came—'Fling 'em overboard!'

Our latest prize tanker refuelled *Scheer,* the *Tannenfels,* and ourselves. Her bounty seemed inexhaustible.

Then later in this remote area of the Indian Ocean, we turned to the more serious work of contacting Italian submarines and refuelling them from our capture. For us this was a most interesting assignment as we had not before had an opportunity of contacting our southern Allies—except, of course, via the odd prisoner escorts to Somaliland. From what we could see of them, however, we gathered the impression—later to be confirmed—that the efficiency, or otherwise, of an Italian crew depended entirely upon the character of the immediate commander. Many submarine commanders of the Italian service were individually brave and skilful, but in general the higher ranks seemed lacking in what the Americans term 'the knowhow', and we were appalled at the wide social gulf that existed between them and their men. As a rule, we found that the Italian officer lived on the very best that could be supplied but his seamen existed little better than animals on near starvation diet. Under these circumstances it was not surprising that enthusiasm, or the general seaman-like virtues, were lamentably absent.

However, at the time we received the priority instruction to refuel the submarine *Perla,* coming out from Massawa, we proceeded to the rendezvous point with eager curiosity, arriving at the meeting place, 35 degrees South, right on schedule. No submarine! Irritated, we steamed around, Rogge grumbling away and our tempers getting shorter as the hours went by. Then, of all things in those days of radio silence, we received a message from the submarine. The confounded craft was wondering why she was being made to wait. She had turned up at 33 degrees South, and now, worst of all, was sending out a signal to guide us in on D/F. We were furious at the carelessness of the Italian. Any inquisitive warship around in the vicinity would have 'homed-in' on us both, and it cost us an effort to maintain a surface appearance of Axis solidarity as we handed over to *Perla* seven tons of lubricating oil. This should have satisfied her completely, but the Italian commander, after lauding our 'wonderful successes' had the bland audacity to ask for 70,000 cigarettes as well!

We said our goodbyes to *Scheer* however with the regret of men who, far from home, know that any morning may bring death, and say goodbye to their compatriots wondering whether they will ever meet again. We felt more alone than we had ever felt before, and *Atlantis* seemed infinitely small, almost puny in fact, as we remembered *Scheer*'s steel decks, those turreted 11-inch guns, and the almost forgotten touch of Kiel discipline and Kiel amenities. But, as Kamenz—always the merchant navy man—reflected, 'It's so stifling hot on those steel ships. *Atlantis* for comfort any time!'

We were only now beginning to realise the wide extent of surface raiding activities, and the extent, also, of the organisation behind them.

We heard news of our gains—and of how our brother raider, *Pinguin,* had completely captured the entire

Norwegian Antarctic whaling fleet. For days on end she had patiently stalked her quarry, warily observing the scattered fleet, yet just keeping out of its range of vision until locating the position of the factory ship. She then steamed straight in, took her completely by surprise, and discovering the secret call sign found it an easy matter to recall the unsuspecting whalers, one by one to the factory ship and capture.

Not a nice trick? Possibly it was not. But one of vital importance to us and unlike many of the other dirty aspects of war *Pinguin*'s deceit did not result in a single casualty. The whole incident is even more remarkable in as much as that the entire fleet was subsequently headed for Occupied France AND got there safely!

In other directions, *Pinguin* inflicted heavy damage, nearly rivalling our own record of tonnage sunk, and being the only raider to approach it. Had we but known it she had only three more months to live . . . We were to hear of losses, too, among them that of the only Italian armed merchant cruiser to put to sea. She had no luck, and ran straight into the waiting guns of a British cruiser. Many of our supply ships had also been captured or sunk, but so extensive was the area of their activities, so imperative the British need for concentrating practically all major forces in the North Atlantic and Mediterranean, that we on *Atlantis* who, incidentally, heard that the British A.M.C. *Ranchi* was waiting for us north of Chagos, still enjoyed a liberty, largely unguessed at by our enemies.

Scheer, on this, her second raider cruise, had not experienced much success. Indeed after the war her activities were much criticised as lacking the audacity that could have resulted in very heavy Allied losses. Those who advanced this view pointed out that the British had not one single ship in the Mediterranean or South Atlantic that would have been capable of standing up to her heavy armament. On the other hand, it was not possible for us at sea to realise things that afterwards seemed so abundantly clear to the armchair students with all documents at their disposal. At all events, her presence caused widespread disruption of Allied communications.

As for ourselves on *Atlantis*—well, we alone had accounted for nearly a fifth of all merchantmen sunk by our surface warships.

CHAPTER NINETEEN

INTERNATIONAL INCIDENT

'COCKROACHES,' SAID the rating at my side, his voice thick with revulsion.

As I peered into the filthy galley, looking towards the spot where his gaze was riveted in morbid fascination, I saw what appeared to be a black stream moving UP-WARDS across the acutely tilting floor.

It was the first time I'd ever been 'behind the scenes' of a passenger liner, and although I had hardly antici-pated the streamlined cleanliness of a luxury vessel, *Zamzam*'s kitchens were the Last Word.

'Cockroaches,' repeated the rating with loathing.

And so they were. Specimens that were two inches long, and now teeming from the unknown and ugly places of the sinking ship into which we had so rudely intruded.

'Phew,' said the rating. 'This place stinks.'

But as we moved towards the staircase to the safety of the deck I thought to myself, 'It isn't the only thing that'll stink, not when the Allies hear about the *Zamzam*!'

'A second *Lusitania* . . .' That's what they said about our victim.

'A new act of barbarism . . .' That's how they de-scribed her sinking.

For weeks to come the story of the liner *Zamzam*, widely publicised as involving 138 American citizens at a time when America was neutral, was to be held up to the Western world as 'yet another example' of Ger-many's 'wanton disregard' for the law of nations—an 'international incident'.

We attacked *Zamzam* on 17th April—from out of the dark Western sky, from out of the fading night, with her outline clear against the dawn's first breaking. We sank her after many hours of patient stalking, a 'special operation' to celebrate our temporary return to the field of our first hunting—the waters of the South Atlantic. The exploit obtained for us the unexpected distinction of a monumentally phrased leader in the London *Times* and, among lesser 'unsolicited testimonials', an article and a number of letters in *Life*.

Said one writer:

'Hell. This has gone far enough. Let's get at 'em!'

'Em, of course, meant US, and the writer, from Brownwood, Texas, added, 'If those birds want to start something with us over here, I think you will find all Texans more than ready to meet them half way . . .'

START SOMETHING! . . . The real story of the sinking of this wretched Egyptian ship is far more fantastic than anything that appeared at the time, and the embarrassments that resulted were such as to make the term of 'doing a Double Sam' synonymous in our jargon with 'dropping a brick'. For the ship we shelled at three miles range was NOT the ship we'd been looking for! *Zamzam* was the victim of a coincidence, a coincidence dating back to the friendly days of 1937, and a visit Rogge paid to England . . .

It had been a Royal summer for a Royal occasion, and Rogge, representing Germany in the six-metre yacht races during the Coronation celebrations of King George VI, was enjoying himself, for Britain had received our German crews with overwhelming hospitality. How different, he'd thought, was the situation in 1937 to that prevailing a few years earlier. Anglo-German friendship. That was the thing. And when he'd seen the contents bill of a Devon newspaper devoted to just five words—'German yachtsmen . . . Welcome to Torbay'—he'd felt so moved that he'd begged the placard from the newspaper seller as a souvenir. It would do the Anglophobes at home some good, he thought.

196

This aura of good fellowship continued to linger along Britain's south-west shores and many a glass was raised and many a friendship established between British and German naval officers, among them one that resulted in Rogge's being invited to visit the Royal Naval College at Dartmouth.

Rogge liked Dartmouth, the professional in him admiring the tradition it represented; the artist and yachtsman appreciating the beauty of its setting, delighting in the broad sweep of the bay, the sight of small craft dancing upon the vivid blue water beneath rolling hills of lush green, and cliffs of grey and red. Only one thing puzzled him—the two merchantmen in this naval anchorage; distinctive looking merchantmen at that, elderly craft with, of all things, FOUR masts.

'You have two strangers here,' he said. 'I'd imagined I'd see only warships.'

His host glanced at the steamers, and with a careless shrug replied, 'Oh, you'll often see them. They belong here. Bibby Line steamers you know. We use them under charter quite a lot. Trooping and all that sort of thing.'

'Ah yes,' said Rogge, and thought no more about it . . . no more, that is, until the night of the 16th April 1941.

'Overhaul at dusk. Attack at dawn!'

Such were Rogge's orders when news of the distinctive fourmasted silhouette came from the masthead lookout to the bridge.

'Overhaul at dusk. Attack at dawn' . . . It was the same old recipe, the mixture as before, the method we'd so often employed in the Indian Ocean—now temporarily a little too 'hot' for us. But this time there was a slight variation. NO WARNING! Our salvoes must hit home without giving our adversary the benefit of delay, and our fire must continue, rapid fire, until the stranger's surrender, or destruction.

'Little do they know,' said Kasch when he heard that our opposite number—blacked out and flagless—was proceeding on course. 'Little do they know the shock they're going to get tomorrow.'

For so long had we been on the run . . . with the British buzzing after us in the waters we'd fanned so impressively into flame that we welcomed the opportunity for playing hunter once again. This was a victim worthy of our shell, a victim probably equipped with plenty of teeth herself, a Bibby liner, either employed as an auxiliary cruiser, or else packed with troops.

Only Rogge, the man who'd given the orders, didn't seem particularly happy. He was thinking back in time, four years in time, to the peaceful waters of the Dart, the waters where he had first seen a ship like this and learnt her purpose . . . 'We use them under charter quite a lot. Trooping and all that sort of thing.'

Our first salvo fell short . . . Our second salvo fell long . . . Our third ripped her wireless cabin to pieces, and our fourth sent a line of fire across her decks . . .

But not a shot back! Unsual for Tommy.

We continued to fire . . . but nine minutes after our opening shot a lamp began to blink out an appeal to us to stop shooting.

'Halt batterie!'

The din now ended. We ran in towards the stricken ship and as we closed we observed that WOMEN and CHILDREN, many of them still in their night clothes, were among the scores of people now congregating in some confusion around the rails, every second bringing its fresh quota of bewildered passengers to join the clamour on her decks.

Bibby liner? . . . Troop transport? . . . What the hell?

Scenes of unprecedented confusion now surrounded the *Zamzam*. The boats were approaching us at speed, but they were occupied mostly by sailors rather than passengers.

'Good God. What next . . . ?' To my stupefaction I heard the strains of a hymn floating across the water, and pathetically, rather ludicrously, someone in one of

198

the boats was playing 'Nearer My God To Thee' upon a cornet.

'Well!' said a voice beside me. 'I've never seen a crowd like this emerge from a British warship!'

His sarcasm was about as acceptable as salt rubbed in an open wound.

'Bring me my pistol. I'll kill the bastard!' bellowed Rogge, pounding his fist against the side of the bridge.

'The bastard'—a slight Arab seaman—was quite calmly climbing to the safety of our deck. The rope we'd flung to him to secure to the crowded boat he had accepted as a personal invitation to save his own skin, and now, swinging gratefully, he had left behind him some forty unfortunates bobbing precariously up and down beneath our sheer iron hull. 'The bastard' safely reached the rail, carefully hauled himself aboard, and beamed his thanks to a shocked marine. Rogge groped futilely for a holster that perhaps mercifully wasn't there!

'Get him out of my sight or I'll fling him back' roared our irate Commander.

The Arab, although obviously quite unaware of doing anything unusual, was hastily and rudely hustled from view.

We flung another rope.

It was then we noticed the flag. Hanging limply from *Zamzam*'s dejected stern it had been hoisted after our initial salvoes. The flag was the flag of Egypt.

We had not realised it but the Bibby liner had changed ownership only a few months before the outbreak of war when Britain had sold her to Egypt, and now, instead of the troops we had expected, she was carrying 202 passengers, many of them women and children.

In the water around *Zamzam* we could see men and women swimming for their lives, among them a woman desperately clutching her child. The Egyptian crew had been in such a hurry to pull away that she'd been forced to jump and had fallen into the water between the boat and the ship. But even after that the crew had continued to row away, leaving her to fight for life until pulled on to a raft by an American ambulance man.

The lifeboats, in many cases, were only half full as a result of the panic of the *Zamzam* crew, and the only saving touch about the behaviour of the ship was the manner in which her passengers helped each other when all other help, it seemed, had failed.

Among the Americans a team of about twenty young volunteers for the De Gaulle French Ambulance Unit behaved particularly well, dragging women and children on to floating rafts until the rescue boats were organised, while, despite the nauseating spectacle of one clergyman whose sole contribution towards maintaining morale was confined to the saving of his own skin and the unctuous shout to his fellows . . . 'It's God's punishment for your sins!' . . . other clerics (many missionaries were aboard the *Zamzam*) endeavoured to soothe the weeping women and children, many badly shocked.

As I climbed aboard *Zamzam* I was confronted by her elderly British Commander, William Grey Smith. He was composed; grim to the point of coldness.

'Why didn't you signal us earlier?' I asked. 'Why the hell did you wait till we'd pasted you like this?'

'Because' said the Commander with a bitter smile, 'your bloody third salvo destroyed our signal lamp.'

In his hand he still carried the torch with which he had eventually managed to stay our fire. Smith was one of the very few really level-headed people on the ship, and beside him—the two forming a sort of oasis of calm in the middle of the panic—stood a young Egyptian cadet who had not left his side throughout the incident, and who, in the days to come when so many of his compatriots were to occupy themselves only with delivering petitions asking for their release as 'neutrals', was to give a very fine example of seamanlike loyalty, staying by his captain, captivity or no.

Before I met Smith I had not realised the rather

frightening extent of our catch. But as he walked he proceeded, with some degree of relish, to detail the type of problems with which we might have to cope . . .

Zamzam carried over 100 clergymen drawn from twenty denominations . . . She carried 76 women, of whom five were pregnant . . . Of the 35 children, some were little more than babies . . . Apart from the American ambulance team, the passengers included also elderly Britons, wives of Service officers, some extremely photogenic Greek nurses, and a French woman.

Smith, I learned later, seemed to have had quite a few headaches as regards his passengers, who, before the advent of *Atlantis,* had been separated into three feuding groups—the American missionaries who WANTED THE BAR SHUT; the American ambulance men who WANTED IT OPEN; and the British who—presumably—wouldn't have minded so long as it CLOSED at 10.30!

Many of the passengers, when they came aboard *Atlantis,* had nothing to wear but the flimsiest of nightclothes, and Rogge had detailed Fehler and me, each with an axe for 'key,' to recover from *Zamzam* as much clothing as we could. I mentioned this to Smith. He smiled somewhat wryly.

'What a coincidence,' he said, 'I was planning a fancy dress party for tomorrow night. An informal affair, you know. Just to get the passengers more matey . . . Rather ironic isn't it?'

'Look out! Here they come!' And over the side of *Zamzam* hurtled a bundle of ladies' underwear.

Kross, the helmsman, looked up from the waiting launch, his disapproval of this rough procedure plainly evident as some flimsy garments in delicate pastels floated like thistledown above his head to be wafted down into the hungry sea.

'Mind how you handle them,' bawled Krass. 'Some people treasure their property.' And as he spoke the shadow of the listing *Zamzam* loomed over the pink lingerie he had just stretched out to save.

There was no finesse about our 'packing'. The sailors simply swept clothes from hangers or scooped them from drawers, rushed them to the rails and bundled them over the side.

The old tub was heeling over and we expected her to go at any minute, so that if neither Fehler nor I went very happily about our tasks, at least we moved smartly! Down in the engine room the water poured in with a roar that deafened us, smashing against the bulkheads like a hammer, swirling around the machinery, eddying and gurgling. The ship was creaking and groaning, its tilt each minute becoming more acute. Yet the odd thing was that when the water reached a level twelve feet high, its weight dispersed in such a way that it actually brought *Zamzam* to an almost even keel, enabling us to spend four or five hours aboard her and—cockroaches or no—to secure something from the larder in the way of lime juice and lobsters, frozen geese and duck. We also stripped the bar.

We'd got the wrong 'baby' but anyhow, it was one worth 'adopting' after all.

When, on their way to Europe in the blockade runner, *Dresden*, the Americans protested about the conditions of their captivity, and in doing so laid particular stress on the fact that they had left the United States 'in an unarmed ship operated by a non-belligerent power.' Similarly, the Egyptian officers submitted a 'somewhat complicated' petition in which they stated . . . 'Egypt is, up to this day, a non-belligerent Sovereign country. *Zamzam* was a neutral unarmed ship by International Law.'

Why then, if *Zamzam* was taken as a result of a mistake, did we carry on with the job and sink her? What right had we to decide her fate? What object had we in destroying a passenger ship? To us the answer was clear cut. Egypt *was a belligerent* in-so-far that she *failed to behave as a non-belligerent*. Her soil provided *bases and fields of manoeuvre for Services at war with Germany*. Willingly, or unwillingly, was another matter and

202

didn't count. This 'neutral' ship was *conforming to Admiralty routine instructions*; was failing to comply with the stipulation that neutrals should be *lit by night*; and was carrying *contraband*, for *Zamzam*'s cargo we found by no means consisted solely of missionaires, ambulance men and nurses. She carried, besides, ten thousand barrels of oil and one hundred American trucks, all destined for the Cape, and all earmarked for use by a country at war with Germany.

Now that we'd gone so far the prize was definitely worth the taking, although Rogge was quick to see the complications that could arise from our action. They were formidable . . . An Egyptian ship was one thing, but a largely American passenger content was quite another, especially when the United States administration was seeking every opportunity of exploiting such situations in favour of its policy of supporting Britain.

We had been partly revictualled by *Dresden* shortly before our encounter with *Zamzam*, and Rogge had arranged a second rendezvous to complete the process. We transfered *Zamzam*'s passengers to her keeping on the 18th.

But, in the meanwhile, we still had our problems with us, and back on *Atlantis* I met them 'face to face . . .'

Some of the 'prisoners', I found, seemed to have the most peculiar ideas about us, one even prophesying in my hearing that we had probably brought them on board so that we could more conveniently MASSACRE THEM AND DESTROY THE EVIDENCE!

I reflected, however, that we had not enjoyed the best of introductions, for reveillé played by a 5.9 is scarcely the happiest method of commencing the day!

Two young American girls came up to me, both very worried. 'Say, we're sure glad you speak English,' said one. 'Can we get any oranges around this ship?'

Oranges! They seemed as remote as sunny Spain itself. Where could they get some? Well, certainly not on *Atlantis*. The girls were dismayed. 'But what'll we do?'

I hadn't a clue. American girls, I was to discover,

possessed an unquenchable thirst for oranges. I could sympathise. Except for our loot from *Tirranna* we had not tasted that succulent fruit ourselves—not for a year.

I wandered along the deck, a deck that was crowded by passengers and their belongings. Some of these people had had extraordinary experiences after the liner's shelling. One mother had pushed her child of six through the water having first attired him in a Mae West. The kid seemed none the worse for his experience and appeared to treat it as a great adventure. But others were still crying from shock.

Down in the sick bay the leader of the American ambulance men was one of the three seriously wounded. A charming New Yorker, and a member of the New York intellectual set, a shell blast had torn the muscles from his thigh, yet his comrades had to force the Egyptians to take him in their boat.

Other distinguished company, fortunately uninjured, included Mr. J. V. Murphy, then one of the editors of *Fortune,* and Dr. D. E. Graffhunter, once chief of the survey of India.

'What are YOU up to?' I asked.

Sandwiched between two triumphant, heavily armed marines, was a rather apprehensive looking passenger.

'He's been taking pictures, sir,' said the senior marine, answering up for him, and handing me a camera as evidence.

'What's your name?' I asked.

'Scherman. David Scherman.'

'What are you? A missionary, ambulance man . . . or what?' A flicker of a smile. 'No, I'm just a cameraman. For *Life*.'

David Scherman . . . *Life* photographer! As a keen amateur I was delighted at this opportunity of observing a gifted professional at work. To the marines' disgust the camera was handed back to Scherman, and we both took pictures, side by side, of the final sinking of the Double Sam.

She went down without a fuss. She almost seemed glad to go.

204

* * *

We raced to our rendezvous with *Dresden* to the accompaniment of hymns from the missionaries, and our own '*Atlantis* special'—an old German folk song, a relic of the sail training ship that Rogge had formerly commanded. Our passengers were silent as we sang and seemed to have some misconception about the theme.

Said one of them curiously. 'Er, would you tell me please which of the Nazi marching tunes that is? And what do the words signify?'

Solemnly I repeated the nonsense rhyme . . .

> Good Evening. Good Night.
> Offered with roses. Covered with carnations.
> Tomorrow morning, if God wills it,
> You will be awoken.

My interrogator was puzzled. 'Fine. Fine. But what does it really mean?'

'Quite candidly,' I replied. 'I haven't the faintest notion.'

Only later, when I pondered a little, did the words seem to achieve a meaning that was peculiarly opposite to our circumstances. Yet none of us had noticed it before . . .

Rogge, realising the probable repercussions that the nature of our haul would have on American opinion, repeated his promise that the passengers would either be transferred to a neutral ship on route, or else landed at a neutral port. For Rogge was acutely sensitive to the 'Bad Press' that would follow our latest exploit.

But our promises were never kept . . . Only three or four days after *Dresden* had left us we 'listened in' to a code message from '*Higher Authority*', a code message overriding all our original instructions and ordering *Dresden* instead to run for Occupied France. Rogge was extremely angry at this sudden switch in policy, feeling his honour committed by reason of his earlier promise, and his point of view, subsequently recorded by me in our official log, resulted in SEVERE REPRIMANDS FOR US BOTH.

But whatever may be said about the military aspect of risking such a supply ship as *Dresden* in a scheme to hand over prisoners to a neutral power, I believe, to this day, that it would have been far better had our original plan been implemented, even at the risk of *Dresden*'s loss through internment or blockade. Quite apart from the purely humanitarian aspect, expediency itself demanded implementation of our pledge. We incurred considerably odium for having broken our word. We were, therefore, inexpressibly relieved to learn of the safe arrival—although in Occupied France—of *Zamzam*'s passengers for we regarded their plight with deep concern.

As Rogge said, 'After all, a submarine rarely lingers to discover what cargo an enemy ship is carrying . . . And a mine is notoriously blind!'

As it was, the 'journey home' was bad enough for the *Zamzam* passengers. It lasted five weeks, during which period they lived on short rations, in unhygienic conditions, and were subject all the time to a discipline necessarily severe, for to control all these thoroughly fed up people we could only spare half a dozen Marines to reinforce *Dresden*'s merchant service crew.

Before *Dresden* sailed I had given Scherman a chit requesting the naval authorities—just in case they changed their minds about that 'neutral destination'—to allow him to keep the photographs I had witnessed him take aboard the raider. They were harmless, I said. Authority did not think so, and confiscated the lot.

Yet certain other pictures he had taken—pictures I was unaware existed, dangerous pictures taken of *Atlantis* FROM THE OUTSIDE, were smuggled by him to America on his return. One of these, indeed, helped the Captain of *Devonshire* to identify us when WE stood at the receiving end of the gun.

Free at last, we said, when the *Dresden* had dwindled into the dusk. Free at last! The *Zamzam* had been a bit too much for us. Almost far too much. The strain of

206

looking after so many women and children—and neutrals at that—had really told.

Commented Pigors approvingly. '*Atlantis* has never looked so tidy or been so tranquil as now.'

You didn't appreciate, he said, the advantages of routine until you'd done without it for a bit. As for the problem of how to feed some thirty-five babies . . . !

But we had not finished with the Double Sam . . . Not quite. For, while we drew deep sighs of relief at *Dresden*'s departure, we were almost as soon to hold our noses to escape the 'aromatic legacy' that *Zamzam* had left behind . . .

'That stench,' I said, 'is becoming progressively worse. It started as a gentle odour, but now, by God, it's terrifying. The air blowers are just sucking it in. What the hell can it be?'

'I wouldn't be surprised,' prophesied Fehler gloomily, 'if it didn't kill us all—eventually!'

'THE SMELL' had become a topic most painfully absorbing and, as the stench increased and the mystery deepened. 'Detectives' had been investigating it for four days now. At first we'd thought that there might be dead rats behind the ventilator, for we'd already discovered a rodent's corpse in a mailbag—a rat that evidently found a copy of *Esquire* insufficient for the maintenance of life. Inspired by this precedent we searched, then searched again, but still found nothing . . . And the smell increased.

I don't know who finally unearthed the cause, but THE SMELL was at last traced to a loot bag, ostensibly holding captured flags, compasses, charts, etcetera, which had been left on the port promenade deck to be sorted out at leisure . . .

Some thirty or forty frozen geese from our victim's ice room had been accidentally included in the heap . . . nearly forty goose corpses lying right across the air intake of our ventilators! And in as revolting a state of decomposition as one would never wish to see!

Phew!

*   *   *

Soon, however, the *Zamzam* episode became little more than an embarrassing memory, lost sight of in the stress of our most nerve-racking encounter . . . thirty minutes of fear in the moonlit night of the South Atlantic.

It was our turn now to experience the full terrors of the hunted . . .

CHAPTER TWENTY

SHIPS THAT PASS

NOT UNTIL 19th May—only a day before her passengers and crew set foot on Occupied France—did the British announce that *Zamzam* was 'overdue'. Yet, though they had kept it so quiet, we were under no illusions as to what our latest 'coup' would entail, and so *Atlantis*, in accordance with the moment's exigencies, made maximum revolutions towards areas less dramatically publicised, anxious for a while to seek obscurity. But the hunt was on, and, barely a few nights after our parting with *Dresden*, the alarm bells broke the silence of sleep, suddenly, harshly reverberating through the ship.

'Action Stations . . . Action Stations . . . !

Through the aftermath of a too-sound slumber I heard the rush of feet under the deck above. What the hell now? Confusedly I tried to sort out the meaning of the clamour that was all around me, even as my fingers fumbled for the telephone.

A voice from the bridge: 'Two ships sighted, Sir.'

I rolled out of my bunk and staggered to the door. TWO ships? Even in my tiredness the significance was plain. TWO ships. That could only mean, at best, a liner so important that she would have the dignity of a heavy armament, *and* a warship for escort, or, at worst, TWO WARSHIPS. A poor prospect for our raider either way. I ran to the bridge where Rogge had already joined the officer of the watch. 'Nice time for this to happen,' he said grimly.

At the time of the sighting, *Atlantis* had been lying stopped; rolling slowly on the sea's smooth surface, only the creak of her port to starboard swing disturbing the silence of her blacked-out solitude. And now after the rush that had followed the warning we were quiet again, our silence no longer the silence of sleep, but the quietness of mounting tension created by the shadows in our night glasses, shadows growing ever wider, even larger.

I looked carefully. Yes. There were two of them all right. Each had the unmistakable pyramidal superstructure of a man-of-war. Each was travelling at high speed—straight for us! A most disturbing spectacle, and one designed to scatter most speedily the sleep from my eyes and the drowsiness from my brain; setting every nerve atingle in the apparatus of self-preservation, and starting a chain of automatic calculations concerning range and closing speed, and our chances, which seemed but slender.

Until this moment the night, by South Atlantic standards, had been particularly dark. But now, behind the advancing silhouettes, the moon broke in all its chilly splendour, cleaving the sombre, heavy clouds, and shining straight upon us, seeming, to us who waited, like a searchlight focusing and holding our ship—a symbol of ill omen. Yet this apparent disability had its happier side. Moonlight, by creating its own shadows on this sea of shadows, would be hindering rather than helping the enemy look-outs; hurling back the colours of *Atlantis* into the greys and blacks and whites of the ocean pattern, merging her into a sort of dappled camouflage of sea and sky and ship combined.

'Number one gun ready . . . Number two gun ready . . . Number three gun ready . . . Torpedo tubes ready.' The reports flowed to the bridge where now we clustered, silently watching our foes' approach.

'Start engines,' ordered Rogge.

'Start engines,' I repeated, my voice unconsciously low. We dare not get under way too rapidly. An obvious flurry would betray us immediately. So we edged away cautiously; just sufficiently to show our enemies our stern.

Another squint through the binoculars. And then another. No. It couldn't be true. I looked again, straining hard. Surely I must be wrong? Someone whistled softly, incredulously, and someone else muttered, 'Heaven next stop . . .' But Rogge just grunted cryptically, and I realised, with an odd sensation, that my guess was right. There were only two ships in the world that even remotely resembled the foremost of the two strangers—the giant battleships, *Nelson* or *Rodney*!

The ship astern of the steel monster could be readily identified—as regards her class at least: a fleet aircraft carrier. There were, I reflected, about two alternatives as regards their reception of us. They might know all about us, and come just close enough to give us a broadside from the secondary armament——not deigning to waste their costly 16-inch shells on us; or, they might have stumbled on us by chance—in which case we would still have the same disagreeable ending, but with merely the distinction of a few minutes' time between their asking for our secret call sign, and our revealing that we didn't know it.

We were, it appeared evident, all destined to die gloriously for the Fatherland, with our 5.9's (now about as futile as peashooters) blazing to the end, and our Battle Ensign still at the masthead when we plunged into the depths. I almost grinned to myself as I thought what the poets of the Propaganda Ministry would make of it! And so we waited, dreading the signal that we could not answer, the challenge heralding the scarlet gun flashes of our foes.

Yet Fortune continued to treat us as her favourite . . .

The carrier passed us so close that we could see the racing waters of her stern spreading their tumbling, milk-white swathe towards us; so close, in fact, that the possibility of a collision began to attach itself to our other apprehensions. But we did not collide, and the clouds at that moment scattered across the moon, spreading a new type of dazzle camouflage to confuse further the watchers to our starboard. For several minutes we continued to wait tensely. Surely, we thought, they could not miss us, moonlight or not? Surely they must be devising an unpleasant variation of cat and mouse?

But the warships passed upon their way, and dwindled into the distance . . .

Unbelievable that it seemed, the plain fact was the British HADN'T SEEN US!

Our tension finally relaxed and worry changed to incredulity. Rogge ordered, 'Full ahead.'

Eager to get away fast, *Atlantis* throbbed into life again, and then—a volley of oaths and blasphemies from every quarter . . . The funnel had caught alight! In a second it was erupting a cascade of sparks, followed by a red column of flame as the soot's blaze spread. Only a miracle, we felt, could save us now, yet how could we dare hope for another? But we got it! In those days *Atlantis* seemed always to get the miracles—even two in one night!

For, once again, the British did not see us and, after fifteen minutes that were like an eternity, the two unwelcome intruders dropped out of sight, leaving us on our own again—and grateful for large mercies. This was the strangest encounter of our cruise, and most of us looked back upon it as the worst, for, even in our sinking I cannot recall a suspense as intense as upon that summer's night.

In our history as a raider we were to see many ships at close quarters . . .

On one occasion we were surprised to see in the far distance the navigation lights of a steamer, followed by a series of other lights winking back into the blackness. 'What ship?' we flashed, and the mystery was solved. The steamer, part of a Vichy France convoy, was on her way to Indo-China and escorted by a flotilla of submarines. So to confuse the issue we sent them a message—'Bon Voyage. Viva la France,' and left them to their thoughts . . .

A piquant situation arose with another neutral—a Swiss ship that I boarded in order to carry out a routine inspection. Her papers were in order. So also was her cargo. Her Captain, however, seemed extra flustered, and I discovered the reason—a crumpled piece of paper, which, when I smoothed it out, revealed the 'neutral' had been on the verge of sending out a Q message.

I tossed it back. 'Yours, Captain, I think?'

The Captain hurriedly tore it up, and with a relieved grin offered me a Scotch. It was a large one!

On 27th January we spotted a liner, later identifying her as the *Queen Mary*. One of our prisoners confirmed our surmise, adding, happily, that she was scarcely our meat. She was, he said, heavily armed—which we knew; usually escorted by a cruiser—which we also knew; and was often employed on this route—which we did NOT know! We had, of course, turned away immediately, having no inclination for suicide. But, if only our prisoner had known that the pocket-battleship, *Scheer*, was almost 'round the corner'—would he then have been so obligingly informative, I wonder? Later the *Q.M.* was taken off this route. Just as well, both for her, and her escort.*

In March, we made a short excursion into the Mozambique channel. Here we had the unique experience of our potential 'victim' answering the signal to stop with a bewildered 'What is wrong? Do you require assistance?' On this occasion the innocent stranger turned out to be French—(the *Chenonceaux*)—so, after replying that we were all right, we let her proceed. Such episodes notwithstanding, however, the *Nelson* and *Ark Royal* encounter, as we later called it—(later we discovered the carrier was really *Eagle*)—remained the most fantastic incident of all.

A general weariness of the business of stalking and sinking had long since begun to settle upon it all. The initial glamour had faded in the memory of our victims. Face to face with our prisoners every day we were developing an awareness of the 'other side' that was lack-

---

* A faulty identification here. The ship was actually the liner *Strathaird* which left Bombay for Cape Town on 24th January. The security moral still remains obvious, however.
                                                                A.V.S.

ing in the huge impersonal battles and bombardments of the land, or among the bomb-laden armadas of the air. We were beginning to feel that, however necessary to our war effort, the business had its pitiful side. And, although we had tried to keep casualties among the merchantmen as low as we could, the fact remained that we had killed over sixty seamen engaged upon their calling.

It is not good to look upon the face of your enemy as he dies. Better by far the long range approach—the bombsight, the periscope, or the inclinometer. It is not good to hear the voice of your enemy as he lives talking of home, of normal things, or the discomforts that you, too, must share. Oh better, far better, to hear his voice in hate across the radio or upon the printed page.

It would be dishonest to pretend that we were overcome by remorse, or that we denied our cause, or had turned traitor to our country. Far from it. We had a job to do and we would continue to do it. It would be idle to claim that the thought of sixty dead would turn us from our purpose, or seem a price unduly high for our 'successes'. On the vast continental fronts, in the cities at home, millions of soldiers, hundreds of thousands of civilians were dying, or about to die, in circumstances worse than those of our so-called enemies, less easy perhaps than the manner too, in which we might perish. It was just that our encounters—often separated by weeks in time, or hundreds of miles in space—seemed to possess a peculiarly personal significance. For when men are opposed to the forces of nature every hour, a feeling of kinship arises, or, at least of common ordeal, even with their foes.

These feelings were, obviously, not shared by those at home. Privileged to listen to the British broadcasts as well as our own, I was astounded at the hate that had been unleashed. However, the B.B.C. news reports, and political broadcasts in the English language, interested me intensely, and I found that they, at least, attempted to be factual when dealing with their own people or their friends in Europe. I could not say the same about the broadcasts to which our countrymen were being subjected by the Party; broadcasts which disseminated the wildest and most dishonest claims, and were a patent absurdity to anyone who knew a little of the facts.

One of the things that particularly annoyed Rogge, myself, and all the other officers, was the persistent statement that the *Ark Royal* had been sunk. I can now reveal that, even at the time these propaganda claims were made, the Intelligence Department of the Berlin Admiralty was supplying us with the carrier's estimated position.

This blunder had its inevitable effect upon the morale of men who had been ordered to listen to their own radio news service only and to rely on it implicitly. Knowing, in this instance, that the claims were not only baseless, but made dishonestly, we doubted other claims, many of which were no doubt true. And although we did our best to conceal it from the crew—such was our loyalty, or our need to bolster self-respect by indulging in self-deceit—the *Ark Royal* scandal soon became generally known, and aroused some fairly cynical comment.

At this stage of the war we had not been compelled to undergo the rigid discipline of the Party, a discipline that, later on, after gradual infiltration, was to secure such a decisive grip upon the Armed Forces. Such was our autonomy—(due perhaps to our comparative inaccessibility)—that I was enabled, while compiling the daily news bulletin for the crew, to draw extensively upon the B.B.C. and neutral radios.

I ran a sort of one-man censorship before sending the information out, cutting out the British propaganda, but employing their 'straight' news. News was what we wanted, and, if our people could not give it—or would not give it——then it was fair enough to obtain it elsewhere. Or that's the way I looked at it. Later, however, our government felt efforts like these insufficient properly to 'educate' seamen. They were to be steeped in the 'philosophy of the New Order'—a subject too holy to be left in the hands of amateurs. An indoctrination officer was thereupon imposed upon many ships, making the task of the command even more complicated, subject as it was on several occasions, to the feeling that one's moves might be reported and criticised behind one's back!

But it was thanks to the B.B.C. that in May, 1941, the *Atlantis* News Service secured two items of information that 'scooped' the Goebbels network—not necessarily by obtaining the news first, but by *publishing* it first! Our 'success' brought us small joy at the time; our 'scoops' were, indeed, of a profoundly depressing nature.

First, came the news of the loss of *Ketty Brovig* (our tanker prize), and *Coburg* (which she was refuelling in the little-frequented shallows of Saya de Malha, where she was pounced upon by the British and Australian cruisers *Leander* and *Canberra*). The next, undoubtedly connected with this misfortune, was the announcement that our brother-raider, *Pinguin* (Ship 33), had been cornered and sunk in the Indian Ocean. The German went down with all guns blazing, and Ensign flying. All but thirty of the crew were killed.

Pinguin, as we have seen, had an exciting career although short-lived, and experienced many narrow escapes. Leaving Germany in June, *Pinguin* was chased for three hours by a British submarine, and later had to dodge again, this time from a British armed merchant cruiser. Operating on the Australian shipping route, the raider sent home her prisoners, 520 of them, on a tanker prize.

Although *Pinguin*'s treatment of prisoners was by no means what it should have been, there was no doubt at all of our 'brother's' valour, and we mourned his loss as a family. This tragedy was a personal affair, involving a ship we knew, a ship sharing the same hazards as *Atlantis*, a crew sharing the same hardships as ourselves, and the loss made us ponder again on our own chances. But, scarcely had we got over the shock of *Pinguin*'s passing than we received from the B.B.C. the news of yet another battle, a battle that was to have an intensely important effect upon our future plans.

Hood had been sunk by *Bismarck* . . .

The announcement, made over the ship's internal communications system, of this event that so shook England, was greeted with little enthusiasm aboard *Atlantis*. We toasted *Bismarck*, of course. But with sadness in our hearts for we knew that *Hood* was the pride of the English, and we knew, too, that the Royal Navy, regardless of how many ships it might lose in the process, would throw in everything to avenge her loss.

In his war memoirs, Churchill records—'Her (*Hood*'s) loss was a bitter grief, but knowing of all the ships that were now converging towards *Bismarck* I felt sure that we should get her in the end . . .'

We officers had a similar belief, and it is impossible to describe the anxiety and the alternating hopes and fears with which we now listened to the new summaries reporting that most dramatic of all ocean searches, or the terrible frustration we experienced when hearing the details of her last stand. After *Bismarck* had received her coup-de-grace from *Dorsetshire* we observed a brief silence for her memory, gripped now by a heavy pessimism that weighed upon even the staunchest of us; stunning the crew, and making many of us consider the wisdom of her Captain's proceeding so far into the Atlantic after his original action.

Bismarck's sinking also meant much more to us on a more selfish level. We had been on our way home that May. Now we knew we should not be able to make it for the North Atlantic would be a hornets' nest. The battlewagon's move would have entailed the presence at sea of a train of supply and weather ships, and there would have been a re-deployment of our U-boats as well. As we considered the situation we realised that all over the North Atlantic the British—now that *Bismarck*'s presence no longer tied down other battleships and the accompanying paraphernalia of cruisers, destroyers, etc.—would be hunting for those, their victim's servants. If we carried on we would walk straight into their guns . . . !

'Clear Lower Deck . . .'

Rogge called the crew together and broke the momentous news. Instead of making a dash for Europe we were to turn round and proceed to the Pacific, then travel around the Horn after the alarm had died down . . .

CHAPTER TWENTY-ONE

THE STRAIN BEGINS TO TELL

To TURN back! To make the decision entailing months and months more voyaging when, with the exception of the brief Kerguelens episode, his crew had not set foot on shore for over a year. It was a hard blow to the ship's company. It was a hard decision for Rogge to make.

Sixty percent of the crew were married, many of them reservists called from good civilian jobs ashore. They were men with families, men worried about the prospects of the bombing raids and the effects of the blockade. Rogge's decision was not popular and he had never expected it would be. Yet his the choice, the Captain's choice; one of the penalties of command.

The turn to the East had followed a brief conference, or rather a brief meeting at which Rogge had transmitted to the navigating officer and myself his orders which we would implement, for his mind was made up.

'Sorry, gentlemen. But my decision is final,' he said. 'A bitter blow for the men, and a bitter blow for me. It's our duty to save the ship, and worry the English as best we can.'

Rogge's reasoning was, as usual, practical. Two-thirds of our heavy ammunition was still intact and *Atlantis*, in excellent shape mechanically, had sufficient fuel to be independent for months of outside help. Command had given him the alternative of slipping into Dakar, but Rogge felt, as he put it, 'Once in never out!' He had no wish to see *Atlantis* idle at anchor for the duration. Our appearance in the Pacific, he said, would confuse the enemy, entail extra ship movements, and maybe enable us to pick off additional victims off the Australian continent. And after that? 'Well,' Rogge, with a wry smile, 'we may try the South Atlantic again in the fall, then take advantage of the winter to break through for the North.'

Atlantis turned in her tracks and headed for the East . . . after destroying *Rabaul* and *Trafalgar*.

It was on 17th June that we sank the *Tottenham*, commanded by Captain Woodcock.

Carrying a cargo of ammunition she erupted like a volcano.

Five days later, on 22nd June, we sank the *Balzac*, robbing the Allies of a cargo that included 4,000 tons of rice, vast quantities of beeswax, and a 'mixed bag' of practically anything from beans to postal mail.

A short while later we transferred our prisoners and soon we were on our own again, and running eastwards, ever eastward, under skies that seemed to match our gloom and over waters so rough that we had to spill oil to placate them. We passed Prince Edward Island. We passed New Amsterdam, while the hail fell like bullets and the rain came like a flood, hitting us as hard as the merciless sea itself; making life a misery and the sleep of exhaustion a luxury. Never had we driven through such a wilderness and for days on end the thunder rolled around us, a constant companion—the perfect sound-effect for this stage setting of storm and gloom.

Strange fancies came over one upon the bridge . . . of the sea ghost legends of long ago, of the *Flying Dutchman* for ever encircling the seas; and sometimes, when spirits were low and life was at its most monotonous one would even speculate as to whether or not we, too, were just the ghosts of some fantastic legend—not living men at all, but sunk, far back in Time; with our ghost ship the only thing left in the world . . . So, in exhaustion, did our imaginings flourish; imaginings that ranged from my own nonsensical speculations to a victimisation complex in one or two of the crew, who, frustrated, and with nerves frayed, believed that their comrades were

220

beginning to plot against them, or that everyone hated them.

In these stormy wastes we began to suffer the inevitable aftermath of our long period of alternating excitement and boredom; our separation from the normal things of life and our too close confinement. All these things, almost unperceived by us, had been steadily building up an explosive force within us and, for a while, it seemed that the role of the weather was to provide the spark.

There we were . . . in the same surroundings day after day . . . month after month . . . and now, apparently, year after year; seeing none but the same old faces; enduring and indulging in, the same old habits. The little things that once had passed unnoticed were now beginning to irritate, and always, in our ears was the sound of the sea, the sea at its cruellest and loneliest, the sea whose song had ceased to soothe, maintaining instead a nagging and fretful accompaniment which rose all too often to a frightening crescendo.

Hitherto we had had the company of the gulls or the small birds of the African shoreline, but now even the gulls had vanished, and the black and white Cape doves had left us too, until only an albatross remained as escort, its wings rigidly straight and wheeling round our masthead as though the old superstition was true and it and its kind housed the souls of departed captains who could not cease to haunt the waters.

The weather was at its filthiest and the peak summer month was symbolised for us by the spectacle of the look-out on the poop, clad in thick yellow oilskins and on the watch for icebergs while once more men filled the sick bay, with fingers crushed, legs broken, and every variety of minor but unpleasant mementoes of the storms.

'Mohr,' said Rogge, as we stood on the bridge. 'I've decided to send the crew on leave.'

'On leave, sir? Where? To the nearest ice-floe?' I joked.

221

'No. The isolation hospital!'

I stared, yet waited silently for further information, knowing Rogge well enough to realise that he had something up his sleeve.

'We can't give them shore leave. So they must have ship leave instead . . . seven days per man. And during that time they'll be free of all duties—even saluting and general ship's discipline. Except, of course, Action Stations in emergency. I'll leave it to you, Lieutenant, to see that the "leave" quarters are made sufficiently attractive . . .'

I smiled. Rogge's scheme would certainly surprise and please the crew, and I am convinced, on looking back on it all, that this novel system did much to prevent the sort of ugly incident that arises between officers and men as a result of change, hardship, and separation from home.

The 'leave' centre was quite attractive when we'd finished with it. There were pictures of relatives at home . . . some lurid pin-ups . . . a ship model or two . . . The crew's reaction was excellent, the first party 'to leave us' providing imaginative ideas of their own to still further the illusion.

'A deputation to see you, sir.'

Rogge frowned slightly. 'Deputation?'

Outside his cabin stood six 'holidaymakers' clad in the pick of our loot, attired in smart lounge suits and gay sports jackets, in shorts and flannels.

'We've come to say goodbye,' they said, and stacked beside them were immaculate suitcases, all carefully labelled to the most expensive hotels and holiday resorts in Germany.

Later the Captain received an unexpected 'mail' . . . 'Having a glorious time here. Weather is lovely!'

Such lighter incidents apart, it was indeed a pretty problem, this preservation of discipline by the so-called orthodox method, but Rogge's methods succeeded in gaining both. Not that we did not have our setbacks . . .

* * *

'Sorry. Can't stop to stow the tables now. Going on duty.'

And the signallers, justly proud of their achievements as lookouts, marched out of the mess with that air of urgency and superiority that of late had so irked their messmates.

A lean and truculent jawed A.B. banged his fist hard upon the signaller's table.

'Comrade,' he shouted to the man nearest him. 'I've had about enough of this. Who the hell do the signallers think they are? I, for one, am *not* clearing up after them. Leave the blasted table where it is!'

A chorus of approval. 'Let 'em do their own dirty work.'

Then, into this flush of independence walked a petty officer.

'Stow that table. Look sharp now.'

Deadly quiet. The P.O. glanced round, impatient to get on with the rest of his duties.

'Well? What are you waiting for? I gave an order.'

Silence.

'By God,' thundered the P.O. 'I said stow that table.'

A couple of seamen made a half hesitant move, and then the lean, truculent seaman spoke. 'It's those signallers,' he explained. 'It's *their* table.'

'Never mind whose table. Put it away.'

The seamen glanced at each other, at the P.O., and then back at their ringleader.

'I WON'T!'

'You *what?*' shouted the irate petty officer.

'I won't' repeated the man firmly. 'Nor I,' said his comrade Inst.

An orderly officer entered. The men were called to attention.

'What seems to be the trouble, P.O.?'

The P.O. found himself in the position of having to explain why several sullen looking sailors were surrounding a table that should have been put away, and wasn't.

223

'You heard the P.O.'s order?' barked the orderly officer.

'Yes, sir.'

'And you still refuse?'

'Yes, sir.'

Oh well, thought the orderly officer, becoming vitally aware of some thirty or forty speculative faces watching curiously from the background, there's only one thing for it.

'Sergeant-at-arms. Put these men under arrest . . . !'

As chairman of the court-martial I found myself with a very delicate problem, though just how delicate I only realised when I delved deeper into our military law.

Two of the seamen were accused of mutiny. That meant they could be shot—or hanged. Third alternative was to set them free, and we certainly couldn't free them, however harmless had been their motive, or however much they had apologised, for undoubtedly they had been proven guilty. To release them, to act leniently and let them free among their fellows on a cruise such as ours would not only be legally wrong; it would also be morally dangerous. I longed for what the English so satisfactorily call the 'happy medium,' and could not find it.

'Sentence deferred,' I pronounced desperately, and went to search the books of law . . . At last! An archaic proviso . . . !

'Bring in the prisoners.'

The men were marched in. I pronounced sentence with solemnity . . . 'Three months "Festung".'

Framed decades before this 'Festung,' or fortress confinement, applied actually to nobly born officers, and was a form of honourable restraint. But it sounded just sufficiently impressive to subdue any imitative spirits among the men's comrades, and, incidentally, made the remorseful signallers jump to it.

'Three months "Festung"?' queried Kamenz, after the men had been led away. 'But that's impossible to execute.'

224

'Precisely' I murmured.

This incident had occurred at an earlier stage in our cruise, and we were able to transfer the men under guard to a supply ship returning to Germany. Only a year later did I learn that our glorious anticipation of what would happen at home when the authorities read our extraordinary sentence was far more than justified.

'Fortress imprisonment? A fortress for two sailors!' Were fortresses then so plentiful? Urgent consultations followed between the historians and the lawyers of the Admiralty. It was ultimately decided that my order should be cancelled as 'Impossible to execute'. Instead the men went to gaol for fourteen days—though why they should have given them this punishment I never could quite fathom. I wondered what Gilbert and Sullivan would have made of it.

But, however amusing in retrospect, it was essential for us to curb even the slightest symptom of disaffection. Examples are notoriously contagious, especially in the small world of a ship where all its petty aggravations are so easily exaggerated into major crises. That is why the only two cases of disciplinary action brought against our prisoners related in each instance to the refusal of a seaman to treat his own officers respectfully—the 'since-we're-all-prisoners-together' and 'he's-no-better-than-me' sort of attitude which almost invariably crops up, and to which I have already made reference.

Then, too, there was a problem among our own crew, a problem which one might have expected to be The Problem—that arising from the frustration necessarily experienced by men so long debarred the company of women. Originally we had feared that the presence of women prisoners would further complicate this difficulty, but, as was subsequently proved, these fears were fortunately not justified—not at least to the extent of any offence being offered or uttered. But certain other difficulties still arose, the first real trouble coming during our New Year's celebration off the Kerguelens . . . We had sanctioned an impromptu cabaret with female

225

impersonations, employed our captured frills, and our feminine disguises as well. An unwise move! Within a few days two cases of homosexuality were tried by the ship's court-martial. In general, however, this problem—so much canvassed on shore—did not assume the proportions we might have expected.

We were now progressing towards the Antipodes, and Rogge, playing every trick to keep our crew's morale high, adopted, in addition to the ship's leave system, another and more disciplinarian-like approach to the job of keeping men occupied . . .

'Captain's inspection!'

The buzz went around the mess-decks.

'What, here?'

'Me . . . ?'

'In the middle of this endless waste of water . . .'

'What for?'

'Never mind what for,' barked the P.O. 'Get those Number Ones shipshape!'

At the appointed hour Rogge appeared, resplendent in full dress uniform, with full decorations, and with me, equally gilded, leading the glittering retinue. Painstakingly, elaborately, he made a tour of inspection that would have gladdened the most exacting diehard. This ritual of his became an institution of *Atlantis*, and, however unpopular with the idle among us, it certainly kept us alert and occupied in the summer filled Pacific waters . . . Saluting drill, boat drill, painting stores, tidying ropes, and generally undergoing the usual laborious process of packing and unpacking best suits of clothing, brushing and pipe claying, splicing and knotting . . . and it left us little time for indulgence in the luxury of personal discontent or its attendant temptations.

In such style, then, did 370 men come again from the Antarctic cold to the heat, and *Atlantis* commenced her voyage in the Southern Bight to meet the victim which was to be her last . . .

CHAPTER TWENTY-TWO

LAST VICTIM

'PRETTY LITTLE things aren't they?' And Kross held up for his mate's approval one of the grotesque little idols from Bali.

Not all of the boarding party thought so.

'They'll bring us bad luck. It's an ill omen,' protested one. 'I'd ditch the evil things,' said another.

Kross laughed, and flung the wooden figure back among the hundreds of similar effigies that we'd found crammed together in fifty wooden cases in the holds of the *Silvaplana*.

We'd taken her on 10th September 1941. It was a date worth recording, the date of our twenty-second encounter, the date of the conquest that was to be our last.

Our evasive journey into the South Pacific had involved our crossing the Southern Bight, making a wide detour around New Zealand and finally turning yet once more before setting course for the sun-bathed Kermadecs, seven hundred miles to the north. This unorthodox route—described by Rogge at the time as 'a blatant contradiction of the mathematical theory that the most efficient method of reaching B from A is by way of a straight line'—was due to the need for dodging the East Indies-North Australia 'screen', and the embarrassment of Allied patrol forces. Involving a 'flank march' (nautical variety) that was thousands of miles in extent. Rogge's decision was based on the interesting philosophy that it is far better to be cautious than to be sunk, with which we heartily concurred.

We passed the Antipodes Islands in late August,

sighting in the distance their black and lonely cliffs and experiencing a very strange occurrence that caused us to christen the area The Zone of Silence. For some strange reason or other ether went 'dead'. Our radio operators could not obtain a single whisper. They tuned in to every wavelength, but in each case the result was the same, a silence as dead as if the set itself had ceased to function. An atmospheric freak? We never knew, but we steamed for over 200 miles before hearing, once again, the faint whisper of the world outside, and we did not like the sensation at all, it was something completely outside our ken.

We cruised so far to the south, partly because of the experience of our brother raider *Orion,* which, although 300 miles to the south of the Australian shore had been located and subsequently 'looked for' by aircraft of the R.A.F. *Orion*'s escape had been made possible by her being able to hear the enemy's D/F bearings and take refuge accordingly in a providential squall. But you can't just bank on the weather, and *Atlantis* luck couldn't last for ever.

Silvaplana was carrying a cargo as romantic as one would expect in this world of sapphire seas and whispering waters, enchanted isles and still lagoons. In addition to the idols we found her laden with coffee and wax, vanilla and teak, while the air of the hold was heavy with the aroma of woods and spices.

But our catch had more than romance about her, I reflected. That 100,000 lbs. of coffee would have been worth as many pounds in sterling on the black markets of the Continent, and for a moment I spared a wistful sigh for the days when romance and money-making would have gone hand in hand.

Rogge, too, had an affection for *Silvaplana.* She was a beautiful ship. Modern and fast and taken without bloodshed. She was our best catch since *Ole Jacob* which Authority had christened *Benno*—a near diminutive of his Christian name. She did her duty for the Reich did *Benno,* but, having slipped out of Germany on a blockade bursting operation a year or two later, incurred the violence spared her in the Pacific, being sunk by a British bomber when off the coast of Spain.

'The Rattlesnake of the Ocean! That's what we are,' said Fehler with enjoyment.

'Rattlesnake?' I queried.

'Yes,' said Fehler, looking up from the captured newspaper he was studying from the wardroom's best armchair. 'That is the endearing title that our friends from Down Under have been graciously pleased to bestow upon us. Still, it makes a change!'

'For rattlesnakes,' I said, 'we seem to be extremely unfortunate. A U.S. radio station has just put out the yarn that thirteen raiders have been sunk in these parts. Sounds like the Reichsminster in reverse.'

The Admin. Officer sourly intervened. 'If they call us snakes,' he said, 'then maybe we'll get a chance to use our venom.'

Rogge called me to his cabin. 'We are going to establish a base for a new series of operations,' he told me. 'I intend to select an island where we can use our seaplane for long range reconnaissance. Anything she finds, we'll follow.' He added, 'Anyway, sand and palm trees won't do the crew or any of us much harm. Give us all something new to think about. We can do with a change.'

I went away cheerfully to start the buzz throughout the ship, and as we drove to Vana Vana in Captain Cook's Low Islands, the crew, whose ideas of this part of the world remained, even under the Hitler régime, largely Hollywood conditioned, looked forward to meeting dusky maidens with swaying hips, grass skirts and floral garlands. The radio might still turn out its martial music for the raider fleet, but in the ears of the men who manned it was wafted the twang of guitars, the lilt of women's voices . . .

As the Arado's wing tips tilted across the foaming white that marked the coral reef, Bulla shouted to his pilot, 'it looks more like the fringe of a pond than an island.'

It was a good description, for behind the palm trees and the glittering white beach lay a vast lagoon, in area far greater than the circle of land that enclosed it; a lagoon of the deepest of blues, limpid and clear, refreshing, inviting.

Bulla throttled down and the seaplane almost glided in, pilot and observer silent, making a sort of mental inventory for the benefit of Rogge upon their return . . .

Reed huts . . . a village . . . a large building . . .

'My God!' said Bulla suddenly. 'It's a steeple!'

And so it was, a steeple as they later discovered, made entirely of palm leaves and raised above a little church.

Funny there's no one about, thought the observer as the plane made a second run in. 'Do you think they've got wind of us?' he shouted.

Bulla laughed. 'They don't get the newspapers in these parts. They'll probably take us for a visitation from heaven.'

And as the wing tips shadowed the village once again a host of men and women swarmed from the church and, awestricken by the noisy bird, promptly fell flat on their faces in attitudes of veneration.

Bulla was too surprised to take any credit for his prophecy.

'Well' . . . said the observer, as the kow-towers kow-towed, but the rest of his unprintable sentence was drowned by the roar of the engines, as the plane swept back over the reef to fulfil the main task of its reconnaissance, namely, selecting a landing point for the boat parties now waiting eagerly upon the deck of *Atlantis*. As he came in Bulla reflected that the long barrelled gun trained diligently upon the shore looked almost anachronistic or at least a little over-done!

A plum job they'd said, when Fehler and I were ordered to attempt a landing, and certainly, if we'd taken everyone who had wanted to come *Atlantis* would have been left as empty as the *Marie Celeste*. But now, faced with the business of manoeuvring through the gap in the reef, the reef against which a high swell now threw the waters fountain high, we weren't quite so sure about the nature of the fruit. Both launch and float set dramatically a-dance by the suck and pull of the current and the force of the breakers that threatened every second to hurl them against the jagged coral, we were held for long on the doorstep and when we did get in it was in a most undignified fashion—stern first, with the bows of the float held seaward by a line attached to the launch, and ourselves frantically paddling while the launch crew paid out the line. By the time we arrived we were glistening with spray, breathless with exertion, but almost incredibly triumphant; elated at feeling again that firmness of the land. The beach was warm beneath our feet, and, studded with coral pebbles, almost blinding in the sun. Plum job!

'Hollywood,' said Fehler, 'has nothing on this. Coconuts . . . lagoons . . . swaying palms!' Then, suddenly, 'But where's the girls?'

Well, wherever they were, they certainly weren't in the two reed huts near our landing place. Our orders were to make a thorough search . . . we decided to implement our orders.

From the gloom beneath a thatched grass roof came a whimper. We looked inside the hut and in a corner found a litter of ten young puppies. Nearby was a cooking pot. Its contents were still warm.

'Well,' I said. 'They've obviously panicked. We'd better do something to put their minds at rest.'

So we left a gift of knives and several packets of the world's universally accepted currency—cigarettes.

Twenty natives waited on the beach when we returned the next day, a friendly people headed by the chief and a lady of uncertain age who wore an apron over a gay print frock, and a stetson shading a faintly moustached face.

Hissed Fehler, at my elbow, 'what price Dorothy Lamour now?'

Ignoring him I made my neatest bow and smiled a smile as gallant as I could muster. The chief and his lady seemed to view us with approval and gravely the doctor set the seal on the occasion by removing from his haversack a Red Cross flag and proffering it to the chief with the formality of a diplomat from the Wilhelmstrasse. It was well received. Despite the language difficulty—the natives only knew about half-a-dozen words of English—we were soon on friendly terms, and on our indicating that we needed coconuts, they promptly produced five hundred! We gave them several hundredweights of flour in exchange.

We were shown a slightly better place to land and organised a sort of chain ferry service from launch to beach—our rubber float being attached to two lines, one on shore and one on the ship, and manually manoeuvred through the gap.

The only ship that called at the island I gathered was a trading schooner, which visited there twice yearly to barter stores for copra. Vana Vana possessed no landing jetty of any sort and its little church, built with such loving care by these so strangely isolated Christians, had not had the benefit of a white pastor for nearly half a century. My eye caught the sheen of the belt clasp of one of my landing party. 'Gott mit uns' . . . and a holster at the side. Maybe it would be convenient I reflected to leave our automatic pistols behind when we came next time.

Bulla, back from yet another fruitless patrol, eyed the hook of the seaplane hoist with distaste. It was never a happy business this returning to *Atlantis*. First, you had to taxi slowly up on the beam while the ship attempted to create a 'duck pond' of smooth stern water. Then you had to prove yourself an acrobat, climbing out of your seat and kneeling on the outside of the cockpit fuselage, with your toes dug in as though you were riding a mule.

Next, you had the juggling job, of trying to catch a hook, a hook gyrating crazily at the end of a steel cable and then—without getting your head bashed in of course—you fumbled to fit the steel into the bracket on the top of the wing.

Not that one minded the snags if the job gave you something to show for it. *Mandasor*, for example . . . Back in January it had been the Arado that had made possible this English freighter's capture. Bulla, fed up with the present monotony of scouring the empty seas, thought wistfully back to that assignment; how Rogge, up against a cleverly handled opponent, had told Bulla to bring her aerial down with a hook swung from the belly of his plane, and then delay her until the raider could come up. A dicey job. He'd thought at the time that he'd never want that sort of excitement again. But now, taxi-ing in, in the Pacific calm, he recalled it all with some nostalgia. There was a war on—THEN! A stubborn fire from the Englander's guns, one four-inch, one three-inch, and two m.g.'s had met him on the way, yet he'd severed her aerial on his first run in and on the second he'd raked her bridge with cannon shells and bombs. But the British fire had never faltered—even though the gunners were wounded—and in the end they'd given him such a warm good-bye that he'd landed up in the drink, sitting on the wings until the raider picked him up . . .

Bulla woke from his daydream and a few minutes later was cursing with his customary vehemence for the clumsy fools who, with their bamboo poles, were responsible for fending off the seaplane from crashing into *Atlantis*'s side, miscalculated their thrust and nearly knocked him flying from his perch.

Our last night on Vana Vana was a sentimental one. We sat around camp fires singing the songs of the homeland. Yet we were reluctant to leave this friendly oasis for the barren, hostile sea for indeed the homeland seemed more remote than heaven itself.

Last night . . . The ship's Bad Character was found in the undergrowth hand in hand with a native girl. 'I was lost, sir,' he explained . . .

Last day . . . I acquired a collection of bruises when the rope that was towing my float broke and I was hurled with stunning force against the coral.

As *Atlantis* moved off, Fehler and the doctor waved back to the singing natives on the shore. Said the doctor, who had become an especial friend of the populace as he had treated them for a rare eye disease to which they seemed much afflicted, 'Not another doctor for hundreds of miles! It's barbaric . . . I wish I had more time . . .'

Said Fehler: 'Disappointment that . . . about the dancing maidens I mean. But the coconuts were good!'

Slowly *Atlantis* proceeded to the East in a zig-zag questing for potential victims. But her search was in vain. Indeed quite a few of us were almost glad that it was so, the Pacific serving to intensify the strange feeling of remoteness from the world's affairs that had periodically attacked us ever since the early stages of our cruise.

We came to Henderson Island, one of the high volcanic islands of the Pitcairn group, famed for the legend of the *Bounty*. So high and so steep were the cliffs that we had to cling to the roots of trees left jutting outwards where the soil had crumbled. So thick and tall was the undergrowth at the top that, when only twenty yards inland, I had to climb a tree to find the way back. On Henderson Island we saw no sign of animal life let alone human life. But we did find a signpost.

Yellowing under the impact of the sun and the wind its faded lettering announced, 'Henderson Island. This island belongs to King George V'. More than a little out of date of course, but equally so was the inscription scribbled upon it. This recorded the arrival of a British cruiser, the occasion, we thanked our destiny, being removed by some ten years from our own.

On board *Atlantis* Fehler proceeded with his pet

schemes for maintaining morale—maintaining Fehler's morale. On one occasion we filled the Admin. Officer's cabin with toilet paper—thousands of rolls of it. On another he placed there a prize speciment of a kelp—sixty feet long, slimy and wet and possessed of a strange odour. The Admin. Officer was devoted to a pet canary, so Fehler seized on the opportunity to temporarily kidnap the bird and squeeze into the cage instead the ship's cat!

In these narrow surroundings things that would normally be dismissed as too petty to worry about tended to become magnified. For example the case of the ship's doctor and the whisky that tasted peculiar.

'Well, I'm damned,' Reil said, pushing aside his plate and rising indignantly to his feet. 'I've never been so insulted . . . !'

The peace-makers intervened. 'Now, now, Doctor . . . of course he didn't mean it . . .'

But Reil was unplacated. 'If there's anything wrong with the whisky, then you'd better blame the manufacturers not me.'

Reil felt he had good reason for annoyance. As ship's doctor he had charge of the spirit store, and he felt that the criticism levelled at the quality of the Scotch reflected upon his integrity.

'But Doctor,' said the offender, pink-faced. 'I had no intention at all . . .'

Reil said nothing and walked out of the wardroom.

For days he was missing from his quarters for long periods of time, and we became genuinely worried fearing that he had taken mortal distress at our references to the undoubtedly queer taste of our favourite proprietary brand. Then the rumours began to trickle out. The doctor was at work at the dark hole that constituted the soda water factory of the ship, glistening with damp as he conferred with the Wagnerian and simple giant who manipulated it and making extensive, mysterious tests of the quality of the distilled water.

Eventually he emerged triumphant. 'It's not the

whisky, it's the water,' he said. 'I'm trying out a new formula—mixing a minute proportion of seawater with the fresh.'

When, after another 'run of trials' the doctor tried out his experiment upon us, we had to admit that the whisky tasted perfect . . . Thus do great scientific discoveries arise from minor accidents. After all, if Newton hadn't been insulted by an apple . . . !

We were to rendezvous with *Komet*, the raider that had broken out with Russian connivance from the Bering Straits, and was now at large on the seaways between Japan and the Western seaboard of America.

For one of those inexplicable reasons there had long been a rivalry between our two ships, and now that Eyssen, her Commander, had been promoted to Admiral, we decided that it would be an appropriate occasion for a lighthearted diversion. Accordingly, when we sighted the 'flagship'—a smaller vessel than our own—we fired a solemn salute with our pompoms and dressed ship, while Rogge, in spotless white, and heavy with gold braid, went across to pay a courtesy call, just as though he was a cruiser Captain calling upon *Bismarck*. But alas for our sense of fun. Eyssen took it all at face value and received us with the dignified formality of the C.-in-C. himself.

Of far more personal interest to us was the reappearance of Kamenz, our navigating officer, fresh from his round-the-world trip via Japan, Russia and Germany. This was indeed a great day for the ship, and when we heard that Kamenz, emerging from his U-boat, had to receive a typhoid and cholera injection, we arranged for the 'operation' a somewhat dramatic setting.

Kamenz's dislike and suspicion of Freemasonry was a byword on the ship, so, when he walked into the wardroom he was confronted by three hooded figures wearing silk aprons and sashes, and waiting for him at the head of a table dimly lit by candles. The rest of us, attired in a garb reminiscent of the Ku Klux Klan, stood silently in the shadows. It took quite an effort on the part of the two doctors and the doctor's assistant to give our Odysseus the dose required.

Morale soared when we first heard that we were to round the Horn. The South Atlantic, we realised, was frequented by our foes, but its waters also marked the way back, waters that were almost familiar, the threshold as it were of home. We'd gone the long route round, the way of the old sailing ships, dodging the Falkland Islands and keeping just north of the South Shetlands, travelling through the fog and ice of the Antarctic. When we turned to the north again, *Atlantis* travelling at speed on her last lap, the lap we'd intended to lead to home . . .

'Proceed to Flower Point Daffodil to refuel U-68.' Rogge read the message and turned to me.

'We're going to be busy after all,' he said.

He looked at the chart and checked the point assigned him. 'They're crazy,' he said in astonishment. 'Quite crazy.'

A few minutes later *Atlantis* was signalling back, 'It is suicide to send us to this position.'

U-68's Commander was equally indignant, backing Rogge's protest with a terse 'agreed', for the rendezvous that High Command had chosen for us was the middle of the crowded traffic lane between Freetown and the Cape.

At length we were granted an alternative point, but even this was still too frequented for comfort, and the refuelling was noteworthy for the haste displayed by both of the two major contracting parties.

'Thank God, that's over.' I thought when U-68 had disappeared. But no sooner had we started on our way than we received another signal.

'Proceed to Flower Point Lily Ten to refuel U-126.'

'Where's Lily Ten?' asked Rogge.

Kamenz made a few calculations. 'Just . . . here . . . !' he said, placing the pencil point neatly upon the chart. 'Just here,' repeated Kamenz.

It will be easy for me to claim today that I had some

subtle premonition of disaster, or that the words Lily Ten troubled me. But nothing like that happened. Point Ten? We glanced at the little black cross that the pencil had marked upon the linen, and not one of us thought for one moment that it might conceivably mark the site of *Atlantis*'s grave . . .

CHAPTER TWENTY-THREE

'FEINDLICHER KREUZER IN SICHT!'

'FEINDLICHER KREUZER *in Sicht! Feindlicher Kreuzer in Sicht . . . !*'

The alarm bell's staccato clamour followed within seconds the lookout's hail . . . breaking through the dreams of those off duty, rousing the quiet ship into action and sending the gun crews to their stations for this, the last and fatal meeting.

'Feindlicher Kreuzer in Sicht! Feindlicher Kreuzer in Sicht . . . !' The shout came to us like an agitated whisper through the telephones, linking the watchers and the bridge, then transforming itself into a vibrating note of urgency that reached into the bowels of the ship as the fingers of the watch jabbed down the buttons of alarm.

So came the warning of the end of *Atlantis*—the warning that we all knew would some day come, *must* some day come, much though we relegated it to the back of our minds in the long sequence of our ocean cruise, preferring to seek no further than the immediate; taking thought for the day alone . . .

The early morning of 22nd November 1941 had been dull but clear. Our rendezvous with U-126 made, we lay stopped, refuelling our grey companion for her mission, but otherwise almost idle; relaxed. Everything was so tranquil that morning in the South Atlantic; tranquil as a street in the city before the first rush of traffic; quiet and chill and clear as before the first footsteps stir the fallen linden leaves in autumn. Yawning, I looked around me as I emerged on deck . . .

U-126 lay alongside, the oil pipe linking her with us

239

like an umbilical cord; *Atlantis*, tall and broad-beamed; U-126 lean, urgent, and possessing it seemed a silent, trustful dependence as the life-blood flowed into her.

From Rogge's cabin I caught the murmur of voices. The U-boat Commander had come aboard and the two men were exchanging information and gossip over a glass of sherry; rival departments of war conferring with the quiet geniality of friends met in peace. From somewhere else I hard the snatch of a song, typically sentimental. A quiet morning. Yes, and a cold one too. And for me the sequel to an unsatisfactory slumber . . . For the tenth time I had experienced the dream that had been persistently recurring ever since we had left the atolls of the Pacific behind us. Account for it how you will—premonition or subconscious funk—the dream was invariably the same, a vision of a British cruiser, three-funnelled and long-hulled, appearing two points to port. There my dream would suddenly end . . . I could never seem to reach the climax.

The officer of the watch grinned his good-mornings. 'Thank God yesterday's panic is over,' he quipped. He was referring to the fluster that had followed an accident to our seaplane. After a routine patrol she had caught her floats in a precipitous sea, and promptly sank. This was a grievous loss. Our 'eyes' had gone just when we happened to be in an undesirable locality! Small wonder that Rogge, after his previous misgivings over the neighbourhood's 'security', had not been pleased.

'Oh, well. Can't be helped. A lot more peaceful now,' I said. A light breeze played across the decks which were deserted by all but the working party. Only a slow swell disturbed the surface of the sea, grey at the moment in its morning livery; soon, as we knew, to sparkle into blue. For a while, and not for the first time by any means, I forgot about the war and gloried anew in the pleasanter aspects of this life upon the waters; the rare opportunities it afforded of appreciating the 'little things' that otherwise, in the automatic rush of existence, so speedily lost their meaning. The coffee tasted good, and even the reek of the fuel oil—when divorced from the U-boat and her mission—seemed a not unpleasant companion, just part of the background as it were, wholesome, and of the sea.

Then came the warning! *'Feindlicher Kreuzer . . . Feindlicher Kreuzer in Sicht!'*

Everything started to happen at once . . . In a second the pipe-line had been disconnected. A second more, and the U-boat's Captain had come running to the side to rejoin his command. Too late! His young Number One had reacted so promptly that only a surge of bubbles and foam now marked the spot where U-126 had been, leaving her Commander, storming with anger, stranded on our decks.

'Bastards. The bloody bastards! . . . To dive like that when she couldn't even SEE the enemy!' But there was another foe for U-126 to fear, and soon we became aware of this—we who had so prided ourselves on seeing our enemy first! The cruiser's seaplane was overhead, diving around us, photographing and recording our every movement.

'Give the swine a burst,' shouted one of our seamen. But Rogge shook his head. The Walrus continued to encircle us, an infernal buzzing menace; an inquisitive wasp with poison for us all. But still we were instructed to hold our fire. Our motor launch came up to us like a frightened chick to its mother, and, as it cut neatly alongside, someone jested, 'No good visiting us now!'

A hurried conference followed at which Rogge made preparations for the wrath to come, his usual calm masking the worries that were buffeting his mind. Briefly, his plan was to try one last and desperate bluff. 'We'll play for time,' he said. 'We will pretend that we are British.' A fantastic notion? Not a bit of it. There was just the chance that the cruiser, puzzled by our bluff, might come in closer to investigate, in which case we could at least attempt something, with our torpedoes.

'We've got the U-boat as well,' said Rogge. 'She must be up to something by now. I'll try and buy all the time

241

I can, but, for the present—well, remember! Not a gun must be exposed!'

Through our glasses *Devonshire* made a majestic sight, her bow waves bringing to life an otherwise creaseless sea and giving some indication of the high speed at which she was travelling. But we were in no mood for admiring her graceful, classical silhouette. We could scarcely see the barrels of her guns, and this, as we were only too horribly aware, meant that they were trained upon us; that she was heading right for us, and that, unless a miracle should occur, she would shortly be claiming her reckoning.

Our opponent made his introduction at far range—brief, and to the point; pregnant with emphasis as to what we were entitled to expect in the future. *Devonshire* most certainly did not believe in wasting time! An orange flash splashed vividly her long grey hull. With the roar of an express train an 8-inch shell came hurtling above our masts, twisting crazily into the sea behind us. Another flash, and another shell, but this time in front of us, raising a great and angry geyser of discoloured, tortured water. The inference was plain, and our reactions rapid.

'Stop ship!'

Now that the accustomed diesel's throb had died, a stillness fell upon *Atlantis,* a stillness that seemed to wrap every man in its embrace. Not that we had lost the power of speech—we were talking. Not that we were paralysed with fear—we were moving. But our talking and our moving seemed alike subordinated to the thinking process that every one of us was undergoing . . . Would we have a chance to settle the Britisher? It did not look like it. Yet by this time, our luck—*Atlantis* luck—had become almost as accepted in our lives as the rising of the sun or the waning of the moon. *It* just could not happen to us! Not to *Atlantis*!

Silence—except for the creaking of the ship as she rose and fell on the slow, slight swell, and the shuffle of feet as men fidgeted behind their guns. I thought of our twenty-two kills. I thought of the date. Twenty-two kills; twenty-second day of the month. Certainly a coincidence. Maybe an omen! Good? Or bad? Meanwhile, reflection on these matters did not unduly impede enterprise . . .

From a captured British signalling lamp we sent out the name *Polyphemus*, and, from our radio, as an innocent British ship would, we sent out a squawk to the world: 'RRR . . . *Polyphemus* . . . RRR . . . Unidentified ship has ordered me to stop . . . RRR . . . *Polyphemus* . . .'

It was a very slender chance. We knew that. But it was our only chance, and again we repeated our message in a desperate series of dots and dashes—our last bluff chattering out into the world with all the indignant, helpless frenzy of a stopped merchantman calling for aid and support. And then we waited.

'Wonder what they'll make of that on Tommy?' said a signaller. We soon found out!

Tommy told us to stay where we were. We stayed! Someone remembered the old blasphemous prayer of Nelson's men while awaiting an enemy's broadside . . . 'For what we are about to receive may the Lord make us truly thankful!'

Our radio shut down, for even the most short-sighted and ignorant of sailormen would scarcely continue to mistake the distinctive *Devonshire* for a German! Although our ruse had obviously made the enemy reconsider (the real *Polyphemus* had left Spain at a date that could have placed her in this area) it became evident that she was not going to give us the chance we needed. She was 'checking up', but not checking up by personal close-range experience as we had hoped she might. Instead, she was radioing the Admiralty for advice on the real *Polyphemus*'s movements. Her eyes had obviously glimpsed the wolf's fangs for all our deceptive fleece.

Refusing to relax her vigilance she was performing instead a series of intricate naval evolutions in the far distance; pursuing a zig-zag course, never slackening speed, and never approaching nearer than 16,000 yards—far beyond our utmost range.

The seaplane continued to annoy us, her buzzing curiosity being apparently insatiable; her presence precluding us from all but the most cautious movement on deck. This aerial watch did the strangest things to one's mental make-up, inducing in me, at any rate, a most absurd feeling of self-consciousness, like a boy developing pigeon toes when embarrassed by the eyes of a critical master; making us all pray heartily for a chance to knock her down!

Would one ever live to recall the stage setting of this strange climax to our adventuring, I wondered. There we were, the captain, gunnery officer, torpedo officer, navigating officer, and myself, all together on the bridge, an assembly of naval gentlemen, expensively trained, and yet about as powerless (bar a miracle) as sheep before the slaughterers; watching rather hopelessly the persistent blinking of the big searchlight of our opponent, now sending a signal whose meaning we did not know—obviously something to do with a secret call sign to which we should have sent an appropriate reply.

Behind us, waiting desperately for our hoped-for opportunity, stood three torpedo ratings, three artillery ratings, three signallers, and the I/C range finder. Of us all the U-boat Commander was outwardly the most perturbed. Furious at being away from his command, frustrated at not having any practical work to do, he paced up and down the bridge, becoming steadily more angered at U-126's apparent failure to shine. But, even at such a desperate moment we could not help but chuckle at the nature of his grouse, so typical of the service he represented . . . 'Me!' he snorted. 'Me! To be caught on a blasted merchant ship. To be sunk on the surface after all I've endured. Makes me feel naked—absolutely naked!'

What next? Rogge saw the appeal in our eyes and answered it. 'She will find we are not *Polyphemus*, of course,' he said. 'Then we can expect her to be *really* rude! Even so, I'm still not going to fire.'

Not fire? We were astonished. We knew, of course,

that our 5.9 inch guns would never be able to reach the enemy at the distance she so skilfully maintained. Equally well we knew that, even could they do so, we still would have had no chance against an armoured ship carrying 8-inch guns.

'But surely a shell or two?' pleaded Kasch. 'Just for the sake of prestige?'

'No,' said Rogge. 'Maybe we can bluff them yet. We'll keep on hoping. If they shell us, and we don't fire back, there's still the chance that they may take us for a supply ship. In which case they'll probably close with us discovering their mistake too late!'

So, still we played for time, the hardest discipline of all now enforced upon us; the discipline that refused us even the childish relief of making a vulgar noise at our tormentors. Half an hour went by. Then my batman appeared, all eager deference, and at his most formal before this glittering brass. 'You would like your best uniform, sir?'

My best uniform? . . . At a time like this? I glanced at the earnest, solicitous face before me, and remembered, with a queer reproach, the part I had to play. Whether the bluff should succeed or fail, here was another bluff, a social bluff, arranged by joint agreement, a bluff that tacit, instinctive, was well understood between both parties. 'Yes. By all means,' I replied.

This philosophy of taking the best had its points, I reflected, and immediately I started to do some organisation on my own account. I asked the administrative officer to free the dollars that we carried for 'emergency use only.' If shipwrecked, there was always the possibility (very problematical though it seemed at this stage!) that we might make the coast, or (even more problematical) be picked up by a neutral, or . . . well, money was MONEY! But where to put it? Finally, I placed the greenbacks between my shoes and the soles of my feet; a bulge of wealth most comforting in happier circumstances—if only one knew for certain that one would find a place to spend it! Such a nuisance, said one or two of the others, to go swimming with your shoes on!

And what makes you think you'll be fortunate enough to need the money?

Meanwhile, where was the U-boat? Her Captain's remarks by now were quite unprintable. So too, were ours! Yet, in actual fact, we knew that our annoyance was partly a feeble attempt to excuse our own humiliating discomfiture, for we realised well enough the *Devonshire*'s manoeuvres left small scope for U-126.

How long before *Devonshire* would confirm her suspicions? So unpleasant was this suspense, this awaiting unmasking, that we were almost impatient for the wrath to break. I suppose, looking back on these isolated reflections, that one could say, for the sake of the literary record, that the scene was 'drenched in drama'. At the time, however, most of us were too preoccupied to be unduly dramatic, or cinematically emotional! There were so many things to think about . . .

09.35 and the game was up! A spurt of red and yellow flame jumped across our opponent's turrets. Kasch leaned over from the rail above us, his teeth bared in a grin. With professional appreciation he shouted, 'They'll be here in twenty seconds!'

As *Devonshire*'s first salvo sang around us the sea suddenly sprung into fountains of spray from which steel splinters poured, and above the wailing and crashing of the shells came Rogge's order:

'Start ship! Full ahead!'

Atlantis began to move—but *Devonshire*'s shells caught up with her like a grip on the neck of a runaway.

'Up Battle Ensign,' roared Rogge.

For the last time the Red, White and Black shot upwards to the peak, and *Atlantis* was in her true colours—defiant and unashamed; a warship receiving her reckoning.

The British shells hit us again, and the whole ship wilted and trembled. For the first time I had that old sensation known only to those whose ship is under fire—that of the deck recoiling physically from under one's feet; of the wooden planks literally straining in the contraction and expansion of their hurt.

246

'Make smoke!' An acrid cloud of billowing white spread around us, drifting out to form a wall between us and our foe. Yet, from nearly ten miles off the shells continued to find us as in the last attempt to lure *Devonshire* to destruction, we twisted and wriggled desperately to the south-east. If the U-boat could not get to the cruiser, then perhaps we might persuade the cruiser to come to the U-boat. But *Devonshire*'s Captain was far too wily. Our manoeuvres were fruitless. Within minutes we were using our screen merely as a cover to get our crew away, confusing *Devonshire*'s fire, and drawing it from us—for a salvo or two, as if striking home would create a massacre among our sailors, now filing as coolly into the boats as if they were carrying out routine drill. Accordingly, we made one-and-a-half knots, just sufficient speed to operate the rudder and stay within the smoke screen; indeed by this time we could not make more for we were hopelessly battered, though just how battered I did not at first realise.

While the men were leaving—one of them carrying a protesting Ferry in his arms—I rushed down to my cabin to deal with the codes, picking up a camera as well for I was determined to get a picture of our ship's ending. I dallied a minute or two, thrusting some shaving gear and one or two personal mementoes into my pockets, and then, with films and camera, I reported back to the bridge.

How speedily our ship had changed her coat! Her once trim decks were reduced to a shambles of twisted ventilators, of fallen derricks, and shattered rafters. The 'stage props' had gone down before the shell blasts like corn before a hurricane. 'Stanchions' and packing cases' lay splintered, and the smell of burning hung heavy over *Atlantis*. Black smoke wreathed her masthead like a funeral pall. A dozen small fires were leaping from the deck and our seaplane hold was a raging inferno. By now all the crew had left except Rogge, C.P.O. Pigors, myself, and Fehler's demolition party, whose job it was to plant and fire the explosive charges that would destroy our ship. I slipped as I stepped towards the bridge.

There was blood on the deck. The enmy's fourth salvo had brought us the first of our 'action dead' . . . now there were more of them—eight in all.

Pigors, an old friend of Rogge, with whom he had served in the sail training ships days, was trying to persuade him to leave the bridge, 'I won't go without you,' he said.

Another shell hit us. Then another. The ship was listing heavily to port. So this was it!

Atlantis was dying and dying without an answering shot being fired from the long barrels that now lay exposed through the torn decks which once had been their camouflage. Pretence and menace alike irrevocably past, the five-point-nines useless, silent, pointed blindly at the sky. Our last bluff had failed and, remote as heaven itself, the *Devonshire* continued to probe and search for us.

Fehler and his party, their mission completed, dived over the side. So did Pigors—persuaded at last that we, too, would escape.

Now only Rogge and myself were left. Above the roar of the flames, he shouted. 'Jump, Mohr! Jump! I follow you!' I jumped . . .

CHAPTER TWENTY-FOUR

AND SO WE SINK

As I hit the water an enemy shell crashed into the sea nearby, sending its tremor through the ocean, a pulsating physical 'echo' followed by a surging, angry wave. For the first time I felt the panic of the hunted, the terror that comes when you feel the enemy is after YOU, not after you and the others . . . but after YOU personally. Another shell. Twisting like a corkscrew, growling like a hound it came. An idiotic sensation temporarily swept over me; a mad yearning that I could not resist—a yearning to plunge my head underwater for 'protection' as the shells came down; to behave like an ostrich before its enemies. Another shell . . . and another . . . 'near misses' as the smoke screen blinded both *Devonshire* and *Atlantis*.

By now, however, I had recovered my scattered wits. I jerked up my head as I remembered the fatal fuel oil that could swamp and clog the lungs. I even began to worry if anyone had noticed me and hoped they had not! So does convention, instilled down the years, govern one's external reactions even though the inner self be gripped by fear. An appropriate theme perhaps for a doctor of philosophy? Candidly I wasn't much interested in developing it at the time. I was far too busy with the problem of keeping alive . . . !

A new crescendo of sound, muted and different, reached me as the explosive aboard *Atlantis* blew up, sending thundering shock waves to buffet and clutch up at me. When the smoke from the screen and the burning drifted, *Devonshire* saw the full state of her victim. There was no further need to fire—nor did she attempt it and, as I splashed around in the water I heard what, hitherto, the whine of metal and the tumult of the up-flung seas had blanketed—the shouts of swimmers drifting about the dying ship. For now that the guns had slaked their fury it seemed as though we were men who had been deaf, and now heard again. Another rumble echoed from *Atlantis*. Smoke began to pour from her, not this time from her screening but from the second explosion of Fehler's charges. She began to shiver. The end was near . . .

We watched as she started to fall back into the sea, going down rapidly by the stern. And, as her bows began to rise, we saw for the first time (the fact registering even in spite of our predicament), the great raw scar that she had carried with her as a memento of the Kerguelen days.

Atlantis, our home for nearly two years, was now following the path of her victims, leaving us loving her and hating to see her distress, yet preoccupied with the business of survival; the simple urgency of keeping one's nostrils clear of the oil, now spreading around us in a choking, stifling circle. But, even at this moment, old loyalties awoke, and I saw something incredibly fine, a scene that I could not have imagined happening outside of fiction . . .

There in the middle of twenty swimming men, Rogge was dragging himself painfully upright, and, treading water as *Atlantis* took her final plunge, he remained erect, his hand meticulously at the salute. Not only oil, and smoke, and sea water stained his face, but tears as well. The Commander in tears! I too swallowed hard for a moment as came the last cry from our ship—the sickening groan of timbers straining and breaking, the tremendous hiss of hot metal flopping down upon the cold sea. A surge of steam, and then *Atlantis*, mortally wounded, slid beneath the surface.

Our rescue boats were too far away to be seen, but surely even now they would be struggling to meet us, although we knew it would be a long while yet before we should feel their planks beneath our feet. We started searching for 'strays' among the flotsam where men, still fuddled by shock, clung gratefully to floating driftwood, the debris of disaster.

I noticed a man a few yards away. He was sagging in the water, his head bowed down in front of him. In my own dazed state I had the quaint notion that he didn't know the cruiser had ceased firing, and was still seeking the protective cover of the waves as I had done, so I called to him, to tell him all was over. There was no answer!

'Come on man. Get your head up' . . . Still no response. I closed with him, grabbing his shoulders, jerking him up. Only to look into a face that, once so familiar, was now an eternity away. Yet still I held on to him, urgently, still not understanding, until I heard the threshing of water a few yards away.

'SHARKS!' and a man's scream . . .

The weight in my arms increased and tightened . . . a terrible force was dragging his shoulders down, tearing him from my holding hands with a sudden shock and violence of the pull. It was then that I caught a glimpse of the underside of a black and white belly—a shark was taking him to the depths. I struck out, splashing for all I was worth, cursing, shouting, praying, all at the same time. Blood began to stain the water in my vicinity and I realised with a surge of horror that it was not the blood of my dead companion. It was my own blood—my right hand was covered in it. Had those needle teeth caught me as they snapped shut on the body of my comrade? Impossible . . . my hand was still in one piece. I remembered then, the razor blades I was carrying in my pocket. The water had seeped open the packets, and the blades had cut through my skin as I recoiled from the shark's onrush. But such reassurance was, I knew, only momentary. The blood would merely act as scent to the pack beneath.

God! A man was pounding the water beside me . . . Sweat seemed momentarily to drain all strength from me and a strange numbness held me. Then I was shuddering, laughing, panting as a cry of desperate fright

251

came from the swimmer floundering past me . . . 'For God's sake—sharks!' His voice, pitched higher in his terror, stirred my senses and I struck out again; clutching hold of a drifting plank until at length, reaching a float, I clung to its edge.

A droning noise, and the enemy seaplane appeared over the scene; the infernal buzzing that had haunted us during the action now changing to a steady roar as she swept along but a few feet above us. I remembered thinking what a strange gulf separated us—only a few feet between the comparatively safe life in the cabin above us, and the uncertainty in the water of any existence at all. We could see the pilot's face quite clearly as he throttled down—a face that was as remote as a god in Olympus. We could see the camera, its lens focusing on our defeat, the celluloid, dispassionate, recording mechanism that modern war required!

Again and again she encircled us. I cursed her presence for I knew that so long as she remained overhead, there was no hope of the U-126 surfacing. But, in one respect, at least, we were lucky. Sharks or no, this was a not unreasonable sea. Here were no boat-capsizing North Atlantic rollers, and most of our craft had fortunately been left intact. We hoped too, that eventually the U-boat would give us some aid, for *Devonshire* had left us. She would, by this time, be but a faint streak on the far horizon, ever dwindling, and now her seaplane also turned away, and we of *Atlantis* were alone—except for the sharks!

How we hated and feared those flesh-tearing teeth. In the centre of the raft squatted one of our number as lookout against our enemies' savage thrusts.

'Sharks! Sharks;' . . . In near panic we would force our heads under water, expelling the breath from our lungs with a noisy puffing, knowing that the louder we could manage it, the more likelihood there was of it frightening the fish. Yet even in this macabre situation man's discipline prevailed and the sharks, to our infinite relief, gave up the struggle.

* * *

Two hours later I was hauled into one of our whalers. As I felt the touch of the hard, dry wood, it seemed the greatest luxury in the world.

I looked around me. We were a pretty bedraggled lot, peering anxiously at each fresh arrival, wondering how many of us were safe. Where's Schmitt Hallo, Ernst . . . Oh, and there's Werner . . . Christ, you look a mess, chum. Make way there . . .

Everyone started to inquire about their comrades. I looked around for Kross, so often my helmsman. But he was not with us. He was dead. Gradually I pieced the story together. It was his politeness that had killed him. He was going to the staircase leading to the boat deck when he met an officer. Dutifully standing aside to let him pass, Kross said. 'After you, sir.' Two seconds later a shell burst upon him . . .

Pigors, that veteran sailor, had survived. It was good to see him toughly grinning his relief, but alas, the war was later to claim him also—when serving with a submarine. Keuhn, the second in command, had been wounded, and Surgeon-Commander Reil was already at work amongst the men, patching wounds and treating shock.

Such are the oddities of human experience, the paradoxes of life, that from out of the misery around arose one or two lighter aspects raising a laugh, a flicker of humour . . . There was, for instance, the story of Bulla and his wardrobe. He'd found it drifting by the float, by some freak undamaged and with its door uppermost. "Hallo, old friend,' he said, and hardly realising what prompted him he opened it to find his clothes still dry! He seized a pullover and his pipe—the latter an English Dunhill—saying, 'Well, these at least will come in useful.' Ferry also had fared uncannily well. The sailor who had jumped with him had placed the quivering Scottie on a plank, and held him there as he swam alongside.

Of us all, Kapitänleutnant Bauer, the U-boat commander, seemed the least gracious to Providence, appearing to find no consolation at all in being saved. He

253

was for too preoccupied with other considerations— scanning the sea for the reappearance of his command, and occasionally mumbling to himself as though we were all involved in some fantastic plot to bring the submarine service into dispute, and deceive and make a fool of him personally. When, at length, to his relief and ours, U-126 reappeared, she came up in her usual jaunty and self-assured fashion, a 'real' warship with the knowledge that the waters of the earth were hers, but this 'relax-we-are-rescuing-you' attitude was drastically deflated as the conning tower and the first officer emerged, her marooned parent unleashing his feelings in a spate of language that was not only coarse and sailor-like, but quite original as well! But our own wrath soon died. After all, the youngster could not have done much more—not against a ship as alert as our opponent. He had at all events, the intelligence to keep himself intact to save us—a factor of some importance!

We then went into conference. Perhaps the strangest conference ever held, its board-room a cluster of lifeboats and whalers round the U-boat; and packed by over 300 men awaiting the decision as to how they were to get to safety. We considered our two alternatives . . .

One. We could set a course for Freetown. Travelling in an easterly direction we would, at least, have the advantage (if the journey was for our rescue alone) of striking the main trade routes and making use of the easterly currents.

Two. We could head for Brazil. This was a project considered at the start as being the most fantastic of all, for Brazil was nine hundred miles away . . .

The first plan, however, was rejected immediately by Rogge. He did not want us to end up as prisoners—not if it could be avoided, and this objection of his, I am proud to say, was shared by us all.

One of our C.P.O.'s, Frochlich by name, helped make Brazil sound even more attractive. Originally he had served with *Langsdorff* and was with the *Graf Spee* at the time of the River Plate action. Interned by the local authorities, he later escaped, and was concealed for several months by the German settlers—being passed from office to office, and farm to farm until smuggled on to a blockade runner.

When *Atlantis* subsequently contacted this ship Rogge's personality—('I need a man like you,' he said)—and our combined hospitality, took the edge off Frohlich's surprise when he was ordered to join us without even the opportunity of a glimpse of home. Later he became a virtual tower of strength, not only as an efficient radio-room C.P.O., but also as an expert on 'how to escape in Latin America', and his idea appealed particularly to me. My dollars were now drying rapidly in the sun, and I was confident that we would have more than a sporting chance . . . once we had surmounted the navigational hazards involved in getting there!

So Brazil it was to be, and U-126 now had the responsibility of taking our wounded inside—much to the disgust of her Commander, who protested, 'I might just as well run a hospital ship or a tow boat.' However, he arranged for forty members of our crew, suffering from shock and exposure, to rest upon the narrow decks, and said he would take the chance of towing us. 'But,' he warned, 'if the Tommy sees us then you'll have to jump for it! And when you jump, jump quick, for we'll be going down fast. And you'd better swim fast too or you'll be sucked under with us.'

After this encouraging address, we tied our boats to the submarine and, in line ahead, like some sprawling, untidy caravan, commenced our slow pilgrimage across the 900 miles of this most changeable and treacherous of all deserts. A pleasant prospect! It did not take more than a hour or two before I began to wonder if we had not over-estimated the advantages of a 12-day cruise to Brazil. For this was no restful interlude in which rescued sailormen sprawled peacefully on the boards of their boats as the U-boat did the donkey work. Far from it. The tow-ropes kept on breaking, leaving the whalers and floats to wallow blindly, until rowed back by tired men, once more to be secured, but only part time and again. I do not remember how many times this happened, or how often we had to wait for and gather in the stragglers, but the process was real hard labour for the rowers, since boats designed to carry forty men now carried seventy and over. Our progress was painfully slow.

By day the sun beat down upon us with the full force of the tropics. Our salt-infected clothes rubbed against our bare skin, forming unpleasant sores. Slight cuts became major discomforts when exposed to the heat of the sky and the salt of the spray. Lips cracked and eyes became swollen beneath the unrelieved monotony of the broiling rays and the heaving waters. The woodwork of the boat became blisteringly hot to the touch, an agony to lie upon, while possessing my shoes I was the envy of my companions, some of whom tore strips from their clothing to make 'socks' as a protection for their bare feet against the scorching planks.

Yet by night we nearly froze. With our teeth a-chatter, our bodies numb, we huddled together and slapped ourselves for warmth. Merciful dozes had unmerciful endings. One would wake in the utmost discomfort, feeling as though consigned to a refrigerator and at such moments of acute misery we almost envied our wounded. At least they had warmth in the cramped mystery of the U-126's interior. I found just three days of this life sufficiently wearying. So did most of us. Not that our agonies were really epic. Not that our privations were really extreme. In comparison with the ordeals experienced by other shipwrecked crews in these waters our sufferings were fantastically light, and in most respects we could still regard ourselves as fortunate. Of our original company, ten were dead, but, considering the punishment that *Devonshire* had given us this was a lower figure than we had any right to expect. We were given daily reports of our wounded, who were thriving, and at any rate we were spared enduring the distress of hearing those most pitiful sounds of all—the groans of men who can do nothing for themselves, and for whom nothing can be done.

For seventy-six-hours—it seemed far longer—we

continued our journey, with Brazil appearing daily to grow more and more remote, and even its mirage fading in our hearts. We still might jest about the black-eyed wenches and lush groves of the shore, but our jokes were forced and heavy, even the greenbacks beneath my feet ceasing finally to provide a topic for the humorist. But our luck, *Atlantis* luck, still held. Relief arrived—guided to us by the U-boat's call for aid. We could scarcely believe our eyes. We knew about the signal of course, but so many things were happening at sea . . . A ship! And one of ours—the 3,660 ton merchantman *Python*, now engaged on refuelling German submarines . . .

We came alongside. Some of the men of *Python* leaned over the rails and there was the odd jest, the odd cheer. But otherwise there was almost a sense of anticlimax about the way in which we boarded her. Someone said, 'Well. We're here.' A sailor muttered behind me, 'Won't be long before you get your head down now, Franz.' And Rogge, although incongruously attired in officer's cap and jacket, plimsolls and shorts, kept his dignity to the end, climbing rather stiffly to the deck, and saying, with a most proper salute.

'I report myself and the crew of the auxiliary cruiser, *Atlantis*, aboard *Python*.'

Trust Rogge! Just the cool, correct, professional naval officer.

'Glad to have you, sir,' said *Python*'s Captain.

And that was that—or so we thought . . .

Python took us straight to her hospitable heart. We were made comfortable, and I enjoyed, with two others, the luxury of a cabin and stateroom.

But when we started hoisting the whalers aboard her comparatively untried crew's reaction to the future seemed of a far more recklessly heroic calibre than that of our men. 'Why bring those along with you,' one youngster asked. One P.O. answered grimly, 'Because, son, you never know when they will come in useful!'

During the next few days I had plenty of leisure time in which to reflect upon our recent experiences, and the

257

end of our ship. And now that the mental mists of battle had cleared I was able to get a truer perspective of several of the factors surrounding our defeat.

Prominent among these of course was the question of the young submarine officer not engaging the enemy more closely. Actually *Devonshire*, steaming and manoeuvring at between 25 and 30 knots, had left few loopholes for torpedo attack. Her aloofness had been most intelligent for if she had closed with us, she would, after all, have been playing into our hands, and might have received the same rough treatment that *Sydney* got from our brother, *Kormoran*. While, had she lingered on the scene a little longer, U-126 would undoubtedly have seized her chance.

We bore *Devonshire* no grudge. Indeed her Captain must have found his decision a painful one, for, as I later read in an Admiralty communiqué, he had thought the British prisoners were aboard *Atlantis* at the time.

In actual fact we had but one prisoner aboard when we were sunk; most of the others having been transferred to a supply ship a few weeks earlier. The exception was Frank Vicovari, who was badly wounded during the *Zamzam* incident, and whom we had decided to keep for treatment in our own ship's hospital. Vicovari was one of the first to be put aboard the boats during the action and was to survive all the vicissitudes of the long journey home.

It was on the fifth day of our stay aboard *Python* that she received the order 'Refuel submarines'—halfway between *Rose* and *Dandelion*.

'Let's hope we'll have better luck this time,' said Fehler. 'After all you know the old superstition that a shell never falls in the same spot twice ... .'

CHAPTER TWENTY-FIVE

AND SINK AGAIN . . . .

BACK IN KEIL my father, in his professional capacity, had been one of the first to hear that Atlantis was in action. His feelings can probably be well imagined especially at the time of our sinking—knowing, as he did, all the hazards and nothing of our good fortune, yet powerless to do anything and forced, as a matter of honour, to say nothing and mask his fears from his colleagues. He later told me that it was the most terrible period of waiting he had ever experienced. Naturally the number of survivors was not known for hours after the sinking. Nor indeed was it known whether there were any survivors at all. In all this he feared the worst. Only when, days later, the signal from U-126 arrived, did he learn that I was aboard *Python*. Never, he told me, had he felt so thankful or relieved . . . But there was more bad news to follow. The English had sunk *Python*! This, he thought, was definitely the end—and was deep in remorse that he had ever helped me to leave the mine sweepers! He felt he would never be able to face mother again.

This, our second upset, took place on a Monday afternoon—a languorous Monday afternoon, as *Python* rolled gently in the slight sea swell, two U-boats at her side. On deck the Trades blew gently, yet with just sufficient force to remove the full burden of the sun from the half-naked men who manned the pipe line.

Below, we of *Atlantis* lounged or napped according to whim. Happy to be relieved of the responsibility of making decisions, content to leave the arrangement of our fortune in the hands of others, ours was but the rule of idle guests, a part much to our liking after the excitement of the last two years, and one of which we were determined to take full advantage.

I had been reading earlier, but now I lay on my bunk in a delicious torpor, neither fully awake nor fully asleep, but peacefully adrift in a limbo of reminiscence . . .

The bumbling of bees in nodding heads of wheat . . . the softness of lush clover . . . the warmth of the friendly earth creeping up through the scented heather . . . this delightful half consciousness I lived again in the happy days of Peace; a trick acquired during our voyage, of drawing upon images far from the present, now achieving more than its usual success; a process of self-hypnosis aided on this occasion by the apparent tranquility of even one's real life surroundings. I nodded on . . .

A day of days on the glittering waveless mirror of the Alster . . . white sails framed against trim lawns and tranquil water . . . gay striped umbrellas blossoming mushroom-wise across the cafe tables . . . and a lovely girl . . .

But what the H . . .

Into a million fragments fled the dream, the girl, the yacht, the land. The alarm bells hammered. Our peace had ended. Doors opened and slammed along the ship's grey corridors. Boots thudded overhead. Harsh male obscenities echoed through the cabin, and shouts, orders, and complete confusion broke through our illusions and brought us at the double up on deck. 'Three funnelled steamer in sight.' Three funnelled . . . ! For a second or two the significance didn't register. For a second or two longer, when it had, we tried to bluff ourselves. COULD be a mistake on the part of an overexcitable look-out. COULD . . . But the optimist pursued his argument no further, his comfort drowned by the urgency of a new cry from the masthead, that cry we'd heard on *Atlantis* just nine days before . . .

'*Feindlicher Kreuzer in Sicht! Feindlicher Kreuzer in Sicht!*'

A new thought took hold of us. Could this be merely

the remembrance of an evil dream? A delusion based upon fears but recently remembered? In the eyes of my companions I could see the mad hope born, only to flicker, then waver and die in a moment's passing. For this was no subconscious throw-back, no psychological switch to the advent of *Devonshire*. Our fellows were real, and not the phantoms of a dream encounter. And *Dorsetshire* was real as well, carving her way towards us with the triumphant belligerency of a hound that has cornered a fox, the urgency of her purpose reflected in the speed that churned the wake of her passage into a maelstrom of foaming leaping water. We started to run . . .

'Free oil pipe!'

The U-boats parted from us, jerking back as our stern slewed round towards them, then diving like porpoises beneath the sea.

'Full ahead . . .' *Python* shuddered and shook with the sudden strain of her departure. 'Maximum Revs. . . .' And the voice from the depths reflected the strain that now made the engine room perform the impossible, raising the knottage to fourteen, sending the ship shuddering forward, as though temporarily endowed with the strength that had accompanied the trial runs of her youth.

I joined Rogge and *Python*'s captain on the bridge— all of us pretending to hope, when all reasonable hope had gone, that our foe might make some stupid mistake, and that the submarine, now far to our rear, might yet achieve a prayed-for miracle. For otherwise, despite the engineers, the end was certain. Fourteen knots on our part, twenty-eight to thirty knots on the part of our adversary . . . such a mathematical equation left no scope at all for optimism, but merely served to indicate the precise minute of our reckoning; a simple relationship between space and time, between an enemy closing and the clock hands turning.

Met by a warship, the drill of a supply ship's crew was to abandon ship when hope of escape had gone, then scuttle her rather than permit her to fall into British hands intact. In this case we had taken the chance of running, in the faint hope that the *Dorsetshire* would cross the U-boat position and so give them a chance for attack. But, as there was no hope at all of our 'making a fight for it' the men of *Atlantis* made the best of things and showed what hardened campaigners they were by preparing for as comfortable a retreat as possible. A strange spectacle. Among the bustle that otherwise prevailed on *Python*, certain of our lower deck comrades displayed the phlegmatic calm of professional burglars, as, while examining the open till, they calculate to a nicety the arrival of the police.

Our best 'scroungers' had early disappeared into a galley, and returned on deck laden with hot rolls and tinned meat. Without waiting for orders they had methodically ransacked the larder, and now proceeded to load the boats with their 'requisitions', stolidly ignoring the drama around them, and innocent of 'loot' that, however attractive in more civilised surroundings, would be more of a menace than a comfort in an open boat. Yes. They had actually left the liquor well alone. Not a single Scotch were we to take on our ocean wanderings! Instead, the search parties had concentrated on water which they carried in every type of receptacle. Such provisioning we noted with approval . . . theirs was quite obviously, most painfully obviously, the most useful activity of any of us aboard.

For half an hour the pursuit continued. And then, over all our action and reflections wailed the first eight-inch shell from *Dorsetshire*, strident as a factory hooter's warning, presage that leisure time was passed and gone. Another shell, and the sea fountained up once more—this time on our opposite quarter. The hint was there: we were quick to take it. 'Hard over . . .'

There was no one at the helm. The *Python* sailor who had been there only a minute earlier had left. I grabbed the helm myself, and put her hard over. Too much so! With the speed still in her *Python* developed a frightful list. My mistake was overlooked in the astonishing confusion which now prevailed, a confusion not due to panic but to a general aimlessness—well exemplifying the contrast between comparatively untrained civilian personnel, however brave, and a naval crew welded together by experience and discipline. Yet even as I thought approvingly of how well our own men's reactions justified Rogge's oft-complained-about and irksome adherence to 'regulations', a tragi-comedy was proceeding (unknown to us then) in the ship's stores.

Python carried, amongst innumerable supplies for the U-boat fleet, a vast quantity of leather jackets. With such recent memories of freezing nights in the boats, some of our men went down to collect as many as possible. 'What's all this?' asked the storeman. 'You can't touch these without the signature of an officer.' In vain the men protested. The elderly storeman (proud of his former career in the regular navy) just stood by the book and sent them packing. I did not hear of this episode until we were in the boats when I asked why it was that no one had done as I had done. The indignant complaints—maintained through bitter weather by shivering men—made me reflect subsequently that even naval discipline had its practical drawbacks and wish that a merchant sailor had been in charge of the jerkins' issue. Certainly I had no reason to complain of the hospitality of *Python*'s Captain. A true and philosophic comrade in misfortune, he turned to me as the men were filing to the side, and said, 'If you care to take a walk I will have great pleasure in showing you my wardrobe and inviting you to share it!'

Well, maybe I *was* wearing that navy best of mine but I'd only one shirt, and a change is sometimes desirable, so I eagerly complied with his suggestion and a short while later emerged the richer by a smart silk shirt, that I have kept to this day as a souvenir of an exceptional host.

The minutes ticked by. The boats were three-quarters full. We were almost ready to cast away when smoke, white and choking, shot up from *Python*, causing a furious outcry from us all: 'That bloody fool. That accursed stupid idiot . . .' A seaman had turned up the valve operating *Python*'s smoke screen. Blasphemies fell rich and fast upon the unhappy man, whose action was indeed the limit. The making of smoke would give the Briton every reason for suspicion, every reason to re-open fire and, as even a near miss would create havoc among the defenceless, crowded boats, our anger was well justified. I waited, tensed for the roar of the enemy's shells. But nothing happened. *Dorsetshire*, performing a clever and unending series of anti-submarine manoeuvres in which she turned figures of eight at 28 knots, evidently felt sure enough of herself to be benevolent and spare the fool-hardy. For our part we felt quite fond of her—with the gratitude of men reprieved from sudden death. She was certainly not out to kill for the sake of killing; the end of our ship was what *she* desired, and the end soon came.

I saw *Python* sink from a more comfortable point of vantage than that from which I had witnessed *Atlantis* die. As the charges exploded I photographed her from one of the whalers that our pessimistic intuition had saved from the previous occasion. How right we'd been when he said, 'You never know when you might need them . . .' At the time *Python*'s officers had argued that they were too heavy for davits. But Rogge had insisted. Idly I now wondered how our crews would have fared had he not argued the point for *Dorsetshire* was leaving us, wisely deciding that there was no point in her lingering as a target for the submarine which her smart look-outs had reported, and even now our boats were sufficiently crowded and our lot sufficiently parlous.

Soon after the disappearance of our adversary, one of our U-boat friends surfaced. We clustered around her—(yet another flashback to the episode of 22nd November)—and her Commander told us he had fired at the cruiser but it had been quite hopeless. 'He fooled me about his speed. A totally impossible target and we could never guess his next manoeuvre.' Then the other U-boat joined us. Her Commander had had even worse luck. At the time of the action his torpedo tubes were immobilised and he had been unable to do anything at all, only watch impotently at a stage when *Dorsetshire* (he said) would have been otherwise open to his attack . . .

Definitely our luck was out, but we were all intact. That was the main thing. And once again the U-boat men decided to help us on our way. By this time, however, we were beginning to feel somewhat depressed, for an idea of the scope of the mission to which both *Atlantis* and *Python* had been so recently assigned and so speedily lost, had begun to penetrate. In these remote waters we had encountered four U-boats in a fortnight. And there were more about. This activity had its ominous aspect—inevitably implying British countermeasures! The more we thought about it the clearer the plan became. Both ships had been instruments in a scheme for re-fuelling a U-boat pack designed to launch a mass offensive against the Cape convoys. All well and good. But distressingly evident was the fact that the British had known what our activities were all about long before we did. This, in turn, gave rise to other reflections, obviously disconcerting . . . if the supply chain in general was being looked for and dealt with as effectively as we had been, then there seemed less hope than ever of our making the journey home . . .

'Enemy aircraft! Enemy aircraft!'

Shouts from the submarine's conning tower jolted us back to the perils of the present. In the time that had elapsed since *Dorsetshire*'s departure we had grown more than a little careless. Too careless. And though the cruiser couldn't see what we were about she'd sent the seaplane as her proxy, a visitor almost as unwelcome as herself. The U-boats crash-dived in a violence of movement that sent the whaler dancing crazily askew on the fringe of a tell-tale tumbling whirlpool, while only a few seconds later the shadow of the British aircraft swept over the boats. Instinctively I flinched. So did the others. Wait for it! Wait for the bombs that, following the sub, would send our quivering flesh and splintered bone sky-high in the water's upward rush.

265

Wait for it! The aircraft banked, then ran in low, her engine deafening. I clutched the gunwale, my eyes half closed. But the rain of death did not fall. The seaplane circled round, only a few feet above the water, but not a bomb fell. When she left us we waved her goodbye. Was our immunity the result of some lingering trace of chivalry coupled with the sense that the submarines might now be too deep to hurt? Or was it just due to plain necessity, the seaplane being perhaps merely on a sortie of reconnaissance, or not sufficiently equipped for attack? Or hadn't she seen the subs, thanks to our screen of boats and rafts? We did not know the answer but in our new-found relief were only too eager to believe the best.

It was a long while before our underwater friends surfaced again, and this time their appearance followed an ultra-cautious periscopic inspection of the sky, while our eyes and ears alike remained alert for danger. Life, we reflected, was becoming really hectic in the hitherto comparatively tranquil South Atlantic, with the sea about as populated as Portsmouth harbour during Navy Week, and home even further than the map indicated. Only later did we learn that the unmasking of *Atlantis* had caused two other ships to meet in fatal rendezvous. The cruiser *Dunedin* and the U-124 had both hastened to the scene of the action. Their lines of approach and fate converged. But in this case the German was the victor. *Dunedin* was torpedoed and sank with heavy loss of life.

CHAPTER TWENTY-SIX

HOME BY THE UNDERWATER ROUTE

You'll die like rats in a trap,' he screamed. 'You'll die slowly . . . slowly I tell you!'

The frenzied cry, the words tumbling over each other, cut through my half doze, waking me again to the discomfort of my uneasy perch on the red hot gunwale of the lifeboat.

'Shut up!'

'Stow it!'

'Keep that loony quiet or I'll bash his teeth in . . .'

But the majority of the man's comrades—sixty-five of them, herded together in a boat designed for thirty—sat silent and apathetic, worn down by the heat and the strain, their faces wooden in their weariness.

'I can't stand it . . . I won't. Damn you, I won't . . . I've got more guts than the lot of you . . . I'm NOT GOING TO WAIT!'

His voice broke into a half sob, he jumped to his feet, the secret terror that had lain in him since the shells of *Devonshire* had sliced his comrade into a mass of blood and skin, now triggered off, exploding into violence. His face was contorted, swollen and red. His eyes were burning, their lids puffed and smarting with the heat and the brine. He swayed as he shouted at us. 'Creeping death? . . . You can have it . . . It's me for the drink!' And he turned to the side.

'Stop him!' I shouted, then. 'You maniac! Don't do it!'

But even as I shouted the man had jumped.

'My God,' said someone. 'He's gone!'

He fought us with all the strength of the lunatic, spitting out curses and salt water, and clawing at the arms that reached out to save him until, all fury spent, he lay limp, inert and whimpering in the well of the boat.

'Poor devil,' said a seaman.

'Poor devil you say! Be damned for that,' I said, and grabbing the would-be suicide by the shoulders I shook him back to coherence. 'You useless bastard,' I bawled. 'Who the hell do you think you are—the only ship-wrecked sailor in the world? Try that again and I'll take you at your word and leave your stinking, jellied carcase to the sharks!'

Passions on this, the third day of our journey, were running as hot as the sun that set the sea a-steam, the sea that in its deadly, expectant quiet seemed more and more to possess the ominous boding of a waiting and open grave dug outside a sick man's window. Wearily I climbed back to my place, linking again the sweating arm of a comrade, a comrade asleep within seconds of the disturbance's ending, and swaying backwards towards the sea. We on the side of the boat sat in line, arms linked in a human chain we had formed for safety . . . dozing, nodding, and swaying . . . each man subconsciously alert to jerk his fellow back should he overbalance in his stupor.

We were lucky, very lucky, to have the U-boats with us . . . We were lucky, very lucky . . . But it's diffi-cult, sometimes, to count your blessings when your eyes are swimming with the glare of the sun, and the blood in your head is beating like a hammer, and your stom-ach is sick, and the wound in your hand is throbbing . . . It's difficult to be philosophic when there are blisters on your seat . . .

For Fehler, the sinking of *Python* had brought new re-sponsibilities—the duties of watchdog, waiter, messen-ger and boat commander and he shouldered them all with a grin. Not for nothing had he been labelled Dyna-mite.

As watchdog he chased in his launch the six life-boats—now secured to the submarines in two tows of three—and cosseted the stragglers when the confounded cables broke. As waiter, he carried through the freezing night soup and coffee from the submarines' minute canteen, and as messenger he acted as go-between for the submarine commanders, for Rogge, and for the officers in general, performing these duties with an exterior verve and dash that became the commander of a very elegant officers' launch, a craft originally designed for purposes no more exacting than the conveyance of parties from ship to jetty.

Inside him, the enemy Sleep fought to break through the barricades of willpower, but whenever he felt that he, too, must succumb, he considered the crowded misery of the towed . . . No room to lie down . . . hardly enough room to sit up . . . No chance to sleep except for the odd doze followed by an awakening of acute discomfort . . . stiff joints, swollen ankles, fresh arrows of pain to wound anew their burning and aching backs. Crews who had no tarpaulins to rig as awnings suffered unremittingly the violence of the sun, while those who had panted for air, cursing the stuffiness and the stench beneath their canopy. And around them all the heat haze hovered, an agony to the eyes, and vanishing only when the stars came out, the clear hard stars that heralded the cold.

'It's unique,' said Rogge. 'Quite unique. You will always have the satisfaction of knowing that, Mohr . . . if it works of course!'

I sincerely hoped 'it' would.

Our enforced odyssey had entered on a new and rather dramatic phase. Task Force South Atlantic had been broken before it had even properly begun to operate. There was no doubt of that. Not now . . . Not now the *Atlantis* and *Pinguin* had been cornered and sunk; now that another two U-boats had arrived . . . short of oil, short of torpedoes, short of fuel . . . motherless.

What started this chain of disaster? A leak from Group West? Or clever Allied Intelligence work? We did not know what caused Berlin's plans to change, but changed they were, and our personal fortunes with them. For the U-boats had been ordered home. Furthermore, they had been ordered to take us home; the whole way home; home by the underwater route; with a hundred weary passengers on each small U-boat.

'Unique. Quite unique. If it worked, of course . . . !'

'To think,' said Fehler a trifle sadly as the officer's launch took a last, fastidious plunge, and from the upper deck of the U-boat we watched the destruction of the whalers. 'To think that that pretty pansy carried us for seven hundred miles.'

We had 'burned our boats' . . .

The U-boat's Number One indicated the cubby hole of a wardroom built, presumably, for four very small officers. 'This,' he told us, 'is where, somehow or other, we are all expected to sleep.' Nine very large officers exchanged glances of dismay.

'Sharing' in these circumstances, entailed my snatching barely ninety minutes' sleep before rising, half dead, to make way for another, until after three most harrowing nights, I discovered I could make a better 'berth' beneath the table, the steel plates for mattress, my life jacket for pillow, and Ferry—who had nowhere else to go—acting as 'blanket' across my hunched-up legs.

Our arrival had presented the U-boatmen with an extraordinary variety of problems, and to pretend that we were always regarded by them with a comradely affection would be more than misleading. What damnable nuisances we must have seemed—five officers, ten petty officers, and eighty-five ratings—suddenly unloaded on a craft designed to provide but sparse accommodation for a crew of forty! Nor were we only nuisances. We were menaces as well, for, with our extra weight, and the crush we created, the U-boat could be expected to be almost unmanageable in the event of attack.

To accommodate our crew the torpedo room had to be converted into dormitories where the men could only

270

sleep bolt upright, on wooden benches built around the torpedo racks, and the trim dive became a daily hazard, with ourselves, although doing our best, inevitably getting in the way of the crew. We were short of food. We were short of water. And, as surface sailors, we hated the claustrophobic atmosphere around us, spending all the time we could on deck, lying on the gratings, and thanking God for the beneficence of the Trades which, in the twelve days of our surface wanderings, brought to us relief from the overwhelming heat, the gentle winds presaging the blasts of Europe.

Vicovari, our American legacy from *Zamzam,* sat on the wooden seat that encircled the machine gun on the conning tower; a perch habitually reserved for him on account of the leg wounds he had sustained eight months before.

As I approached him he looked up with his usual friendly greeting, and then, as though he had read my expression, his smile became suddenly wary, as if masking an instinctive apprehension. He recognised that my visit was not just for gossip; he knew that I intended to break some news that concerned him vitally. Might as well get it over with then, I thought . . .

Formally, as instructed, I announced, 'A state of hostilities now exists between Germany and the United States of America. As from now you will have to consider yourself a prisoner of war.'

The date was 8th December 1941.

Dorsetshire had sent us wandering on 1st December, and it had taken us three weeks to reach the Cape Verde Islands, to rendezvous with the four Italian submarines that were to reinforce the rescue flotilla and carry scores of us on the last and most critical stage of the journey home. From now we would be travelling mostly beneath the surface, running through Biscay and the British air and sea patrols, to reach the U-boats' most southerly lair, the Gironde River where *Tirranna* had met her end.

Rogge and I shook hands before I climbed into the

271

float that was to carry me over to the Italian, *Tazzoli*. I don't think either of us felt particularly cheerful, but Rogge had arranged that we should separate 'in the interests of history'. Each of us carried written records of the cruise, and each of us also carried much that was unwritten. If one should fall the other might still remain. So we wished each other good luck, each, such is human optimism, quite confident that he would get through all right; each rather wistful and worried about the chances of the other chap.

A high swell was running as I climbed up from the float to the *Tazzoli*'s propeller guard, pausing there for a second before stepping on to the deck. That pause very nearly cost me my life . . .

A mass of water surged around me, covering my head and leaving me dazed as the hull of *Tazzoli* rose again from the waves into which the swell had plunged her. I heard a shout. Someone was pointing in alarm at something behind me. I looked over my shoulder to see that hateful long, black shape tearing at me like a torpedo. My damaged hand registered its warning pain, and before the submarine plunged again, panic had lent me the agility to spring upon her deck.

Life on an Italian submarine appeared to have everything . . . A gracious commander, with a fine collection of valuable first prints, mostly of French erotic literature . . . A cuisine of rich and exciting Italian delicacies . . . An accommodation that was roomy, comfortable. But such delights were confined to officers only. For the men it was a vastly different matter, and I was surprised to observe how wide was the social gulf existing between the two, a gulf that pleased our sailors not at all, especially when they compared notes with us regarding the meagre seaman's diet they shared, and our own renaissance repasts. That submarine could possess two galleys, one for officers and one for men, each with its separate cook, and, furthermore, its separate menu, was a new experience. But still, they agreed, it was no use being too critical, not of people who had pulled you out of the drink and were risking their necks to get you home. And *Tazzoli*, for all the bewildering distinctions of class, was a happy ship, her Commander, Fecia di Cossato, being followed worshipfully by his crew.

During my first few days aboard I took full advantage of the Commander's library, dipping deeply into his treasure of books which included, I found, a most comprehensive description of every form of Chinese torture!

Two days before Christmas and the most colossal row echoed through the ship as everyone went to Action Stations in a confused but dramatic scramble. I stared in some bewilderment as the orders came, in a flurry of volubility in accents rapid . . . A merchantman had been sighted, *Tazzoli* was going in to the attack . . .

The Italian doctor came running to me, a bottle of champagne in his hand.

With sublime optimism he said, 'For us, the little drink to celebrate our victory!'

Victory? Let's have a bit of Peace, I thought, as I was called to the periscope and allowed a privileged peep. I could see but little, and my surface enthusiasm I felt must appear a little thin, for I regarded the whole attempt with considerable misgivings, longing for the open deck of *Atlantis,* and only cheering up when an (apparently) disappointed Italian officer informed me, 'Alas. She is neutral. Sailing with navigation lights. A Spaniard.'

But we had the champagne just the same!

Christmas Day, and one of the *Atlantis* crew built a rather pathetic replica of a Christmas tree, the second since we'd lift the homeland to be fashioned from broomsticks, bits of wire and coloured paper. An indescribable nostalgia gripped everyone, our thoughts reverting to that other Christmas in the wastes of the Kerguelens, and of the grave that now seemed so pathetically remote, and we were thinking, too, of the

273

folk at home, now so near in space, and yet so separated by hazard, for we were in the middle of the Bay of Biscay, about to encounter the full force of the British blockade. Both Germans and Italians were singing carols, and as I listened I pondered on the ironies of fate . . . We, of *Atlantis*, had come over 100,000 miles. Say we, too, should meet Friend Hein upon the homeland's doorstep? . . . I remembered *Tirranna* with a shudder.

Christmas night, and as the *Tazzoli* tried to take advantage of the darkness to travel upon the surface, a questing British aircraft located her and came into the attack . . .

'Crash dive!'

We plunged so fast that I was thrown off balance.

'Crash dive!' And my spirits dived too.

The impact of the enemy's bombs shook the ship. The effect was shattering to the morale although mercifully missing the target, and in the hours that followed I developed a healthy hatred of submarines, a dread of underwater war where a man might die in the dark in a coffin ready-made.

New Year's Day, and still bewildered that we'd really made it, we stood on the quayside of St. Nazaire, our journey ended, nearly two years of hazard behind us.

We were dirty, bearded, and ragged, with faces pale and thin. We bunched together almost protectively as we surveyed the world that had lain for so long outside the orbit of our lives, hardly crediting that this, the moment to which we had looked forward so long, should seem to us possessed of so strong an element of anticlimax.

Houses . . . streets . . . the sound of a car . . . the laugh of a child . . . the sight of a flower . . . dead leaves . . . a torn news page in the gutter . . . we of *Atlantis* felt like space travellers returning to earth after a sojourn on the moon.

The U-boats had come in twenty-four hours earlier

than the Italian flotilla, and Rogge was waiting to greet us, together with the Admiral in charge of coastal command. One of the submarines had received a severe mauling from British aircraft, but there had been no casualties.

We were safe. Our luck . . . *Atlantis* luck . . . had held.

We went to lunch . . . a miracle of crystal goblets and precious china spread lavishly over white, crisp table-cloths. And, to this luxurious setting, we, the banqueters, all guests of the harbour commandant, were figures as incongruous as a bunch of Aborigines, many of us shoeless, all feeling incredibly dirty, bearded, haggard, and ravenous for the French cooking.

We went to our billets—a commandeered hotel that should have seemed a paradise but did not for it was almost completely unheated and we men from the tropics and the depths found the northern weather unbelievably harsh and bitter.

We went to get cleaned up . . . savouring the delicious experience of sitting in a barber's chair relaxed and drowsy beneath the warm and soothing lather—sequel to a session in the public baths where, to the stupefaction of some . . . the delight of others . . . and the embarrassment of a few, women acted as attendants!

A week later, and we were numbered among the heroes of the Reich . . . the officers of thanksgivings, the recipients of the cheers. At Nantes Cathedral Rogge read the Lesson. At the Kaiserhof in Berlin I carried the bejewelled baton of Grand Admiral Raeder, inspecting us at a banquet where each of the crew was honoured as 'a guest of the German Navy'.

The heroes' return!

I went on leave . . . to Berlin, a city full of foreigners, a place where fortunes were made while men died at the Front. I fled to Bavaria to pass through station after station crammed with troops resting wearily, un-smilingly, before the start of their journey to the all-absorbing East. I read the posters and the exhortations . . . to sacrifice and struggle. And I read them while the Zurst, the wealthy industrialists, lived lavishly as kings in the 'unspoilt beauty spot' to which I was a visi-tor.

A hero's welcome . . . !

In Berlin, in the tiny room where he had said good-bye to his wife two years before, and she had wept so bitterly as they parted, one of the best and most com-radely of our crew came home—to find his wife living with a party boss, a boss who jeered at him and cli-maxed the encounter by a threat to send him packing to the Eastern Front.

'My wife just laughed at me as I stood there,' said the seaman to Rogge afterwards. 'And then, sir, I took off my wedding ring, and I threw it at her feet.'

We had come back to Germany.

EPILOGUE

By Captain A. W. S., Agar, V.C. D.S.O. R.N. RTD.

The story related in this book is told with great frankness. It demonstrates again most forcibly the simple truth that maritime nations like ourselves and the Commonwealth, who depend on the broad oceans as their highways for commerce, will always be vulnerable in war unless adequate measures are taken to safeguard our ships from every form of attack. The Raider type of sea-warfare described in these pages is not new, nor was it unexpected, as we had previous experience in World War 1 from the German Raiders *Moewe*, *Seeadler* and *Wolf*. In the last war however, they were much more effective and dangerous because of the ingenious methods used for disguising themselves at frequent intervals which made recognition almost impossible until the fatal moment when they disclosed to their victims their true identity leaving no chance for escape, or of giving warning by radio to friendly shipping in the area, except at very great risks, before a murderous fire at point blank range swept their decks.

It cannot be denied, even by those who had the odious duty of carrying it out, that the character of this type of sea-attack is not only ruthless and horrible but contrary to all sea tradition, for it is directed by ships in disguise with well-trained service crews against *unarmed* ships except those mounting a small anti-submarine gun on the stern: yet the story of *Atlantis* and the conduct of her Captain and officers to a certain extent mitigates some of these horrors, though there must be some unhappy memories of *Zamzam*, *Tirranna*, *Kemmendine* and *King City* (the evidence of which is supplied in the book itself) when human lives might otherwise have been spared. Nor can one excuse the conduct of the prize crew of the *Durmitor* for failing to call for help from other ships, when they knew that the chances of their large number of prisoners reaching port were very slender.

The successes achieved by *Atlantis* against our merchant shipping was obviously due to the high professional ability of her Captain and the personal discipline and comradeship by which he controlled his officers and crew. To voyage twice round the world and remain at sea for twenty months without calling at port is in itself no mean achievement, and however much 'luck' may have been with him, it is to his credit that he turned his back on a way of escape, when offered the chance of reaching(what was for them at the time) the friendly port of Dakar, though it is by no means certain he would have got there. He chose instead to pursue his course and in doing so showed a high sense of duty to his country.

Captain Stephen Roskill, R.N., in the *Official History of the War at Sea,* Vol. I, gives a most clear and lucid account of the problems which this form of attack on our shipping presented to the Admiralty and our countermeasures against it. The use of aircraft by Raiders widens of course their scope of attack, and indeed the *Atlantis* used hers whenever possible; but equally it enables a cruiser to search by day a much larger area. Even more important, it makes easier the problem of identification whether a merchant ship is genuine or not, so that a warship can stay at some distance while her aircraft investigates, thus reducing the risk of attack by U-boat should one or more be in attendance on the suspect ship.

All merchant ships encountered at sea at the beginning of war can be regarded as sailing on a *bona fide* voyage.

At this stage a disguised Raider's task is easy because merchant vessels normally follow recognised trade routes. As war develops, however, ships are gathered into convoy thereby making attacks by Raider more difficult because of the escorts; but it is on the long voyages across wide oceans when ships have to sail independently (as escorts cannot be provided everywhere), which offer opportunities such as the *Atlantis* took advantage of; and if this type of sea-attack is well planned at headquarters to cover widely separated areas like the Indian, Pacific and South Atlantic oceans, the result and effect, even if small in sinkings, is most harmful generally on a maritime nation's war effort such as Great Britain's in the last war.

The best counter-measure is to organise in each area 'hunting groups' of warships powerful enough to deal with a well-armed Raider; but this takes time. In the meanwhile, our merchant ships had to take their medicine, and gallantly they did, often at great sacrifice of life, while these measures were being put into operation by the Admiralty.

In the autumn of 1941 in the South Atlantic I had command of one of these groups in H.M.S. *Dorsetshire* under the general direction on shore of Admiral Sir Algernon Willis (now Admiral of the Fleet). We knew that German commerce raiders—and also warships—had been in the area earlier in the year and were expecting a return visit. But our admiral was even more concerned at this time about the safety of our large troop convoys, then passing through the area bound for North Africa and Malaya via the Cape. It was anticipated that a long range U-boat attack would be planned against them, using both Raiders and supply ships for refuelling. To frustrate this and prevent the loss of thousands of our troops which such a U-Boat concentration threatened, was our great anxiety. The certain way was to destroy both raiders and supply ships and so deprive the U-boats of fuel. This was our immediate task and we spent many weeks and months at sea before we finally accomplished it. It so happens that there are certain areas in this vast ocean where weather conditions are relatively calm compared with others. This knowledge, compiled from years of meteorological data, is of course well known on oceanic charts; anticipating that they would be chosen for the refuelling rendezvous we were especially vigilant in these particular localities.

It was in this way that H.M.S. *Devonshire* sighted and destroyed *Atlantis*, and my ship, H.M.S. *Dorsetshire,* the supply ship *Python* with the result that the group of U-boats, destined for this attack on our Cape convoys had to jettison their torpedoes and return home with the survivors from both ships. *Atlantis'* luck had turned.

When sinking a commerce raider or supply ship with U-boats suspected in the vicinity, the first consideration is the safety of one's own ship. No chances can be taken; and the business despatched as quickly as possible so as to allow the U-boats no time in which to gain a favourable position for attack. Captain R. Oliver, R.N. in H.M.S. *Devonshire* had the added difficulty of waiting to establish the real identity of *Atlantis*. I was more fortunate with *Python* who scuttled herself very quickly immediately after the warning shots were fired which left me in no doubt as to what she was, and relieved my mind of the possibility of causing loss of life amongst our own British seamen (many of whom I thought were prisoners on board), and had I been obliged to destroy the ship by gunfire.

For myself, personally, the story ends here; *Dorsetshire* was transferred soon afterwards to another operation area where, alas, we ourselves were to suffer the fate of being sunk with heavy loss of life by Japanese dive-bombing aircraft. Such in war is the turn of fortune's wheel.

For generations, international lawyers have striven to regulate, by convention and otherwise, the conduct of war at sea; yet experience of two World Wars proves that nations engaged in a vital struggle will turn to any weapon or method, if the end will justify the means. The disguised commerce raider is only one example, but whether the same technique will be used again, or to what extent it can or will be improved, is a matter only for speculation. What stands out so clearly is that when the new technique first appeared in this horrible form of *disguise* our British officers and seamen stood up to it in their merchant ships with the same fortitude and courage as those who faced the U-boat war in the North Atlantic; no wonder we can say with just pride that but for them, we in these islands would not have survived.